DAY HIKING
New England

Autumn foliage surrounds Kettle Pond, Groton State Forest.

Meadow Pond, Great Brook Farm State Park

Previous page: *Hamlin Ridge, Baxter State Park*

Discovering Dodge Point

Forest shades the Metacomet Trail, Penwood State Park.

Sandy Neck Beach, Cape Cod

Morrison Brook, Caribou Mountain

Boundary Trail, Bradbury Mountain
State Park

The Pogue, Marsh-Billings-Rockefeller
National Historical Park

Mount Adam's impressive silhouette from Mount Jefferson

Crawford Notch winter splendor on Mount Avalon

Painted trillium

Palm warbler

Falls Brook Falls, Tunxis State Forest

Maine's Baxter State Park contains prime moose habitat.

Squeezing through Devils Corncrib, Purgatory Chasm

Next page: *The Presidential Range towers above Imp Face.*

DAY HIKING
New England

Maine · New Hampshire · Vermont
Connecticut · Massachusetts · Rhode Island

Jeffrey Romano

MOUNTAINEERS
BOOKS

MOUNTAINEERS BOOKS

Mountaineers Books is the nonprofit publishing division of The Mountaineers, an organization founded in 1906 and dedicated to the exploration, preservation, and enjoyment of outdoor and wilderness areas.

1001 SW Klickitat Way, Suite 201 · Seattle, WA 98134
800.553.4453 · www.mountaineersbooks.org

Printed in the United States of America
Distributed in the United Kingdom by Cordee, www.cordee.co.uk

First edition, 2015

Copy editor: Christy Karras
Layout: Peggy Egerdahl
Cartographer: Pease Press Cartography
The background maps for this book were produced using the online map viewer CalTopo. For more information, visit http://caltopo.com.
All photographs by author unless noted otherwise

Cover photograph: *Trail to Big and Little Moose ponds* (Hike 109), *Maine*

Library of Congress Cataloging-in-Publication Data
Romano, Jeffrey.
  Day hiking New England : Maine, New Hampshire, Vermont, Connecticut, Massachusetts, Rhode Island / Jeffrey Romano. — First edition.
     pages cm
  ISBN 978-1-59485-884-0 (pbk.) — ISBN 978-1-59485-885-7 (e-book) 1. Day hiking—New England—Guidebooks. 2. Hiking—New England—Guidebooks. 3. Trails—New England—Guidebooks. 4. New England—Guidebooks. I. Title.
  GV199.42.N38R67 2015
  796.510974—dc23
2014041440

 Printed on recycled paper

ISBN (paperback): 978-1-59485-884-0
ISBN (ebook): 978-1-59485-885-7

Table of Contents

Overview Map 6
Map Legend 7
Hikes at a Glance 8
Acknowledgments 17
Introduction 19

Southeastern New England

1. Pamet Trail 33
2. Sandy Neck 34
3. Myles Standish State Forest 36
4. Weetamoo Woods 38
5. Trustom Pond 41
6. Great Swamp 43
7. Rome Point 45
8. Long Pond and Ell Pond 47
9. Tillinghast Pond 50
10. Pachaug State Forest 52
11. James L. Goodwin State Forest 55
12. Nayantaquit Trail 57
13. Mansfield Hollow 59
14. Wells State Park 62
15. Purgatory Chasm 64
16. Blackstone River 67
17. Borderland State Park 69
18. Noanet Woodlands 72
19. Middlesex Fells 74
20. Great Brook Farm 77
21. Bradley Palmer State Park 79
22. Great Bay 82

Monadnock-Metacomet-Mattabesett

23. Sleeping Giant 86
24. Chauncey and Lamentation 89
25. Falls Brook Trail 91
26. Penwood State Park 93
27. Chester–Blandford State Forest 95
28. Mount Holyoke 98
29. Mount Toby 100
30. Mount Grace 102
31. Pisgah State Park 105
32. Pack Monadnock 107
33. Willard Pond 110
34. Mount Sunapee 112

Berkshires

35. Kettletown State Park 116
36. Mattatuck Trail 118
37. Pine Knob Loop 121
38. Hang Glider View 123
39. Lions Head 125
40. Jug End 127
41. Pine Cobble 129
42. Mount Greylock 132

Vermont

43. Harmon Hill 136
44. Mount Equinox 138
45. Mount Olga 141
46. Jamaica State Park 142

47. Mount Ascutney   145
48. Bromley Mountain   147
49. Little Rock Pond and Green Mountain   150
50. White Rocks   152
51. Glen Lake   154
52. Snake Mountain   157
53. Killington Peak   159
54. Mount Tom and the Pogue   161
55. Brandon Gap   163
56. Camels Hump   166
57. Niquette Bay   168
58. Missisquoi Wildlife Refuge   170
59. Mount Mansfield   173
60. Jay Peak   175
61. Mount Hunger and White Rock   178
62. Elmore Mountain   180
63. Owls Head Mountain   182
64. Mount Monadnock   184

Northern New Hampshire

65. Belknap Range   188
66. Ossipee Mountains   190
67. Mount Cardigan   193
68. Mount Osceola   195
69. Mount Moosilauke   197
70. Lincoln Woods   200
71. Mount Pemigewasset   203
72. Franconia Notch   204
73. Potash Mountain   207
74. Boulder Loop   208
75. Middle Sister   210
76. North Moat Mountain   213
77. Green Hills Preserve   215
78. Arethusa Falls and Frankenstein Cliff   217
79. Tom, Field, and Avalon   219
80. Middle and North Sugarloaf   222
81. Mount Jefferson   224
82. Mount Madison   227
83. Mount Washington   230
84. Imp Face   232
85. Percy Peaks   234
86. Dixville Notch   236

Maine Coast

87. Mount Agamenticus   240
88. Wells Reserve   242
89. Bradbury Mountain   245
90. Dodge Point   247
91. Camden Hills   249
92. Holbrook Island Sanctuary   252
93. Champlain Mountain   254
94. Dorr Mountain   256
95. Norumbega Mountain   259
96. Acadia Mountain   262
97. Beech Cliff and Mountain   264
98. Tunk Mountain   266
99. Petit Manan   268
100. Bog Brook Cove   270

Northern Maine

101. Androscoggin Riverlands State Park   274
102. Kennebec Highlands   277
103. Speckled Mountain   279
104. Caribou Mountain   281
105. Rumford Whitecap   283
106. Little Jackson   285
107. Sugarloaf Mountain   288
108. Bigelow Mountain: Avery Peak   290
109. Big and Little Moose Ponds   292
110. Borestone Mountain   295
111. Chairback Mountain   297
112. Niagara Falls   299
113. Brothers and Coe   302
114. Traveler Mountain   304
115. Mount Katahdin   307

Appendix I:
Contact Information   310
Appendix II:
Conservation and Trail Organizations   313
Index   315

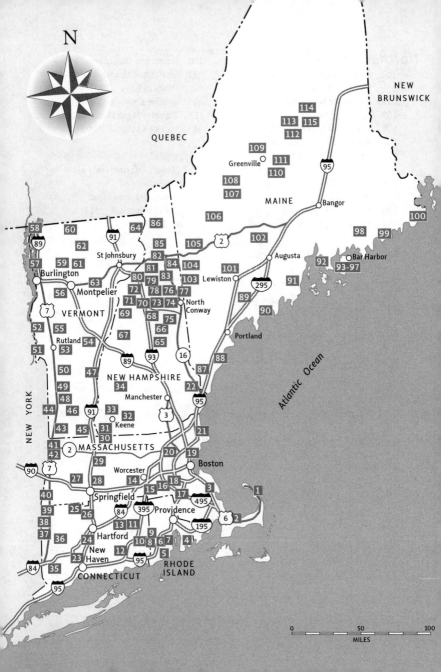

LEGEND

84	Interstate Highway
197	US Highway
14	State Highway
	Secondary Road
=======	Unpaved Road
== 24 ==	Forest Road
--------	Hiking Route
....	Optional Route
- - - - -	Other Trail
	Park/Forest/Wilderness Boundary
1	Hike Number
T	Trailhead
P	Parking
P	Alternate Parking

■	Building/Landmark
	Ranger Station/Entrance Station
禾	Picnic Area
Δ	Campground/Campsite/Shelter
▲	Summit
) (	Pass
~	River/Stream
~#~	Falls/Cascade
	Lake
⸽	Wetland/Marsh
) (	Bridge
→←	Tunnel
🗼	Lookout
I	Gate

HIKES AT A GLANCE

HIKE	DISTANCE	DIFFICULTY	HIKEABLE ALL YEAR	KID-FRIENDLY
SOUTHEASTERN NEW ENGLAND				
1. Pamet Trail	3.3	1–2	•	•
2. Sandy Neck	4.3	2–3		•
3. Myles Standish State Forest	3.9	2	•	•
4. Weetamoo Woods	5.6	3	•	•
5. Trustom Pond	2.4	1	•	•
6. Great Swamp	5.1	2	•	•
7. Rome Point	2.6	1	•	•
8. Long Pond and Ell Pond	2.2	3	•	•
9. Tillinghast Pond	8.4	3–4	•	
10. Pachaug State Forest	9.4	4	•	
11. James L. Goodwin State Forest	7.6	3	•	•
12. Nayantaquit Trail	3.6	1–2	•	•
13. Mansfield Hollow	5.6	3	•	•
14. Wells State Park	6.5	2–3	•	•
15. Purgatory Chasm	2.6	2		•
16. Blackstone River	4.7	2	•	•
17. Borderland State Park	5.2	2	•	•
18. Noanet Woodlands	5	2	•	•
19. Middlesex Fells	4.6	3–4	•	
20. Great Brook Farm	4.1	1	•	•
21. Bradley Palmer State Park	3.7	2	•	•
22. Great Bay	4.5	1–2	•	•
MONADNOCK-METACOMET-MATTABESETT				
23. Sleeping Giant	5.8	4	•	
24. Chauncey and Lamentation	4.2	3–4	•	
25. Falls Brook Trail	1.8	2	•	•
26. Penwood State Park	4.2	2–3	•	•
27. Chester–Blandford State Forest	4.5	3	•	
28. Mount Holyoke	3.2	3	•	
29. Mount Toby	4.5	2–3	•	•
30. Mount Grace	3.4	2	•	•
31. Pisgah State Park	8	3–4	•	

DOG-FRIENDLY	BEACH-COMBING	WILD-FLOWERS	BIRD-WATCHING	WATER-FALLS	WET-LANDS	GEOLOGIC	HISTORICAL	FIRE LOOKOUT
							•	
	•		•					
•					•			
•						•	•	
			•		•			
•			•		•		•	
•	•		•					
		•			•	•		
			•		•	•	•	
•		•		•		•		
	•					•		
•			•					
•					•			
•					•	•		
				•		•		
					•		•	
•					•	•	•	
•			•				•	
						•	•	
•			•		•		•	
•					•			
			•		•			
		•				•	•	
					•	•		
				•				
•					•	•		
•				•				
						•	•	
•								•
•								•
•			•		•			

HIKE	DISTANCE	DIFFICULTY	HIKEABLE ALL YEAR	KID-FRIENDLY
32. Pack Monadnock	8	3–4	•	
33. Willard Pond	3.5	3	•	•
34. Mount Sunapee	6.2	3		
BERKSHIRES				
35. Kettletown State Park	6.5	3	•	
36. Mattatuck Trail	5.2	3	•	
37. Pine Knob Loop	2.5	2–3	•	•
38. Hang Glider View	5.2	3	•	
39. Lions Head	4.8	3	•	•
40. Jug End	4.4	3	•	•
41. Pine Cobble	5	3	•	
42. Mount Greylock	7.6	4	•	
VERMONT				
43. Harmon Hill	3.6	3	•	•
44. Mount Equinox	6.2	4	•	
45. Mount Olga	1.9	2	•	•
46. Jamaica State Park	7	3	•	
47. Mount Ascutney	7.3	3–4	•	
48. Bromley Mountain	6	3	•	
49. Little Rock Pond and Green Mountain	7.3	3		
50. White Rocks	5.4	3		
51. Glen Lake	4.4	2	•	•
52. Snake Mountain	3.8	2	•	•
53. Killington Peak	7.6	4		
54. Mount Tom and The Pogue	5.2	2	•	•
55. Brandon Gap	6.8	3	•	
56. Camels Hump	5.8	4		
57. Niquette Bay	3.5	2	•	•
58. Missisquoi	4.4	1	•	•
59. Mount Mansfield	7	4		
60. Jay Peak	3.4	3		
61. Mount Hunger and White Rock	6.4	4		
62. Elmore Mountain	4	2–3	•	•
63. Owls Head Mountain	3.2	2	•	•
64. Mount Monadnock	5	3	•	

DOG-FRIENDLY	BEACH-COMBING	WILD-FLOWERS	BIRD-WATCHING	WATER-FALLS	WET-LANDS	GEOLOGIC	HISTORICAL	FIRE LOOKOUT
•			•			•		•
			•		•	•		
•					•	•		
•				•		•	•	
						•	•	
•						•		
•		•						
•		•						
•						•		
		•				•		
•		•			•		•	
•								
•		•						
•								•
•				•		•		
				•		•	•	•
•			•					
		•	•		•			
•						•		
•			•		•			
•						•		
•			•					
			•		•		•	
•						•		
		•		•		•		
•		•			•			
			•		•			
		•	•			•		
•						•		
		•	•			•		
•						•		•
•						•	•	
•								•

HIKE	DISTANCE	DIFFICULTY	HIKEABLE ALL YEAR	KID-FRIENDLY
NORTHERN NEW HAMPSHIRE				
65. Belknap Range	4.6	3	•	
66. Ossipee Mountains	14.5	4	•	
67. Mount Cardigan	3.8	3		•
68. Mount Osceola	6.4	4		
69. Mount Moosilauke	7.9	4		
70. Lincoln Woods	8	2–3	•	•
71. Mount Pemigewasset	3.6	3	•	•
72. Franconia Notch	6.2	3	•	
73. Potash Mountain	4.4	3	•	•
74. Boulder Loop	3.2	3	•	•
75. Middle Sister	8.6	4	•	
76. North Moat Mountain	10.5	4	•	
77. Green Hills Preserve	5.6	3	•	•
78. Arethusa Falls and Frankenstein Cliff	5	3–4	•	
79. Tom, Field, and Avalon	7.2	4	•	
80. Middle and North Sugarloaf	3.4	3	•	•
81. Mount Jefferson	10.2	5		
82. Mount Madison	9.3	5	•	
83. Mount Washington	9.3	5		
84. Imp Face	6.5	3–4	•	
85. Percy Peaks	6.7	4		
86. Dixille Notch	5.2	3–4	•	
MAINE COAST				
87. Mount Agamenticus	6.7	3	•	•
88. Wells Reserve	4.5	1	•	•
89. Bradbury Mountain	3.2	2	•	•
90. Dodge Point	4.2	2	•	•
91. Camden Hills	6.5	3	•	
92. Holbrook Island Sanctuary	7.6	2–3	•	•
93. Champlain Mountain	5.5	3		
94. Dorr Mountain	6.5	3	•	
95. Norumbega Mountain	3.8	3	•	•
96. Acadia Mountain	4.5	3		•
97. Beech Cliff and Mountain	4	3–4		

DOG-FRIENDLY	BEACH-COMBING	WILD-FLOWERS	BIRD-WATCHING	WATER-FALLS	WET-LANDS	GEOLOGIC	HISTORICAL	FIRE LOOKOUT
•						•		•
•						•	•	
						•		•
•						•		
		•					•	
•				•	•			
•						•		
			•	•	•			
						•		
•						•		
•						•		
•		•		•		•		
			•			•		
				•		•		
•				•				
•						•		
		•		•		•		
		•		•		•		
		•		•		•	•	
•			•			•		
		•				•		
				•		•	•	
•			•					
	•		•		•		•	
•			•				•	
•	•						•	
			•			•		
	•		•		•			
					•	•		
						•	•	
					•			
						•		
			•			•		•

HIKE	DISTANCE	DIFFICULTY	HIKEABLE ALL YEAR	KID-FRIENDLY
98. Tunk Mountain	4.5	3–4	•	
99. Petit Manan	5.5	2	•	•
100. Bog Brook Cove	4.7	2–3	•	•
NORTHERN MAINE				
101. Androscoggin Riverlands State Park	5.2	2	•	•
102. Kennebec Highlands	4.5	3	•	•
103. Speckled Mountain	8.6	3–4	•	
104. Caribou Mountain	6.9	3–4		
105. Rumford Whitecap	5	3	•	•
106. Little Jackson	9.1	4		
107. Sugarloaf Mountain	6.6	4		
108. Bigelow Mountain: Avery Peak	9	4–5		
109. Big and Little Moose Ponds	4	2–3		•
110. Borestone Mountain	5.2	3–4	•	•
111. Chairback Mountain	11.2	4		
112. Niagara Falls	2.8	2		•
113. Brothers and Coe	10.9	5		
114. Traveler Mountain	10.9	5		
115. Mount Katahdin	11.7	5		

	DOG-FRIENDLY	BEACH-COMBING	WILD-FLOWERS	BIRD-WATCHING	WATER-FALLS	WET-LANDS	GEOLOGIC	HISTORICAL	FIRE LOOKOUT
						•	•		
		•		•					
		•		•		•	•		
	•			•		•		•	
	•			•			•		
	•		•		•		•		
	•		•		•		•		
	•		•				•		
			•			•	•		
							•		
			•				•		
	•					•	•		
						•	•		
	•					•	•		
					•				
			•				•		
			•			•	•		
			•			•	•		

Acknowledgments

I would be remiss if I failed to acknowledge the many people who played a part in the evolution of this book, especially those who joined me on the trail, posed for photographs, and reviewed draft material. I wish to thank Richard Romano, Judy Romano, Craig Romano, Doug Romano, Blake Romano, Austin Stebbins, Dr. Ned Graham, Abuela, Kara Tudman Walker, Devin Walker, and Andy Walsh. Special thanks also to Jacques Tremblay and Richard McGovern for providing a home away from home in Vermont.

Lastly, extra-special thanks are due to my wife, Maria, and son, Anthony. Both provided the essential support needed to make this book a reality. Thanks for your patience when I was away, both physically and mentally. I hope you remember most our many adventures together, both on the trail and the enjoyable meals afterward. I know I will never forget the sunning black racer snakes we found in eastern Connecticut, the majestic barred owl we spooked near Great Bay, the late spring snow-sliding adventure down Mount Mansfield, the photography session atop North Percy Peak, bracing against the fierce winds on Sugarloaf, or the peaceful afternoon visit of Old Mans Head.

Upper Hadlock Pond, Acadia National Park

Western views from Pine Cobble Preserve

Introduction

The hikes described in this guidebook showcase the breadth and diversity of New England's picturesque landscapes: from the sand dunes of Cape Cod to the lofty summits of the White Mountains, from the sweeping ridges of the Berkshires to Maine's rocky coastline, from the traprock cliffs of the Connecticut River valley to the lush forests of Vermont. Taking advantage of the patchwork of conserved lands protected over the past century, this book showcases the region's premier hiking destinations.

Arriving at these 115 day hikes in New England was a challenge—there are so many trails and destinations from which to choose. In addition to capturing the region's varied landscape, the final list includes hikes with diverse degrees of difficulty and multiple interesting features (natural and/or historic). When possible, it opts for trailheads that offer a multitude of options (from short half-day hikes to full-day adventures).

The final list of hikes, organized into seven regions based on geographic features and other considerations, was assembled in a way that complements the adventures outlined in *100 Classic Hikes: New England*, also published by Mountaineers Books. The two books include completely different destinations, although a few of the highest peaks are covered in both books but from different trailheads. Together, these two books capture more than 210 day hikes within New England, providing multiple suggested itineraries for every corner of the region.

New England is noteworthy for a number of reasons, not the least of which is the cycle of the seasons. Whether they are covered in snow, sprouting with wildflowers, buzzing with songbirds, or vibrant with foliage, adding these 115 hikes to your to-do list will undoubtedly lead you to discover what I did long ago: New England is a hiker's paradise that beckons the adventurer throughout the year.

HOW TO USE THIS GUIDE

This book is designed to introduce you to 115 of New England's best day hiking destinations. Extra care was used to choose those locations that not only exemplify the region's most scenic features but also offer you the greatest variety of trip choices. While each recommended hike includes a description of one specific itinerary, many of the hikes provide information on other optional excursions (of various lengths and difficulties) from the same trailhead or a nearby starting point. Each hike also lists its managing agency, and that agency's contact information is in Appendix I. Visit the websites listed there for more detailed maps and other information to plan future hikes. Rather than an end, use this book as an introduction to New England's most special places.

Each hike begins with an information block that rates the hike and provides helpful facts. Use this section as an initial step to decide whether the hike makes sense for you.

What the Ratings Mean

Every hike begins with **two ratings**. The first rating uses 1 to 5 stars to measure the

Chestnut-sided warbler

hike's overall appeal. The **appeal rating** is subjective, but as a general rule it is meant to capture the following experiences:

   ***** Unmatched hiking adventure, great scenic beauty, and wonderful trail experience

    **** Excellent experience, sure to please all

     *** A great hike, with one or more fabulous features to enjoy

      ** May lack a signature feature but offers lots of little moments to enjoy

       * Worth doing as a refreshing nature walk, especially if you are in the area

The second rating measures the hike's **degree of difficulty** and also uses a 1 to 5 scale. A hike's final number is based primarily on an evaluation of the following factors: length of hike, steepness of trail, exposure, and trail surface. In this book, here is what the difficulty ratings mean:

5 **Extremely difficult:** Excessive elevation gain, steep rough trails, and/or significant section of trail is above tree line

4 **Difficult:** Considerable elevation gain, some steep sections, rough surface in places, and/or more than 10 miles round-trip

3 **Moderate:** At least a 5-mile round-trip hike with some elevation gain and rough footing, but no major obstacles

2 **Moderately easy:** Minor ups and downs on an easy-to-follow trail

1 **Easy:** A relaxing walk in the woods

To provide more context for the difficulty ratings, the information block also contains **overall mileage**, as well as the hike's elevation gain and high point. The distances are not always exact mileages—the distances were not measured with calibrated instruments—but the mileages are those used by cartographers and land managers (who have measured many of the trails). Keep in mind, the **distance** refers to the length of the entire described hike and always includes information as to whether the journey is **round-trip** (using the same route both ways) or a **loop**. In other words, a hike that leads 2.3 miles to the final destination and then returns along the same 2.3 miles of trail will be listed as round-trip: 4.6 miles. If, on the other hand, the hike returns on a different trail or trails, it will be listed as loop: 4.6 miles.

The **elevation gain** included for a hike is an approximate calculation of the cumulative difference between low and high points on the hike—in other words, the total amount you will go up on a hike. It is worth noting that not all **high points** are at the end of the trail. For example, a coastal hike may begin a couple hundred feet above sea level and descend to the shore.

The recommended **season** listing is another subjective tool that is intended to be a guide—not an absolute. Anyone who has lived in New England knows that the weather can be quite unpredictable. The amount of snow and ice on a given trail or access road varies from year to year. In most cases, hikes that have trailheads accessible twelve months a year are listed as year-round destinations. However, some hikes with year-round-accessible trailheads are recommended only for times of the year when snow and/or ice are typically not a factor. This does not mean that these hikes are not possible with proper equipment and experience other times of the year.

With each hike you will find a **contact** and **notes**. The **contact** represents the landowner most responsible for the management of the trail or trails along the described route

(some hikes take place on lands owned and managed by more than one organization, individual, or governmental entity). Each contact's phone number and website are listed (alphabetically by agency name) in **Appendix I**. While the vast majority of land in New England is held privately, most of the hikes in this book occur exclusively on publicly owned and managed lands. However, the book also includes hikes accessible over private roads, hikes crossing sections of private land, and hikes on conservation land owned by nonprofit conservation organizations.

Each landowner and manager associated with hikes in this book has unique missions and regulations. Some of the more important of these are captured under **notes**. For your enjoyment, and to ensure that others that follow can enjoy these same special places, it is important to know and obey all regulations and to be especially considerate of private landowners. For the most up-to-date information on fees, trail conditions, camping requirements, and regulations, call the landowner or visit its website.

Every hike includes the names of the **USGS 7.5-minute topographic maps** that cover the area. It is important to note that in many cases the USGS topographic maps may be out of date in regard to trails, roads, and other manmade features; however, they provide a good illustration of the area's natural features. For additional mapping material, visit the website of or contact the landowner listed. For many of the hikes in this book, the landowner offers a useful complimentary map.

There are also **GPS coordinates** (using the WGS 84 datum) listed for every hike's trailhead or parking area. Use these coordinates to get to the trail and to help get back to your car if you wander off-trail.

Lastly, **icons** included for each hike offer a quick highlight of the trip's features. The following icons are used:

Kid-Friendly: Generally easy hikes that include natural features that should engage young naturalists or slightly more challenging trails with terrain enticing to older children.

Dog-Friendly: Dogs are not only allowed, but this hike will also be easy on their paws and not too popular with other hikers.

Beachcombing: Visits an ocean, either a sandy or rocky beach. Be sure to leave all living organisms for the health of our coastal ecosystems and for others to enjoy.

Wildflowers: Has especially abundant and diverse seasonal wildflowers.

Bird-Watching: Provides optimum locations for viewing birds and often the opportunity to spot a large diversity of species.

Waterfalls: Visits exceptional waterfalls or cascades.

Wetlands: Travels to significant lakes, ponds, or other freshwater habitats.

Geologic: Features impressive cliffs, ledges, large boulders, or other unique geologic features.

Historical: Travels through an area noted for its human history, often with evidence that is still on display.

Fire Lookout: Includes a fire tower with exceptional views.

WEATHER

New England's weather is as diverse as its seasons. While each season offers unique attractions, all four require different considerations.

Spring hiking: Spring hiking can be deceptively winterlike. Warm weather at lower elevations and in southern parts of New England does not mean spring has arrived everywhere. In fact, it is not unusual for snow and ice to be abundant throughout April and May (sometimes into June) in northern New England, especially at elevations over 3000 feet. Proper equipment like snowshoes, crampons, and warm clothing may be necessary additions to your backpack. When considering a spring hike, keep in mind that slopes melt faster, especially south-facing slopes, and that flat areas, particularly when shaded by evergreens, stay snowy longer.

While winterlike in some respects, spring can also be like summer. The sun's rays, for example, can burn as quickly in April as in August. Adding to the sunburn threat is the reflection of light off snow and the lack of leaves to provide shade. Be sure to add sunscreen to your pack by March. Insects are also a concern on spring hikes. The arrival of the swarming, biting, and eye-, mouth-, and ear-filling blackflies usually begins in late April in the most southern areas described in this book. By Memorial Day most places have ushered in their arrival. Although short-lived, the blackfly season can be frustrating. Spring also marks the start of prime tick season, and these blood-sucking parasites seem to be spreading farther north each year (see the Ticks and Insects section, later in this introduction, for additional information).

Finally, spring can also be very springlike, and nothing says spring more than water. A constant issue on many spring hikes is the number and size of water crossings. It is hard to hike in New England without encountering running water. To ensure that the worst-case scenario is only wet boots, it is essential to use caution at all stream crossings and be prepared to turn around if necessary. The increased water also creates muddy trails that lead to wet feet and increased erosion. To avoid mud, pick hikes in the southern and coastal areas earlier in the spring and slowly work your way north.

Summer hiking: Few things put a damper on a summer hike more than swarming insects. Clouds of mosquitoes lurking in shady, moist areas and deerflies circling on the hottest, most humid July days can be annoying and painful. To ease the situation, be prepared with effective bug repellent; avoid low, wet areas; and remind yourself that without the insects we would not be blessed with so many different and colorful songbirds.

Summer heat and humidity are other factors to consider. This combination, most common in July, quickly saps your energy. Try to start hikes early in the day and make sure to drink plenty of fluids. Heat and humidity may also trigger thunderstorms. Many of the hikes in this book describe trails with a lot of exposure. These are excellent hikes when the weather cooperates but potentially very dangerous when lightning is in the air. Storms most frequently hit later in the day but often come on suddenly. Be alert and seek cover quickly at the sound of thunder. Lastly, heat and humidity tend to mix with smog from the Midwest, diminishing views that can be far more impressive at other times of the year. If you are looking for the optimum summer day, wait for the day after a strong thunderstorm. Storms are often followed by cooler, cleaner air from Canada.

Autumn hiking: While autumn hiking can be very enjoyable, remember that the days shorten quickly. Conditions may tempt you for long adventures, but be prepared to finish before the sun sets. Unlike the summer, in autumn, once the sun goes down the temperatures quickly follow. In addition, it is not uncommon to experience winterlike conditions during the day, especially in northern New England. Be sure to have plenty of warm clothing, including a hat and gloves. The cool temperatures often make water crossings more difficult, too. When crossing rocks that look icy, step on sections slightly submerged by water rather than wet spots exposed to the open air.

A final consideration for the autumn is that while it is excellent for hiking, it is also prime hunting season throughout the

Hollingsworth Trail, Petit Manan Point

Winter snow blankets Middle Sister Trail.

region—for deer and a variety of other wildlife, each with different times when hunting is allowed. (Note: Not all hunting takes place in autumn; consult with the state's fish and wildlife agency for specific information on hunting laws, schedules, and regulations.) Many of the trails described in this book occur in areas open for hunting. Although it is quite uncommon to encounter hunters near many hiking trails, it is good policy to wear bright colors such as blaze orange (required in some places, as called out in a given trail's notes, as called out in a given trail's notes). To avoid hunters altogether, head for Connecticut, Massachusetts, or Maine on Sundays, when hunting is prohibited.

Winter hiking: Before you choose a winter hike, it is important to keep in mind that many trailheads are inaccessible from November to May. Before heading to a particular hike, make sure to check on the condition of the access road and be prepared to change plans.

The margin for error in winter hiking is slim. It is prudent to carry more than what you think you will need: clothes, water, and food. It is especially helpful to have dry clothes in case you get wet. In winter, the sun sets around 4:00 to 4:30 PM in January and then slowly grows later and later. On cloudy days or on northern, forested slopes, it can get darker even earlier.

Finally, always bring and expect to use snowshoes. Surprisingly, many hikers shy away from using snowshoes and focus more on ice axes and crampons. While ice axes and crampons are essential in certain circumstances, they are needed infrequently, even while climbing 4000-footers. On the contrary, snowshoes are required on the vast majority of winter hikes. When choosing snowshoes, opt for narrow, oval-shaped ones with metal grips below. This design will allow maximum control and maneuverability, particularly in mountainous terrain.

OUTDOOR ETIQUETTE

With more folks enjoying hiking and backpacking each year, the need for outdoor ethics has never been greater. Few things on a hike are more frustrating, for example, than encountering improper or inconsiderate campers. It is amazing how often tents are perched on the banks of a stream or right off a trail. Similarly, watching a mountainside erode due to hikers taking shortcuts, or having a peaceful day in the woods interrupted by a loud group of people inconsiderate to the enjoyment of others, can leave a sour taste after an otherwise glorious day in the outdoors. In some cases these types of activities violate the rules that govern a particular area; more important, these activities diminish the experiences of other hikers.

To ensure that we all can enjoy the same opportunity to renew our spirits in the wilds of New England, each of us must commit to basic outdoor ethical principles. The Leave No Trace Center for Outdoor Ethics, a national nonprofit organization dedicated to promoting and inspiring responsible outdoor recreation through education, research, and partnerships, has developed seven simple principles all hikers should follow. They are:

Plan ahead and prepare: This includes knowing applicable regulations and special concerns for each area visited; being prepared for extreme weather, hazards, and emergencies; scheduling trips to avoid times of high use; and understanding how to use a map, guidebook, and compass.

Travel and camp on durable surfaces: This means using established trails and campsites, rock, gravel, dry grasses, or snow. Remember that good campsites are found, not made, and should never be located closer than 200 feet from wetlands. Also, walking single file in the middle of the trail, even when it is wet or muddy, minimizes erosion. Remaining on the trail is especially important for the high-elevation hikes described in this book that use trails surrounded by fragile vegetation.

Dispose of waste properly: We should all follow the basic rule of waste disposal: pack it in and pack it out. When depositing solid human waste, dig a small hole 6 to 8 inches deep at least 200 feet from water, camp, and trails. Cover and disguise the hole when finished. Avoid washing yourself or your dishes within 200 feet of streams or lakes and use small amounts of biodegradable soap.

Leave what you find: You are not the first to visit any of these places and likely will not be the last. Preserve the experience for others who follow: examine, but do not touch cultural or historic structures and artifacts; leave rocks, plants, and other natural objects as you find them; avoid introducing or transporting nonnative species; and do not dig trenches or build structures or furniture.

Minimize campfire impacts: Lightweight stoves and candle lanterns have less of an impact than campfires. Where fires are permitted, use established fire rings, fire pans, or mound fires and keep fires small. Only use sticks from the ground that can be broken by hand. When done, burn all wood to ash and then scatter cool ashes. Put campfires out completely.

Respect wildlife: Wildlife is best observed from a distance and should never be fed. Feeding animals damages their health, alters natural behaviors, and exposes them to predators and other dangers. Protect wildlife and your food by storing rations and trash securely. Control pets at all times or leave them at home.

Be considerate of other visitors: Respect other visitors and protect the quality of their experience. Be courteous and yield to other users on the trail. Let nature's sounds prevail—avoid loud voices and noises.

SAFETY

Staying safe on the trail is a matter of preparation and some luck. Keep all the following in mind before you set out.

Lightning: Lightning storms are a common occurrence throughout New England. While most electrical storms occur from May to August, thunderstorms are possible any time of the year. Since many of the hikes described in this book occur on exposed ridges and along other high locations, the threat of being struck by lightning should not be underestimated.

To minimize your risk of being injured or killed by lightning, you should take a number of precautions. First, be aware of the day's weather forecast and avoid hikes with a lot of exposure when the threat of thunderstorms is great. Second, pay attention to the sky and do your best to avoid being caught on exposed ridges, in open areas, or above tree line. Third, if a storm hits, it is wise for your group to spread out so if one person is struck, others can help. Lastly, if you don't have time to get to a lower elevation or out of an open area, squat down to reduce your height, minimize your contact with the earth (only your feet should touch the ground), and avoid metal objects.

Hypothermia: Hypothermia is literally the lowering of your body's core temperature. While most often a threat during colder

months, hypothermia can strike any time of the year. To protect yourself or a fellow hiker from succumbing to hypothermia, it is important to understand the early warning signs, which include poor judgment, a slight sensation of chilliness, and trouble using your hands for simple tasks. Should these early signs go unnoticed or unaddressed, hypothermia can lead to more serious conditions such as uncontrolled shivering, unconsciousness, and even death.

The best way to prevent hypothermia is to wear clothes that keep you warm even when they are wet and to dress in layers. Be sure to wear good wind and rain gear, because your body loses heat three times as fast when it's wet. Finally, it is important to eat and drink properly. Even when the temperature is cold, drinking plenty of water is critical to your health. Avoid alcohol and caffeine, because both can contribute to hypothermia. When eating, opt for many small meals.

Weather above tree line: When you choose a hike that climbs above tree line, weather should be of increased concern. The weather here can be ferocious and, in most cases, there is no safe shelter once you are above tree line. Pay attention not only to the existing conditions but also to the afternoon forecast for that day and any incoming systems noted on the weather report. Remember that weather conditions in the lowlands are not reflective of conditions above tree line. Expect a minimum drop in air temperature of three degrees Fahrenheit for every 1000 feet in elevation gain, combined with the wind chill from increased velocity as you climb. Plan for the best possibilities, but be prepared to change plans to accommodate weather conditions. Do not try to outsmart the weather or push hesitant members of your party if conditions are not ideal.

Bigelow Mountain's Avery Peak and Flagstaff Lake

The mountain will be there another day, and hopefully you will get a chance to try again; this decision will be made all the sweeter by the fact that you have exercised discipline and respect for the elements.

Water: Unless faced with extreme dehydration, you should treat any water before drinking it. In fact, the cleanest mountain streams could be home to microscopic viruses and bacteria, such as giardia, that can wreak havoc with your digestive system. Treating water can be as simple as boiling it, chemically purifying it with iodine tablets, or pumping it through one of the many commercially available water filter and purifier systems. Drinking untreated water is a mistake you will remember for a long time and one that will provide you ample time to sit down to think about your poor decision.

Wildlife: New England is not known as a hiking destination fraught with dangerous wildlife encounters. However, there are a few animal species that can potentially be problematic. Male moose during the fall rutting season and female moose with young can be aggressive if their space is violated. Since they typically do not go looking for trouble, you should remain safe if you are not overly enthusiastic about getting their photo. Similarly, black bear sows with their young are another situation of possible concern; however, more often than not they sense your presence first and are long gone before you arrive. Lastly, some of the southern hikes in this book occur in rattlesnake country. Pay attention to where you step and place your hands. If bitten, you should seek immediate medical attention.

In the end, you should not let your fear of wildlife deter you from a hiking adventure. Use common sense with all animals (view from a distance, do not feed them, and

Spring peeper

respect their space), and you will likely avoid threatening encounters. In fact, the animal you are most apt to be threatened by on a hike will be an unleashed dog, and that can just as easily occur on a walk around your neighborhood.

Ticks and insects: While many people tend to fear an attack from a larger animal, the animals most likely to injure you on a hike are among the smallest ones you will encounter. The most common antagonists are blackflies, mosquitoes, deerflies, ticks, and yellow jackets. Since their presence varies depending on the region, the time of year, and the current conditions, you will not encounter each of these on every New

England hike during the year's warmer months. Still, it is likely you will encounter at least one of them if you go for a hike between April and October.

Frequently, encounters with these critters are manageable with little effort. However, if their numbers are high, you suffer allergic reactions to any of them, or your tolerance is low, consider using insect repellents, hats, long pants, or commercially available gear to help ease the annoyance, threat, and pain inflicted by them. To avoid picking up ticks, which carry Lyme and other diseases, it is helpful to tuck clothes in and wear light colors. In addition, after every hike, you should do a thorough scan of your body to ensure no ticks are present and use fine-tipped tweezers to quickly and thoroughly remove any ticks you find.

Getting lost and found: While the hikes described in this book are located on well-developed trails in areas frequently used by hikers, the possibility of being lost, injured, or stranded after dark is something to consider. The best advice is that you should not rely on technology to save you. For example, cell phones cannot receive signals in many regions covered in this book, and even if they did, their batteries may run out of juice. If you find yourself lost or injured, it is much safer to rely on basic outdoor skills, preparedness, common sense, and a few simple rules: it is always safer to hike with companions; if you choose to hike alone, be sure to let someone else know of your plans; study the area you are visiting beforehand to have a better understanding of the topography; keep all hiking groups together; and always carry and know how to use the Ten Essentials (see the following section).

Staying on the trail: Most of the trails in this book are well signed and clearly marked. Typically, forested sections of trails are blazed to lead the way. Most often the blazes are small rectangular shapes painted on trees at regular intervals. Different landowners use different techniques and colors. Sometimes all trails within a specific park or preserve use the same color, while other times each trail has its own unique color. When you encounter two blazes on a tree, be alert for an upcoming intersection or abrupt change in the path's direction. When trees are not plentiful, the trail blazes may be painted on the ground. Often, cairns are also built in these areas. Cairns are small piles of rocks placed to assist navigation. The trail descriptions in this book provide more specific information to help you stay on the trail for each hike.

BEFORE YOU GO

Before you hit the trails, it is prudent to be prepared with proper gear. While it is often tempting to head up the trail with less, you never know what may occur: injury, change of weather, illness, etc. The bottom line for any hike is to bring more than you think you will need; the worst that could happen may be building stronger back and shoulder muscles. For any hike, it is wise to pack the Ten Essentials, developed by The Mountaineers:

1. **Insulation (extra clothing):** Even on the hottest summer days, at a minimum you should carry a rain jacket and another water-resistant layer of clothing. During colder times of year or while venturing above tree line, lots of additional layers are a must, including warm hats and gloves. The highest locations described in this book can experience wintry conditions throughout the year.

2. **Nutrition (extra food):** Hiking is a strenuous activity that burns calories quickly. Fill your pack with high-energy food and more than you expect to eat.

3. **Hydration:** Begin each hike with at least two quarts of water per person, even during colder months. Few things put more of a damper on an otherwise enjoyable hike than headaches resulting from dehydration.

4. **Sun protection (sunglasses and sunscreen):** Sun protection is a must throughout the year. In fact, the low angle of the sun and the reflection off snow and ice can make sunglasses very important during colder months. Sunscreen is also necessary, especially from March to October. Late winter through mid-spring can be your most vulnerable time of the year, when the sun is strong and bare trees provide little protection.

5. **Tools and repair kit:** A knife or multi-tool with pliers is a handy device to carry. While neither may be necessary 99 percent of the time, the one time that either is needed you will be happy to have brought it along.

6. **First-aid kit:** Cuts, stings, twisted ankles, and other ailments are distinct possibilities even for the most prepared hiker. Bandages, pain relievers, and ointments can help significantly alleviate many injuries in a pinch. Knowledge of first-aid procedure can also help instruct you how to react in certain emergency situations to ensure an injured party receives the necessary help.

7. **Fire starter or matches in a waterproof container:** Having something that will catch fire, even when sticks and brush are wet, can be a huge help in an emergency such as an unplanned night in the woods. Like a fire starter,

dry matches can make a big difference in an emergency situation.

8. **Emergency shelter:** A space blanket or bivy can make a comfortable shelter if you unexpectedly find yourself outside overnight.

9. **Illumination (flashlight or headlamp):** If you are forced to spend the night outdoors or are still on the trail after sunset, artificial light can be a big help in returning to the trailhead safely.

10. **Navigation (map and compass):** Having a map of the area and knowing how to read it provides options in the case of emergency. For example, often there are multiple trails in an area that provide shorter or easier alternatives. Know where you are and how to most quickly get to safety in an emergency. While the trails in this book are generally well marked and easy to follow, harsh weather and snow can sometimes obscure the way. If for some reason you lose your way, a compass can be a valuable tool to help you safely return home.

In addition to these ten items, there are other gear considerations. Many of the hikes in this book and throughout the region take place on rocky terrain. To provide optimum comfort and effectiveness, choose sturdy boots with good ankle protection. It also may be desirable to seal the boots with waterproof material. There are a number of commercially available products that will cause water to bead up and run off boots, leaving your feet dry. Gaiters that wrap around your lower leg are also handy for keeping water and debris out of your boots. When choosing socks, avoid cotton, because it is not the best material to wear when wet.

Carrying a camera and binoculars can add a lot of enjoyment to a hiking adventure. Similarly, bringing books that help in the identification of birds, wildlife, trees, mushrooms, and wildflowers can add many new dimensions to a hiking adventure.

A NOTE ABOUT SAFETY

Safety is an important concern in all outdoor activities. No guidebook can alert you to every hazard or anticipate the limitations of every reader. Therefore, the descriptions of roads, trails, routes, and natural features in this book are not representations that a particular place or excursion will be safe for your party. When you follow any of the routes described in this book, you assume responsibility for your own safety. Under normal conditions, such excursions require the usual attention to traffic, road and trail conditions, weather, terrain, the capabilities of your party, and other factors. Keeping informed on current conditions and exercising common sense are the keys to a safe, enjoyable outing.

—*Mountaineers Books*

Pine Acres Pond (Hike 11), James L. Goodwin State Forest

southeastern new england

This most populated area of New England extends from Cape Cod west across gently rolling terrain, north into southern New Hampshire, and south to Long Island Sound. Scattered throughout the densely populated landscape are countless pockets of conservation treasures that highlight the region's sandy coastline, centuries-old history, lush pine-oak forests, and quirky geologic remnants.

Southeastern New England's predominantly easy-to-moderate hikes are ideal for family excursions, bird-watching enthusiasts, picnicking, and seascape photography.

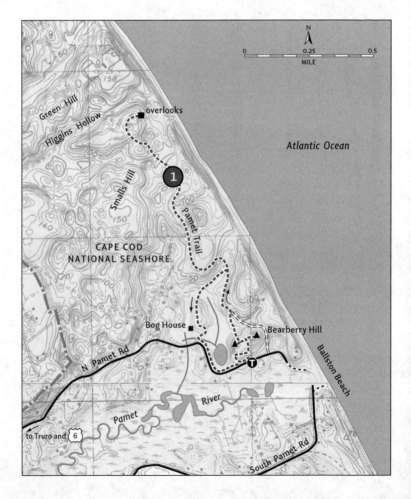

While beautiful and accessible throughout the year, many of this region's hikes are more enjoyable from October to May when crowds, heat, and traffic are less overwhelming.

1 Pamet Trail

RATING/ DIFFICULTY	LOOP	ELEV GAIN/ HIGH POINT	SEASON
**/1–2	3.3 miles	270 feet/ 140 feet	Year-round

Map: USGS North Truro; **Contact:** Cape Cod National Seashore; **Note:** Dogs prohibited; **GPS:** 42.001381, -70.025621

The Cape Cod National Seashore is famous for its incredible sand beaches, but it is also home to a collection of family-friendly trails that explore the region's human history and showcase its abundant natural beauty. Visit the Pamet Trail in Truro for exceptional views of towering sand dunes and enjoy one of the quieter corners of Massachusetts's most famous peninsula.

Hiking along the Old Kings Highway

GETTING THERE

From points south, follow US Route 6 north into Truro and take the Pamet Road exit. Turn left off the exit onto North Pamet Road. Drive 1.5 miles to parking area on right.

ON THE TRAIL

Hike across North Pamet Road. The path heads west very briefly before swinging east and rising 0.2 mile into the saddle between Bearberry Hill's two open summits. Follow the 0.1-mile spur that departs right to the eastern summit. The trail ascends through an open meadow to a wooden platform surrounded by breathtaking shots of the surrounding coastal landscape. Return to the main trail and keep right. A side trail almost immediately leaves left and in a few hundred feet ends atop the hill's western summit. Here, enjoy scenes across the cranberry bog below.

The Pamet Trail descends Bearberry Hill rapidly to the north. In 0.1 mile, level off and then swing sharply left onto the remains of the Old Kings Highway, a major transportation corridor developed in the eighteenth century that connected Provincetown to other parts of the Massachusetts Colony. Proceed 0.2 mile to a well-marked junction where a sandy path leaves on your left for the Bog House. For now, continue straight.

To the right, just beyond the signed junction, arrive at an unmarked intersection. Leaving right, a well-used but unofficial path winds over the dunes to the sandy beach. Stay left on the Pamet Trail. The route ascends in the open at first with pleasant views. Quickly enter a shady pine forest. Across the gently rolling terrain, the path soon tunnels through an area of stunted oak trees. Ahead, the vegetation grows taller. Turn sharply right for the final leg, which culminates at a cul-de-sac.

Two benches at the trail's end offer a modest view south. To the northeast, a slightly overgrown path descends a few dozen feet to a second, slightly more impressive, overlook. While the views from Bearberry Hill are far more stunning, the trek to the overlooks is worth the effort for those interested in more hidden natural beauty.

To complete the hike, follow the main trail 0.9 mile back to the Bog House path. Turn right and hike 0.4 mile up and over a small knoll to the historic colonial structure. Check out the display that sheds light on the history of the region's important cranberry crop. The now-grassy path continues past the house and ends at North Pamet Road. Bear left and follow the pavement 0.3 mile back to the trailhead.

EXTENDING YOUR HIKE

There are many nature trails within the Cape Cod National Seashore that would make perfect additions to this hike. The 1-mile Beech Forest Trail in Provincetown and the 1.2-mile Atlantic White Cedar Swamp Trail in Wellfleet are two nearby ones to consider.

2 Sandy Neck

RATING/ DIFFICULTY	LOOP	ELEV GAIN/ HIGH POINT	SEASON
*/2–3	4.3 miles	50 feet/ 30 feet	Jan–May, Sept–Dec

Map: USGS Sandwich; **Contact:** Sandy Neck Beach Park; **Notes:** Fee charged from May to September, parking lot closes when filled to capacity, dogs prohibited May to September; **GPS:** 41.7384 92, -70.381271

Located on Cape Cod Bay's south shore, Sandy Neck is a 6.5-mile barrier beach that includes more than 4700 acres of dunes, maritime forests, and salt marsh. The bulk

Marsh Trail

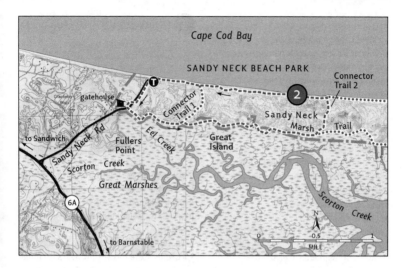

of Sandy Neck is owned and managed by
the town of Barnstable. This is a popular
destination for swimming between Memorial Day and Labor Day, but venture here in
the off-season to enjoy challenging trails,
wildlife-rich coastal habitats, and classic
Cape Cod scenery.

GETTING THERE

From its junction with Route 6A in Sandwich,
follow Sandy Neck Road northeast 0.9 mile
to the Sandy Neck Beach Gatehouse. Continue 0.3 mile to the parking area.

ON THE TRAIL

Near the parking area entrance, find the
paved pathway that leads south toward the
gatehouse. It parallels the roadway 0.3 mile
to the start of the Marsh Trail. Carefully cross
the roadway twice to reach the trailhead.

The 5-mile, aptly named Marsh Trail
hugs an expansive coastal wetland. While
fairly flat much of its way, the route can be

surprisingly challenging. Stretches of soft,
sandy soil can be difficult to plod through.
In spots, the wet marsh also encroaches on
the trail. Lastly, there is little protection from
the elements. While these factors deserve
consideration, they are overshadowed
by the scenic beauty and wildlife viewing
opportunities that abound.

For today's adventure, follow the Marsh
Trail east 2 miles. Easy at first, the footing
is rough near the midway point as shifting
dunes cover the route. The final stretch
is a bit more inviting. In a few spots, the
route traverses privately owned land.
Please stay on the trail and respect the
owners' privacy.

Upon reaching Connector Trail 2, veer
left and hike 0.3 mile up and over the sand
dunes. The path quickly ends at the edge of
Cape Cod Bay. To the right, the sandy shore
continues more than 3 miles. Complete the
loop by turning left and hiking 1.6 miles back
to the parking lot.

The beach is accessible to motor vehicles with appropriate stickers. While not the ideal backdrop for a nature walk, their presence does not overly detract from the experience. Time your hike to coincide with lower tides. This will allow for better footing as well as more space between the beach road and the shore. Along the way be alert for piping plovers and other shorebirds in the sand. In addition, scan the rolling waves for geese, ducks, and grebes feeding offshore. Staircases lead from the beach back to the parking area.

OTHER OPTIONS

Complete a much shorter 1.2-mile hike by using Connector Trail 1, which branches north from the Marsh Trail 0.6 mile east of the gatehouse. Alternatively, extend your hike nearly 4 miles round-trip by remaining on the Marsh Trail as far as Connector Trail 4 (there is not a Connector Trail 3).

3 Myles Standish State Forest

RATING/ DIFFICULTY	LOOP	ELEV GAIN/ HIGH POINT	SEASON
**/2	3.9 miles	250 feet/ 180 feet	Year-round

Map: USGS Wareham; **Contact:** Massachusetts Department of Conservation and Recreation; **GPS:** 41.858272, -70.662903

Myles Standish was one of the original settlers of nearby Plymouth, and he left a lasting mark on the colonial history of the nation. The largest publicly owned conservation area in southeastern Massachusetts, the sprawling state forest that bears his name preserves some of what his fellow pilgrims encountered four centuries ago: acres of pitch pine and scrub oak forests dotted with kettle ponds and abundant wildlife.

Round Pond's reflective waters

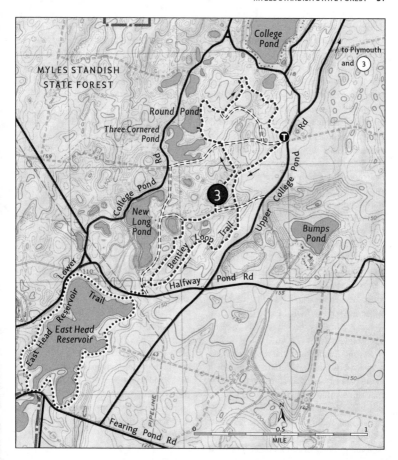

GETTING THERE

Follow Route 3 south from Plymouth and take exit 3. Stay right and in 0.2 mile turn right onto Long Pond Road. Drive 2 miles and then veer left onto Alden Road. In 1.8 miles, turn left onto Upper College Pond Road. Drive 1 mile to Parking Lot 2 on the right.

ON THE TRAIL

Join the Bentley Loop Trail at a large kiosk in the northwest corner of the parking lot. The blue blazes quickly lead left onto a wider corridor and wind 1.4 miles to the southern tip of the loop. En route, the well-marked trail traverses open meadows, weaves through dense pine forests, and passes small wetlands. The trail is mostly level throughout, but there is one minor climb up and over a low ridge.

As the loop begins to swing north, arrive at a junction where a path provides access to the scenic East Head Reservoir Trail. Bear right and remain on the Bentley Loop Trail. In 0.4 mile, approach a secluded pond on the left and then descend quickly to a junction with a dirt road. Turn sharply right and follow this road 0.2 mile. At a signed intersection, bear left into the thick evergreen forest. While being serenaded by a chorus of pine warblers and other resident songbirds, make your way 0.5 mile over the rolling landscape to a junction with another dirt road.

The Bentley Loop Trail crosses the dirt road by veering slightly left. Descend 0.1 mile toward the shore of Three Cornered Pond. The main trail continues right. In 0.1 mile, arrive at an unmarked spur that descends left to the edge of Round Pond. This circular wetland affords excellent wildlife viewing opportunities.

Beyond Round Pond, the route continues a little more than 1 mile before concluding at the parking area. Pay close attention. The trail turns often and passes a handful of side trails. Fortunately, there are ample blue blazes and well-positioned signs to assist navigation. Enjoy the journey as the path pleasantly meanders around the edges of fields, past vernal pools, and over an undulating landscape.

EXTENDING YOUR HIKE

Consider adding the loop around East Head Reservoir to complete a 6.8-mile hike. From the Bentley Loop's southern tip, turn left onto the unnamed path and then left onto a woods road. In 0.1 mile, turn right onto Halfway Pond Road and follow the pavement 0.1 mile to the bottom of the hill. Turn left and cross the road to immediately intersect the East Head Reservoir Trail. Complete the 2.5-mile circuit in either direction. You will encounter numerous intimate views of the large pond along the way.

4 Weetamoo Woods

RATING/ DIFFICULTY	LOOP	ELEV GAIN/ HIGH POINT	SEASON
***/3	5.6 miles	300 feet/ 155 feet	Year-round

Map: USGS Tiverton; **Contact:** Tiverton Land Trust; **GPS:** 41.572320, -71.177298

Weetamoo Woods and the adjacent Pardon Gray Preserve combine to form an 880-acre oasis of forest, fields, and wetlands in the southeast corner of Rhode Island. The area, named in honor of the last sachem of the Pocasset Tribe of Wampanoag Indians, is crisscrossed with hiking trails that pass steep ledges, towering hardwood trees, bubbling brooks, and historic stone structures. This family-friendly hike forms two loops while visiting the area's most alluring natural and historic features.

GETTING THERE

From the junction of Routes 179 and 77 at Tiverton Four Corners, drive east 0.5 mile on Route 179 (East Road). Turn left into parking area.

ON THE TRAIL

Follow the wide path north 0.1 mile through an open meadow to a large kiosk. Turn right and join the Orange Trail for nearly 1 mile.

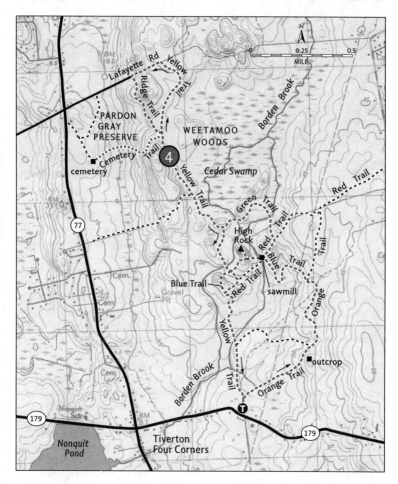

Once you are across a gas-line corridor, the route swings north and passes an impressive rock outcrop on the right. After crossing a small tributary of Borden Brook, arrive at a three-way junction.

Veer left onto the Blue Trail and immediately recross the energy corridor. The 0.4-mile path narrows as it slithers through the shady forest. The footing is a bit rocky at first, but it eases as the route bends sharply right. Reach a four-way intersection where Borden Brook tumbles through the granite remnants of a nineteenth-century sawmill.

Remain on the east side of the brook and follow the Red Trail as it heads upstream 0.2 mile to a junction. Bear left onto the

Scenic meadow along the Yellow Trail

0.5-mile Green Trail. Meandering over the rolling terrain, the path tunnels through thick canopies of mountain laurel and crosses two branches of Borden Brook. The second crossing of the slow-moving water may result in wet feet.

At a three-way intersection, continue straight on the Yellow Trail. This route, which travels the entire length of the Weetamoo Woods property from south to north, is the remains of Eight Rod Way. This and similar roads were designed throughout colonial New England as important transportation corridors. While eight-rod ways were originally 132 feet wide, this one is much narrower today.

The easy-to-follow trail swings north and parallels stone walls and low rocky ridges throughout. In 0.5 mile, arrive at the second of two trail intersections, where the Cemetery Trail diverges left. This junction marks the beginning of a small loop along the day's journey. Remain right on the Yellow Trail 0.5 mile farther, until it ends at the property's northern boundary.

Turn sharply left onto Lafayette Road. Avoid the private property on the right and hike 0.2 mile downhill to a gate. To the left,

find the Tiverton Land Trust's Pardon Gray Preserve. This 230-acre conservation area honors a Revolutionary War hero whose family owned the property for years. From the parking area, pick up the Ridge Trail. It leads 0.4 mile through the young forest to a junction with the Cemetery Trail, a path that gently descends west (right) 0.6 mile to a large field and Pardon Gray's final resting place—a worthwhile extension to the described hike.

Bear left at the junction to return to the Yellow Trail in a few dozen feet and then swing right to retrace your steps 0.5 mile back to the Green Trail junction. Remain on the Yellow Trail as it bends right and winds 0.3 mile to a four-way intersection. Follow the Blue Trail left 0.2 mile into a saddle. Here an unmarked but well-used route rises steeply 0.1 mile to the top of High Rock and serene views of the surrounding landscape.

Return to the Yellow Trail and turn left to complete the final 0.7-mile leg of the journey. After winding around an old cellar hole, the trail straightens and widens significantly. Cross Borden Brook, pass a larger picturesque meadow on the left, and then continue straight to reach the trailhead.

5 Trustom Pond

RATING/ DIFFICULTY	LOOP	ELEV GAIN/ HIGH POINT	SEASON
***/1	2.4 miles	50 feet/ 20 feet	Year-round

Map: USGS Kingston; **Contact:** Rhode Island National Wildlife Refuge; **Note:** Dogs prohibited; **GPS:** 41.383411, -71.585396

Trustom Pond National Wildlife Refuge showcases 787 acres of fields, shrubs, dunes, and forests, as well as Rhode Island's only undeveloped coastal salt pond, a wide expanse that is home to countless species of wading birds and waterfowl. The refuge's gentle terrain and wide paths are suitable for hikers of all ages and invite year-round exploration.

GETTING THERE

From US Route 1 in South Kingston, take the Moonstone Beach Road exit. Drive 1.1 miles south on Moonstone Beach Road and turn right onto Matunuck Schoolhouse Road. Continue 0.6 mile to the parking area on the left.

ON THE TRAIL

In the parking area, check out the small plaque commemorating Anne Kenyon Morse's 1974 donation of the refuge's initial 365 acres. Continue to the small visitor center, where you can find information on the refuge, including recent bird sightings. Join the wide path that leads quickly to the edge of a large field and a three-way intersection. In the 1990s, refuge staff reintroduced native warm-season grasses here, greatly benefiting nesting and migratory birds.

Turn right onto the Farm Field Loop Trail and continue 0.1 mile to another

A bench at Osprey Point affords views of Trustom Pond.

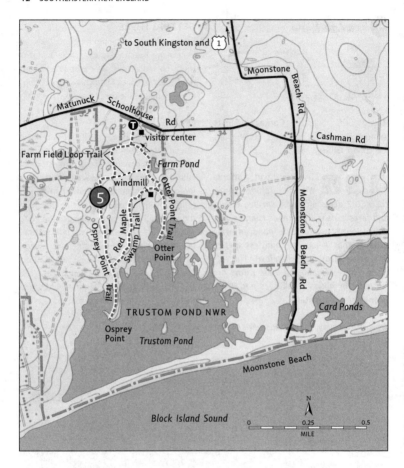

to South Kingston and 1

Moonstone Beach Rd

Matunuck Schoolhouse Rd

Cashman Rd

visitor center

Farm Field Loop Trail

Farm Pond

windmill

Otter Point Trail

Moonstone Beach Rd

5

Osprey Point Trail

Red Maple Swamp Trail

Otter Point

Card Ponds

TRUSTOM POND NWR

Osprey Point

Trustom Pond

Moonstone Beach

Block Island Sound

N

0   0.25   0.5
MILE

intersection. Stay right, once again, and follow the 0.8-mile Osprey Point Trail as it enters the forest and meanders easily past large oak trees and stone walls. At a junction with the Red Maple Swamp Trail, continue straight.

Hike 0.2 mile to the tip of Osprey Point, a narrow peninsula that offers many views of Trustom Pond. From an elevated platform at the trail's end, the sand dunes of Moonstone Beach and the surf of Block Island Sound can be seen in the distance. Trustom Pond, typically isolated from the ocean, can become tidal when the dunes are breached, which occurred most recently in 2012 when Hurricane Sandy pummeled Rhode Island. Whether directly connected to the ocean or not, the sprawling wetland is a great location to spot any number of the 300 bird species that have been observed at the refuge.

Return to and then join the 0.6-mile Red Maple Swamp Trail. As you slowly leave the water's edge, continue through a forest of broken tree limbs and other evidence of recent storms. Swing right along the edge of a field. After passing a small windmill, reach a junction with the Otter Point Trail.

The Otter Point Trail leads right 0.3 mile to a viewing platform near the tip of the scenic peninsula—a great spot to scan the sky and nearby treetops for resident osprey. This impressive black and white bird of prey hovers high above the water before diving in search of an unsuspecting fish below. Conclude the refuge tour by returning north to Farm Pond. Beyond this small freshwater pond, follow the Farm Field Loop Trail north 0.2 mile as it traverses a grassland en route to the trailhead.

6 Great Swamp

RATING/ DIFFICULTY	LOOP	ELEV GAIN/ HIGH POINT	SEASON
**/2	5.1 miles	200 feet/ 180 feet	Year-round

Map: USGS Kingston; **Contact:** Rhode Island Department of Environmental Management; **Notes:** Hunting is allowed in season. There are specific blaze-orange requirements; **GPS:** 41.468887, -71.579670

In December of 1675, a blizzard enveloped the Great Swamp, making vulnerable a Narragansett settlement soon destroyed in one of the bloodiest battles in King Philip's War. Today, this historic site is home to a 3349-acre state wildlife management area that lures those seeking more peaceful pursuits, such as a pleasant hike to forest, fields, and wetlands where wildlife and natural beauty abound.

GETTING THERE
From Route 138 in the village of West Kingston, 0.1 mile west of the junction with Route 110, follow Liberty Lane west 0.8 mile. Veer left onto Great Neck Road's dirt surface and drive 1 mile to the trailhead and large parking lot, 0.4 mile past the management area's headquarters.

ON THE TRAIL
Beyond the gate, follow the gravel path. It remains dry while winding through a swampy landscape. Reach the start of the day's loop in 0.3 mile, at an intersection where a granite post commemorates the Dr. John J. Mulleedy Memorial Trails.

Follow the trail left as it leads through a young forest lined with stone walls. Notice the numerous American holly trees; the spikes of their shiny green leaves are hard to miss and their red berries are desired by robins and other songbirds. The route briefly crosses under utility lines and then past an open area on the right, the site of a recent timber harvest. This habitat may not seem attractive, but it is prime real estate for resident American woodcock.

At a granite post marking the George F. McCahey Memorial Trails, 1.2 miles from the trailhead, follow the path left. Head up the small rise and in 0.1 mile arrive at an unmarked intersection where a difficult-to-follow route descends left toward Stony Point. Continue right on the main trail. At the next unmarked junction in 0.1 mile, bear left and climb gently to a prominent ledge

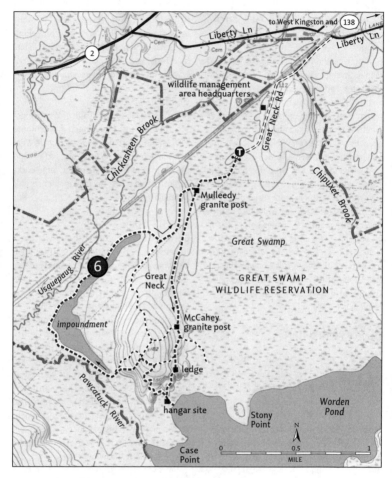

surrounded by towering oaks. From here, the trail descends steadily 0.2 mile to the site of an old hangar. To the left, follow a spur a few hundred feet to Worden Pond's scenic shore.

Rejoin the trail and turn left. The route leads west from the hangar site. While the tread may be wet at first, drier ground awaits as you rise easily across the rock-covered terrain. Approach the high point of Great Neck in 0.4 mile. After passing a series of small fields, the main trail turns sharply right. Stay left here and hike through a large meadow. Follow the grassy path 0.1 mile until it ends at a wider gravel trail.

Wildlife abounds in the Great Swamp's wetlands.

Turn left and head 0.2 mile south down the forested slope. As the incline eases, reach a large manmade impoundment area where a rock seat offers a good vantage point to scan for the abundant ducks and geese that thrive here. For the next 1.5 miles, traverse the large dike as it parallels the narrow water body on the right as well as the impenetrable Great Swamp to the west. Look for nesting osprey, sunning turtles, and the rhythmic flight of belted kingfishers.

Upon reaching the northern tip of the impoundment, follow the main route 0.1 mile to an intersection. Complete the loop by turning left and hiking 0.5 mile under utility lines and past additional fields. At the Mulleedy granite post, bear left and hike back to the parking area.

7 Rome Point

RATING/ DIFFICULTY	LOOP	ELEV GAIN/ HIGH POINT	SEASON
*/1	2.6 miles	100 feet/ 60 feet	Year-round

Map: USGS Wickford; **Contact:** Rhode Island Department of Environmental Management; **Note:** The property has a number of unmarked paths, but it is difficult to get lost; **GPS:** 41.536967, -71.437197

Once a potential nuclear power plant site, the John H. Chafee Nature Preserve at Rome Point was donated to the state of Rhode Island in 2001. Named to honor a former governor and US senator with a passion for land conservation, the preserve offers gentle trails, pleasing views of Narragansett Bay, and the opportunity to observe dozens of wintering harbor seals.

GETTING THERE

Follow Route 1A 2.4 miles south from its intersection with Route 102 in Wickford. Turn left into the large parking area located on the east side of the road.

ON THE TRAIL

The Rome Point Trail descends briefly from the parking area and quickly straightens.

Follow the wide path as it easily ascends a small incline. At 0.4 mile, reach a four-way intersection with a yellow-blazed trail that forms a 1-mile loop in the preserve. The circuit's 0.4-mile southern half leads right, winds up a small hill, and ends just beyond a decorative fireplace. Slightly longer, the 0.6-mile northern half departs left, visits a small holly tree, and swings past an impressive rock ledge. Either serves as an alternative route and both reintersect with the more straightforward Rome Point Trail 0.2 mile ahead.

Beyond the second intersection with the yellow-blazed loop, continue straight on the Rome Point Trail. In 0.1 mile, reach the sandy banks of Narragansett Bay. The towering span of the Jamestown Bridge rises to the right. To the left, Rome Point is visible for the first time. Named for a merchant and British

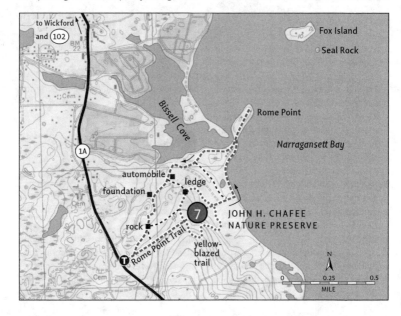

All shores lead to Rome Point.

sympathizer who owned a nearby summer-time retreat in the years leading up to the American Revolution, the rocky promontory is now only 0.5 mile away.

Turn left and head north along the beach. Soon, the shoreline curls right toward the narrowing point and the terrain becomes rockier. Leave the beach and find the well-trodden path on the center of the peninsula. Continue right 0.2 mile to the end of the point. This is the best location for viewing the harbor seals, typically resident from November to April, who tend to bask during lower tides when a number of rocks and other haulout sites are exposed. Take photos and bring binoculars, but be sure to minimize disturbance. These large mammals are easily spooked.

Retrace your steps along the peninsula, and remain on the path that hugs the shore of Bissell Cove. The route eventually leaves the water's edge. In 0.5 mile from Rome Point, the trail briefly follows a former rail bed to the right and then swings left to an abandoned automobile. Here an unmarked path veers left and connects to the yellow-blazed loop. Continue straight and in 0.2 mile reach an old foundation. Follow the tread as it bends left. Pass a large rock and return to the Rome Point Trail in 0.3 mile. Turn right to quickly return to the parking area.

8 Long Pond and Ell Pond

RATING/ DIFFICULTY	ROUND-TRIP	ELEV GAIN/ HIGH POINT	SEASON
****/3	2.2 miles	600 feet/ 390 feet	Year-round

Map: USGS Voluntown; **Contact:** Audubon Society of Rhode Island; **Note:** Hunting is allowed in season. There are specific blaze-orange requirements; **GPS:** 41.506148, -71.764685

Nestled in a landscape of rocky ledges draped in mountain laurel and rhododendron, Long and Ell ponds form the heart of a 1220-acre conservation area assembled by The Nature Conservancy, the Audubon Society of Rhode Island, and the state. This short but challenging route connects to a trail network that extends to several nearby ponds and eventually into Connecticut.

GETTING THERE

From the junction of Routes 3 and 138 in Hope Valley, drive 2.8 miles west on Route 138 to Rockville and then turn left onto Wincheck Pond Road. In 0.1 mile turn left onto Canonchet Road. Continue straight 0.5 mile to a four-way junction. Turn left, remaining on Canonchet Road. Drive 0.6 mile to the parking area on your right.

ON THE TRAIL

Near an old foundation, find the Narragansett Trail sign. To the left, this yellow-blazed route leads 1.1 miles to Ashville Pond. Stay straight and follow the Narragansett Trail as it parallels, from a distance, the southern shore of Long Pond. The path rises gradually up the ridgeline and in 0.3 mile arrives at a large boulder that invites climbing. This is also a good location to observe the area's prolific mountain laurel. Continue over the rolling landscape. In 0.2 mile reach a ledge with limited views of Long Pond far below.

Over the next 0.4 mile, the trail becomes more difficult, dropping three times into

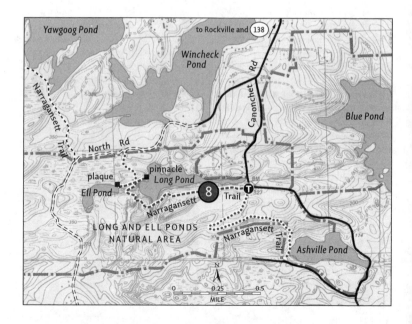

Rocky pinnacle above Long Pond

deep, rhododendron-filled notches and ascending steeply as often. Watch your footing, as the tread is occasionally rocky and uneven. The third climb leads through a gap between two ledges and ends at a four-way intersection. Follow the 0.1-mile path left. It traverses ledge-covered terrain to an open area with restricted views of Ell Pond. Here, a plaque commemorates the 1974 designation of this site as a National Natural Landmark. The pond and much of the fragile wetland ecosystem surrounding it are owned by The Nature Conservancy and are off limits to exploration.

Return to the four-way intersection. Stay straight and head east into the Audubon Society's Long Pond Woods. The 0.1-mile trail leads to an open perch with the day's first unobstructed views. Continue down the path to the base of a large ledge. Swing left and then right. Scramble up to the top of the rocky pinnacle and enjoy breathtaking scenes of Long Pond.

To return to your car, hike back to the four-way intersection and turn left, retracing your steps along the Narragansett Trail. As an alternative, follow the Narragansett Trail right at the four-way intersection. Hike 0.2 mile to North Road (sometimes called Old Rockville Road) and this destination's more popular trailhead . Turn right and follow the road east 0.9 mile to an intersection with Canonchet Road. Turn right to return to the parking area and complete a 3-mile loop.

EXTENDING YOUR HIKE

For an additional 2.2-mile round-trip trek, follow the Narragansett Trail south from the parking area to the shores of Ashville Pond. The path winds gently through an inviting forested landscape of rock walls and scattered boulders.

Tillinghast Pond's picturesque shoreline

⑨ Tillinghast Pond

RATING/ DIFFICULTY	LOOP	ELEV GAIN/ HIGH POINT	SEASON
****/3–4	8.4 miles	450 feet/ 530 feet	Year-round

Map: USGS Coventry Center; **Contact:** The Nature Conservancy, Rhode Island Chapter; **Note:** Hunting is allowed in season. There are specific blaze-orange requirements; **GPS:** 41.645011, -71.756871

   The Nature Conservancy's Tillinghast Pond and Rhode Island's Wickaboxet

Management Areas form the heart of a more than 2750-acre conservation area in West Greenwich. Within this vast expanse of ponds, forests, and former homesteads, a federal, state, and local partnership has developed a hiker's paradise with short treks as well as loops in excess of 10 miles.

GETTING THERE

Take exit 5B off Interstate 95 in West Greenwich. Drive 3.2 miles northwest on Route 102 (slightly longer if using the northbound exit) and then turn left onto Plain Meeting House Road. Proceed 3.9 miles before turning right onto Plain Road. Continue 0.6 mile to the parking area on the right.

ON THE TRAIL

The trail network includes four interconnected loops, each blazed in a different color. This 8.4-mile circuit begins on the white-blazed Pond Loop. Near the large sign and kiosk at the south end of the parking area, the route enters a pine forest, high above the pond. Reach a junction in 0.2 mile and continue straight, joining the yellow-blazed Flintlock Loop. With little elevation change, this gentle trail winds 0.6 mile past a cemetery to the former Ellis Homestead. Near a small pond a trail departs right to Plain Meeting House Road. Veer left and remain on the Flintlock Loop.

Back in the woods, quickly reach the start of the 4-mile Wickaboxet Loop on the right. The first mile of this blue-blazed trail remains in the 2054-acre Nature Conservancy preserve. Rise past small cemeteries, stone walls, and old foundations. As the pine forest shifts to oak, the path descends quickly to a woods road and enters the state's Wickaboxet Management Area. Stay right and follow the route 0.1 mile down to a three-way intersection where a path departs right and leads a few hundred feet to a parking area on Plain Meeting House Road. Veer left and remain on the Wickaboxet Loop Trail as it follows a woods road 0.3 mile to an unmarked spur. This obvious path winds 0.1 mile around and then rises up to the summit of Rattlesnake Ledge. Nearby views are attractive, but not as enticing as the impressive rock itself.

Rejoin the Wickaboxet Loop and continue east, still following a woods road. Soon after, another woods road diverges left. Continue straight 0.3 mile to where the main road

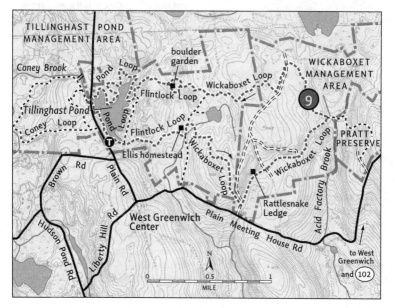

swings left. Here, follow the Wickaboxet Loop Trail ahead, as it departs the road and narrows significantly. For the next 2 miles the well-marked route winds over the rolling landscape, encountering numerous elaborate rock walls and old foundations along the way. At the easternmost point of the hike, stay left at a junction where a path departs right to the adjacent West Greenwich Land Trust's Pratt Preserve. After proceeding west (left) along a dirt road surrounded by giant ant mounds, the blue-blazed trail swings right into the forest to complete its final stretch.

Upon reaching the yellow-blazed Flintlock Loop, stay right and hike 1.1 miles up and over a series of small inclines before dropping toward the shore of Tillinghast Pond. Near the halfway point, the trail splits in two. To the left the path winds through a modest boulder garden, while the route right is more straightforward. The two options rejoin in 0.2 mile.

At the junction with the Pond Loop, bear right and descend quickly to a view of Tillinghast Pond. For much of the next 1.3 miles, the hike parallels the shoreline, passing numerous vistas. Be sure to stay along the edge of the field near the trail's end and away from the private residence to the north. The route eventually intersects Plain Road and follows the pavement left 0.1 mile. Turn left one last time. Hug the pond's shore 0.2 mile before returning to the parking area.

OTHER OPTIONS

Consider adding the Coney Loop to complete a 10.4-mile adventure. Along the way enjoy a small cascade and mill site. Conversely, skip the Wickaboxet Loop and shorten the journey to 4.2 miles. There are countless other options and three other parking areas to use as starting points.

10 Pachaug State Forest

RATING/ DIFFICULTY	LOOP	ELEV GAIN/ HIGH POINT	SEASON
**/4	9.4 miles	700 feet/ 520 feet	Year-round

Maps: USGS Jewett City and USGS Voluntown; **Contact:** Connecticut Department of Energy and Environmental Protection; **Note:** Restroom at the trailhead; **GPS:** 41.593585, -71.867554

 Pachaug State Forest, Connecticut's largest, is a nearly 24,000-acre conservation area with a vast network of hiking trails and other multiple-use corridors. This recommended loop that visits scenic hilltops, old mill sites, wildlife-rich ponds, and cascading streams is a good introduction to this quiet corner of the Nutmeg State.

GETTING THERE

From the junction of Routes 49 and 138/165 in Voluntown, follow Route 49 north 0.6 mile and then turn left onto Headquarters Road. Drive 0.9 mile and veer left onto Cutoff Road. Continue 0.1 mile to the parking area on the left (at the eastern edge of a large field).

ON THE TRAIL

With two brief exceptions, this hike follows three of Connecticut's blue-blazed trails: the Pachaug, Nehantic, and Quinnebaug. Head west along Cutoff Road to start. The Pachaug and Nehantic trails coincide and follow this dirt road 0.2 mile. Pass the campground entrance and then turn left into the forest. The trail climbs methodically to Mount

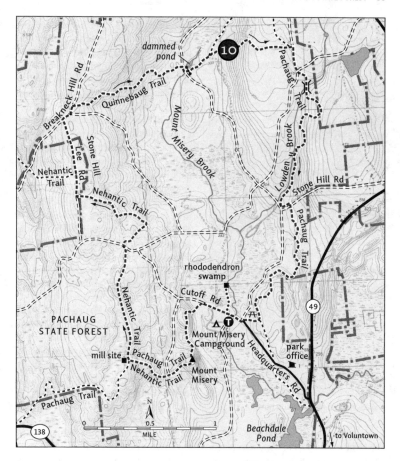

Misery's wooded northern summit. Swing south, descend briefly, and then climb to the mountain's higher ledge-covered southern summit. At 0.9 mile from the trailhead, this 441-foot peak provides expansive views east to nearby hills and wooded ridges.

Descend rapidly to a dirt road and follow it west 0.1 mile. As the road bends right, the blue-blazed trail continues straight and winds 0.4 mile to a major intersection at the base of an imposing abandoned mill site. Turn sharply right, remaining on the Nehantic Trail. This lightly used route proceeds north 1.7 miles over gently rolling terrain and across a dirt road. Make your way to Lee Road, just south of a large privately owned farmhouse. Bear right and hike north along the road. Beyond the farmhouse, the from multiple directions. In this area, the trail turns sharply right and eventually becomes more obvious. Make your way to a major forest road. Turn right and follow the road 0.1 mile to a small dammed pond. At this point, the loop becomes more appealing and easier to follow.

On the dam's east side, near a picnic table, a trail begins at a gate. Follow this flat path 0.2 mile to an intersection with the Pachaug Trail and stay right. Ascend gradually 0.6 mile to a well-marked junction. Continue straight on the Pachaug Trail. In 0.1 mile, the route swings sharply right and leads quickly to a road crossing. On the far side, begin an alluring 1.4-mile jaunt. The trail descends to Lowden Brook, crosses it with the aid of a bridge, and then parallels the running water. At first, it does so from a distance, but the trail soon hugs the cascading brook closely as it winds through a narrow valley.

Upon arriving at a dirt road, follow the blue blazes sharply left up Stone Hill Road. In 0.1 mile, the route swings right once again. Through a white pine and eastern hemlock forest, the Pachaug Trail meanders 1.2 miles across the undulating terrain. At the junction with the Nehantic Trail, follow the path right. The Nehantic and Pachaug trails coincide and lead through a field and large picnic area. Cross a dirt road to the edge of Mount Misery Brook and then follow Cutoff Road right 0.1 mile to reach the parking area.

Hawk-watching atop Mount Misery

Nehantic Trail departs left. Stay straight on Lee Road. In 0.4 mile, bear right onto Breakneck Hill Road. In a few hundred feet, stay left at a three-way intersection, remaining on the main road. It quickly leads to the Quinnebaug Trail, which departs right beyond a gate.

The least attractive portion of the hike, the Quinnebaug Trail is a necessary 0.9-mile connection to complete the loop. Easy to follow at first, the blue-blazed path descends on an old road. As the forest shifts to evergreens, unmarked paths intersect

OTHER OPTONS

Before calling it a day, consider exploring the 0.2-mile trail that leads north of the parking area into a dense canopy of cedar trees and rhododendron. For a shorter adventure, hike out and back to Mount Misery (1.9 miles round-trip) or out and back to the cascading section of Lowden Brook (4.2 miles round-trip).

11 James L. Goodwin State Forest

RATING/ DIFFICULTY	LOOP	ELEV GAIN/ HIGH POINT	SEASON
***/3	7.6 miles	450 feet/ 750 feet	Year-round

Map: USGS Hampton; **Contact:** Connecticut Department of Energy and Environmental Protection; **GPS:** 41.775737, -72.082688

A 1910 Yale School of Forestry graduate, James L. Goodwin was one of Connecticut's earliest conservationists. In 1964, he generously donated lands that became the state forest that now bears his name. Today, hikers can explore this charming landscape of scenic ponds and quiet, forested hillsides.

GETTING THERE
From the junction of US Route 6 and Route 97 in Hampton, drive 1.4 miles west on US 6. Turn right onto Potter Road. Reach the parking area on the right in 0.2 mile.

ON THE TRAIL
James L. Goodwin Forest is the southern terminus of the 18.1-mile blue-blazed Natchaug Trail. Today's hike traverses this route's first 3.6 miles before looping back on two other trails. The Natchaug Trail quickly descends to the western shore of Pine Acres Pond and then begins a gentle 1.5-mile climb. The ascent of less than 200 feet has many intersections along the way. In 0.3 mile, turn right onto the Air Line State Park Trail, a popular destination for bicyclists. Follow the former rail bed 0.2 mile before departing left. At mile 1.1, turn left onto Cannon Road and walk 0.1 mile before leaving the pavement to the right.

Near the top of Bear Hill, continue straight at an intersection with the Goodwin Heritage Trail and hike 0.5 mile to the shore of Black Spruce Pond, a name that no longer matches the surrounding forest. Just before reaching the shore, the Pine Acres Pond Trail departs right. Stay left and follow the blue blazes to the pond's earthen dam. Approach quietly and perhaps spot waterfowl or other critters in the marshy wetland.

The trail swings around the west shore and rises to and then crosses Middle Road in 0.6 mile. Descend to a small stream and then rise to a junction with Nutmeg Lane in 0.4 mile. The

The southern shore of Pine Acres Pond

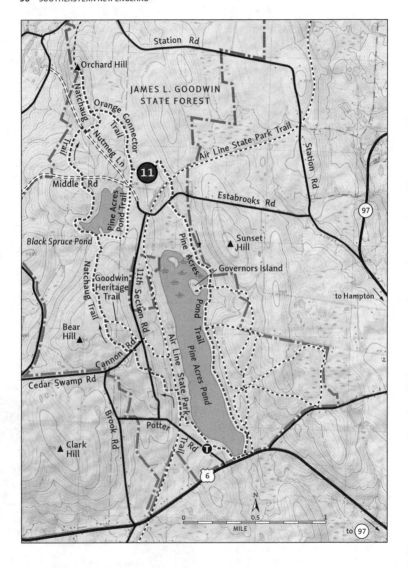

Natchaug Trail coincides with this dirt road right, very briefly, and then swings sharply left. Climb into a dark pine forest before dropping to an intersection with the Orange Connector Trail. This is the route back, but first continue on the Natchaug Trail 0.3 mile farther. After passing two foundations and other remains from an old farm, the path ascends Orchard Hill. Find a modest western vista just beyond the high point.

Return to the 0.5-mile Orange Connector Trail and stay left. It leads east and then south with very little elevation change. Wind through the hardwood forest to an intersection with the Pine Acres Pond Trail. Bear left here. This blue-and-white blazed trail leads 3 miles back to the parking area.

Swing east around a small pond and then veer right before crossing the Air Line State Park Trail in 0.4 mile. The path soon arrives at Estabrooks Road. Briefly follow this paved route right and then turn left back onto a more inviting trail. Over the next 2.3 miles, the route never strays far from Pine Acres Pond. In places the footing is rocky, but the terrain is mostly level. Check out the red-blazed path on the right that leads 0.1 mile to an observation platform on Governors Island. Otherwise, remain on the main trail and enjoy the many shoreline vistas. Near the southern end, hike through a recent timber harvest and then across the pond's grassy dam. The views here are breathtaking. Continue around the southern tip of the pond and then hike 0.2 mile north to complete the journey.

SHORTENING YOUR HIKE

Skip Orchard Hill and instead turn right at Black Spruce Pond to complete a 5.7-mile loop using the Natchaug and Pine Acres Pond trails.

12 Nayantaquit Trail

RATING/ DIFFICULTY	LOOP	ELEV GAIN/ HIGH POINT	SEASON
**/1–2	3.6 miles	680 feet/ 452 feet	Year-round

Map: USGS Hamburg; **Contact:** Connecticut Department of Energy and Environmental Protection; **GPS:** 41.396099, -72.307184

 Exploring the 4222-acre Nehantic State Forest, this trail visits beaver ponds, boulder-shrouded hills, and maturing forest slopes lush with ferns and wildflowers. The changing habitats encountered throughout this 3.6-mile loop are home to a wide variety of birds, amphibians, reptiles, and small mammals.

GETTING THERE

Take exit 70 from Interstate 95 in Lyme and head north onto Route 156. Follow Route 156 north 6.7 miles into North Lyme and then turn right onto Beaver Brook Road. Drive 2 miles and turn right onto Keeny Road. The parking lot is 1.3 miles on the right, 0.2 mile after the pavement ends.

ON THE TRAIL

The trail begins on a gated woods road that departs the parking area to the northwest, but it immediately swings left at a sign. Follow the blue-blazed path, past an impressive boulder on the left, to the start of the loop in 0.2 mile.

Stay right to complete the circuit in a counterclockwise direction. Descending gently, the easy-to-follow trail crosses a small stream before veering left. Make your way up the hardwood-forested slope. Winding past rock and ledge, the trail soon

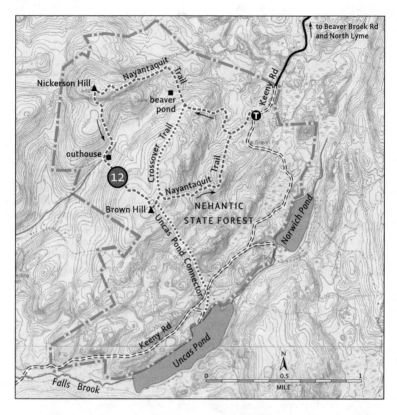

crosses through a gap in a stone wall and in 0.4 mile reaches a junction with the Cross-over Trail. This blue- and yellow-blazed path provides an alternative for hikers seeking a shorter loop.

Remain on the Nayantaquit Trail as it bends right and drops 0.2 mile to the outlet of a large beaver pond. In this area, encounter the first of many woods roads that the trail intersects and joins along its course. While this is potentially confusing, there are ample blue blazes and signs that mark the main route. A wooden bridge leads

across the beaver pond's slow-moving outlet stream. On the other side, begin a steady 0.2-mile climb to the top of a ridge.

Bearing sharply left, the trail proceeds 0.5 mile along the wooded ridge to a semi-open ledge near the summit of 452-foot Nickerson Hill. Draped in small rounded boulders, the ledge offers modest, but attractive, views of nearby hills. It is also an ideal spot for a midday picnic.

The trail descends rapidly down the hill's steep southern slopes, but it soon eases. In 0.4 mile, swing right as the trail

The Nayantaquit loop passes numerous stone walls and foundations.

coincides with a woods road for 0.1 mile. Near an outhouse, the route turns sharply left, starts a gradual ascent, and, in 0.2 mile, joins the former Brown Hill Road. Lined with rock walls and an occasional towering tree, this wide path leads 0.3 mile to the remains of a homestead atop the flat hill. Bend sharply left to intersect the Uncas Pond Connector, a trail leading 0.7 mile to a scenic, narrow pond that is also accessible by car. This is an optional extension to the described hike.

The final 0.9-mile section of the loop continues northeast. Stay right at the Crossover Trail junction and descend steeply down the rocky slope. Past a small stream, rise over a forested ledge. Beyond, the path proceeds more gradually. Upon reaching the end of the circuit, stay right and hike 0.2 mile back to the trailhead.

13 Mansfield Hollow

RATING/ DIFFICULTY	LOOP	ELEV GAIN/ HIGH POINT	SEASON
**/3	5.6 miles	450 feet/ 280 feet	Year-round

Map: USGS Spring Hill; **Contact:** Connecticut Department of Energy and Environmental Protection; **GPS:** 41.764757, -72.178805

Located at the confluence of three rivers, Mansfield Hollow Lake is a 500-acre wetland created in the 1950s when the Army Corps of Engineers constructed a dam on the Natchaug River. Surrounded by a state park today, the area offers numerous miles of trails featuring scenic views of the water and ample opportunities to spot resident wildlife.

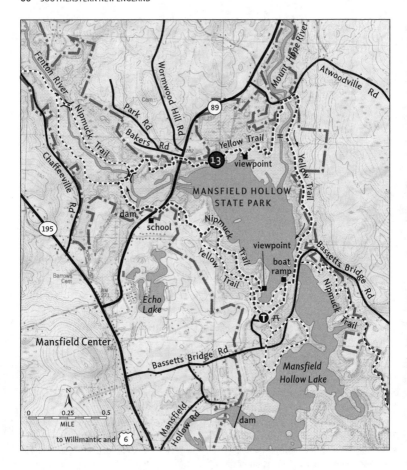

GETTING THERE

From the junction of US Route 6 and Route 195 north of Willimantic, drive 2 miles north on Route 195 and then turn right onto Bassetts Bridge Road. Continue 0.9 mile to the state park entrance on the left. Follow the driveway 0.2 mile to the parking lot near a picnic area.

ON THE TRAIL

Near a large kiosk, pick up the Nipmuck Trail as it swings north through the picnic area. While the route is a bit confusing at first, there are ample blue blazes to follow. Hike 0.2 mile to an unmarked spur that diverges right to the shoreline and pleasant views of the lake. The main route continues in a northwesterly direction and becomes more obvious. Paralleling the water, but mostly from a distance, the Nipmuck Trail traverses the gentle rolling landscape. A little more than 1 mile from the start, swing sharply right as the path coincides with the multi-use Yellow Trail. In 0.1 mile remain right at a fork and, soon after, intersect the Yellow Trail once again.

The two paths pass a ball field and lead to the edge of Route 89. Swing left toward a school. In less than 0.1 mile, look for the Nipmuck Trail sign on the opposite side of the road. Carefully cross the busy highway and then descend 0.1 mile to the base of a large dam. After crossing Schoolhouse Brook, the route continues 0.2 mile to a junction of woods roads. Follow the blue and yellow blazes right and descend 0.2 mile to the slow-moving Fenton River.

Once across the large metal bridge, 2 miles from the start, the Nipmuck Trail veers sharply left and continues its long-distance journey to the Massachusetts border. Stay straight on the Yellow Trail and wind 0.4 mile to Bakers Road. Follow the pavement right a few hundred feet to Route 89. Directly across, the Yellow Trail continues over a guardrail—it's not well marked here. Drop 0.2 mile to Mansfield Hollow Lake's

Mansfield Hollow Lake is a wide expanse of water.

shoreline and the first of many views of its sprawling waters. The route continues left, briefly following an old road. In 0.2 mile, turn sharply right onto a more natural corridor.

The next stretch, nearly a mile, is the loop's most scenic. After stopping at a quiet lakeshore vista, hike to the top of a low ridge. Through a shady hardwood forest, venture north toward the alluring sounds of the Mount Hope River. The Yellow Trail turns right on Atwoodville Road and leads 0.1 mile over a high bridge. Quickly bear right onto a driveway, then back into the state park.

Parallel the river downstream 0.3 mile to a short unmarked spur that leads right to a small cascade. The Yellow Trail continues another mile up and over stone-wall-lined hillsides back to the scenic lake one last time before reaching Bassetts Bridge Road. Turn right and use caution walking along the roadside en route to a large boat-ramp parking area. Look for blue and yellow blazes departing the northwestern corner of the parking area (the Nipmuck Trail also enters the boat ramp from the southeast). Once around a secluded pond, the Yellow Trail continues straight. Stay left on the Nipmuck Trail. It climbs steeply at first but soon plateaus. In 0.3 mile, the loop concludes in the picnic area.

14 Wells State Park

RATING/ DIFFICULTY	LOOP	ELEV GAIN/ HIGH POINT	SEASON
**/2–3	6.5 miles	750 feet/ 860 feet	Year-round

Map: USGS Medfield; **Contact:** Massachusetts Department of Conservation and Recreation; **Note:** Entrance fee; **GPS:** 42.146582, -72.061224

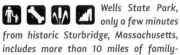

Wells State Park, only a few minutes from historic Sturbridge, Massachusetts, includes more than 10 miles of family-friendly hiking trails through dense forests, past scenic wetlands, and to the top of rocky outcrops. This itinerary combines three separate loops and visits the park's most interesting natural features.

GETTING THERE
From the junction of US Route 20 and Route 49 in Sturbridge, drive 1 mile north on Route 49 and then turn left onto the Wells State Park Road. Continue straight 1.2 miles to the park entrance and day-use parking area on the right.

ON THE TRAIL
Beyond the park headquarters, follow the paved road that leads right, up a small hill. The road drops left and reaches the start of the Mill Pond Trail in 0.1 mile. A Healthy Heart Trail, one of dozens designated by the Massachusetts Department of Conservation and Recreation, this nearly 1-mile path loops across level terrain. After reaching the shore of a small pond, pass the remains of the mill's stone infrastructure, then turn left at a junction with a mountain bike trail. Hike south to return to the park road.

To the left, the pavement descends to the parking area. Straight ahead, it leads to the start of the Mountain Road Trail, a future stop on the day's journey. For now, turn right into the woods and join the yellow-blazed path leading 0.1 mile to an intersection. Stay right on the red-blazed North Trail. Remain on this route roughly 1.5 miles. It climbs moderately to the top of a ridge that is also crossed by power lines. The opening offers views of the wetland below. Descending past small

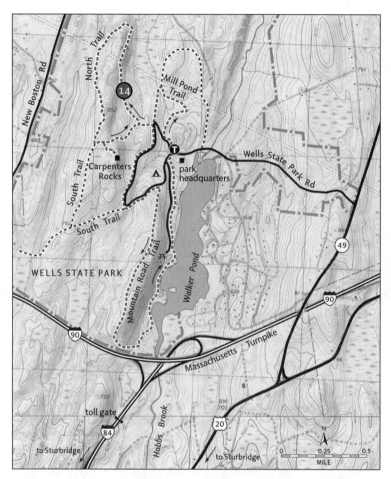

boulders and ledges, the trail veers sharply left and crosses under the power lines once again. After paralleling rock walls, the trail rises moderately, then levels off and reaches a three-way intersection where the South Trail continues straight.

Stay left and rejoin the yellow-blazed trail. Up and over a small rise, arrive at an unmarked junction in 0.1 mile. Follow the spur right and ascend 0.1 mile to the top of Carpenters Rocks. Named for a local settler, this precipitous cliff offers views of the surrounding landscape. Retrace your steps down the hillside and stay right at the unmarked junction. Follow the yellow blazes and descend moderately 0.3 mile through

A young hiker admires Carpenters Rocks.

the rocky landscape. At the North Trail intersection, proceed straight and return to the park road.

To conclude a shorter 3.5-mile hike, take the road ahead to the parking area. To complete a 3-mile-longer adventure, turn right and follow the pavement 0.8 mile. It rises through picturesque forests to the start of the South Trail. Continue on the road as it descends left into the campground. Beyond the first wave of campsites, arrive at a large maple tree and old homestead site.

Departing right, find the orange-blazed Mountain Road Trail. This easy-to-follow path leads pleasantly 1.1 miles atop a high ridge, with minor elevation changes. Approaching the Massachusetts Turnpike, the path turns

sharply left and drops aggressively 0.1 mile to level ground below. Swing north and wind to the shore of Walker Pond. While remaining close to the water, the path visits numerous scenic spots, an impressive scree slope, and many signs of beaver activity before ending at a picnic area. Follow the pavement right nearly 0.5 mile to conclude the hike.

15 Purgatory Chasm

RATING/ DIFFICULTY	LOOP	ELEV GAIN/ HIGH POINT	SEASON
**/2	2.6 miles	400 feet/ 625 feet	April–Nov

Map: USGS Milford; **Contact:** Massachusetts Department of Conservation and Recreation; **Notes:** Avoid this trail during inclement weather. The path is also closed during certain times of the year due to snow and ice; **GPS:** 42.129142, -71.714916

This popular geologic formation in central Massachusetts can resemble an amusement park at times, but its uniqueness makes it a must-see destination. Formed by glacial melt roughly 14,000 years ago, the chasm's steep rock walls drop as much as 70 feet in places. Use caution exploring this uneven terrain and then relax along the paths that wind gently through surrounding forests.

GETTING THERE
From Route 146 in Sutton, take exit 6. If coming from the north, turn right off the exit; if traveling from the south, bear left. Follow Purgatory Road 0.5 mile into the Purgatory Chasm State Reservation. There are multiple places to park.

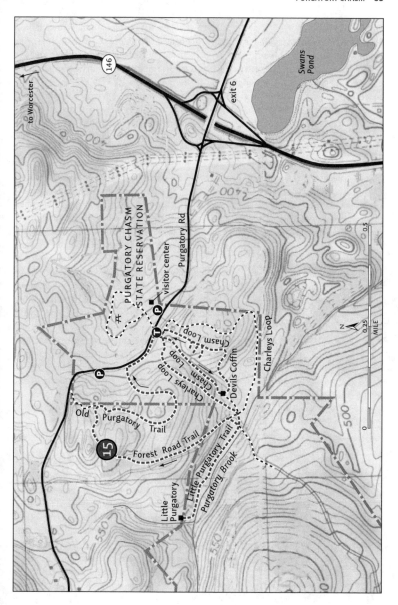

ON THE TRAIL

Follow the numerous signs that lead to the chasm's entrance. The Chasm Loop Trail descends quickly into the impressive rocky passageway. Scramble over ledges and squeeze through the narrow corridors as you head deeper into the abyss. Avoid the temptation to leave the trail, although many others do not. It is enough to marvel at the surrounding walls from the rocky valley floor. Reach the Devils Coffin in 0.2 mile. This tiny cave marks the end of the chasm.

Turn sharply left and follow the Chasm Loop Trail as it rises along the east rim of the canyon, providing a completely different perspective of this geologic oddity.

Looking up from deep within the chasm

Unlike other similar natural features in New England, Purgatory Chasm is not being carved by running water. Today's remains are the result of events that occurred during the most recent ice age.

After swinging right around the base of a large ledge, pass three short spurs that leave to the left. The first visits Fat Mans Misery and the second two explore the Devils Corncrib. Both are narrow gaps in the ledge that invite closer examination. Along the way, watch your step near the many drop-offs.

The 0.5-mile loop soon ends where it began. While many stop their adventure here, there are more places to discover. Head across the chasm entrance and turn left onto the western branch of the Charleys Loop Trail. It parallels the chasm's rim throughout, although from a distance. Climb up the pine-covered slope to a high point. The 0.3-mile path soon descends rapidly to a major intersection. Stay right and follow the flat trail to Little Purgatory.

The path crosses a woods road and then leads easily 0.4 mile alongside Purgatory Brook before ending abruptly. Here a tributary forms a tiny gorge with small cascades. Retrace your steps back to the woods road. To the right the road leads 0.1 mile to Purgatory Brook, a nice picnic location. The journey continues left and quickly joins the Forest Road Trail.

Follow this wide path 0.3 mile up an incline into a dark evergreen forest. Turn right and rise over a small knoll. Drop to an intersection and bear right again. Follow the Old Purgatory Trail 0.4 mile. It weaves across a wooded ridge, passes small boulders, and then descends to the parking area. Look for woodpeckers and other forest birds, but soon their calls will be drowned out by the voices emanating from the chasm.

16 Blackstone River

RATING/ DIFFICULTY	LOOP	ELEV GAIN/ HIGH POINT	SEASON
***/2	4.7 miles	450 feet/ 445 feet	Year-round

Map: USGS Uxbridge; **Contact:** Massachusetts Department of Conservation and Recreation; **Note:** Part of Blackstone River Valley National Heritage Corridor; **GPS:** 42.097998, -71.624181

Blackstone River and Canal Heritage State Park is a 1000-acre natural area that features many miles of easy to moderate hiking trails. This suggested itinerary offers intimate and aerial views of a wildlife-rich river, as well as the remains of what was once a bustling textile manufacturing center.

GETTING THERE
From the junction of Route 122 and Hartford Avenue in North Uxbridge, follow Hartford Avenue east 1.1 miles. Turn left into the grassy parking area (not the private driveway) just before crossing the Blackstone River.

ON THE TRAIL
The day's adventure includes two hikes that begin from separate trailheads: a 2-mile loop over Goat Hill and a 2.7-mile round-trip trek to Lookout Rock. The Goat Hill Trail enters the forest at the northern edge of the parking area. Reach the start of the loop just before approaching the Blackstone River. Turn left and begin the 0.9-mile trek up and over Goat Hill. Remain on the blue-blazed route throughout rather than the many

Water flows past Goat Hill Lock.

unmarked trails departing left. Around the halfway point, the route plateaus near the top of Goat Hill and divides into two paths that quickly reconnect. After heading up one last incline, descend past numerous stone walls and large rocks. Level off, swing right, and proceed to a signed intersection.

The loop continues right, but first turn left and hike a few hundred feet to the remains of Goat Hill Lock. On the lock's east side, an unmarked path leads right 0.1 mile to the end of a peninsula and unrestricted views of the marshy river. Beyond the lock, the

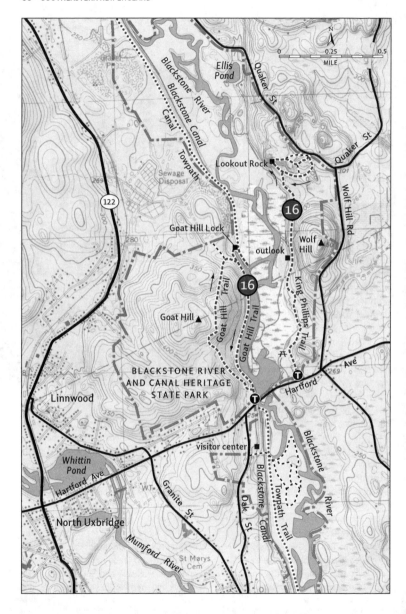

flat Canal Towpath Trail continues approximately 1.5 miles and offers an opportunity to extend the day's journey. To complete the 2-mile loop, return to the Goat Hill Trail and stay left. Follow the slow-flowing river downstream. With little elevation change, the path pleasantly winds past boulders and an occasional vista before returning to the parking area.

The trailhead for the second hike is 0.2 mile east on Hartford Avenue at the Rice City Pond parking area. While it's close enough to walk, driving may be preferable—the busy road has narrow shoulders. Join the King Phillips Trail and hike north 0.1 mile into a picnic area. Follow the white-blazed trail as it departs the pine forest and parallels the water for the next 0.9 mile. Near the halfway point, a short unmarked spur departs left to an outlook on the edge of the meandering river. After crossing a small stream, the trail arrives at a three-way intersection and the start of a 0.7-mile loop.

Stay left on the white-blazed path. It descends briefly but quickly swings right and climbs steeply up the rocky hillside. In 0.2 mile, reach Lookout Rock with sweeping views of the river and surrounding hills. The loop continues on the widest path that leads east (the area around Lookout Rock can be a bit confusing with many unmarked paths). In 0.1 mile, bear right onto a narrower trail that skirts a forested ledge. This route leads 0.1 mile to a parking area on Quaker Street. Just before reaching the pavement, turn sharply right onto a wider trail. Follow this path 0.3 mile to complete the loop. Turn left and hike 1 mile back to Hartford Avenue.

EXTENDING YOUR HIKE

From the Goat Hill Loop Trailhead, cross Hartford Avenue. Take the 1.2-mile Towpath Trail south. This easy path follows the Blackstone Canal and passes other historical remains of the area's industrial past.

17 Borderland State Park

RATING/ DIFFICULTY	LOOP	ELEV GAIN/ HIGH POINT	SEASON
***/2	5.2 miles	270 feet/ 325 feet	Year-round

Map: USGS Brockton; **Contact:** Massachusetts Department of Conservation and Recreation; **Note:** Fee; **GPS:** 42.062575, -71.164767

 *Spreading out over 1773 acres and including more than 20 miles of trails, Borderland State Park in southeastern Massachusetts is a wonderful destination for nature enthusiasts of all ages. The park's dense forests, intriguing geologic features, and sprawling wetlands provide a delightful backdrop throughout the year.*

GETTING THERE

From the junction of Routes 106 and 140 in Mansfield, drive 2.4 miles east on Route 106 and then turn left onto Stearns Road. Continue 1.2 miles and stay left on Stearns Road. In 0.7 mile, bear left onto Massapoag Avenue. Follow Massapoag Avenue 1.1 miles north and then turn right to enter Borderland State Park. Follow the road left to a large parking area.

ON THE TRAIL

Borderland State Park offers many hike options of various lengths. This recommended journey begins and ends along the Bay Circuit Trail, a path that leads more than 200 miles around Greater Boston, connecting conservation areas from Ipswich to Duxbury. The Bay Circuit Trail's journey through Borderland takes advantage of existing state park trails.

Pick up the Bay Circuit Trail as it coincides with the Pond Walk near the park's visitor center. Descend 0.1 mile to a stone lodge and enticing views near the shore of Leach Pond.

Staying close to the water's edge, continue 0.1 mile north to a sign for the West Side Trail. This intersection and most others encountered along the way are clearly marked, often with small maps. Bear left and gently wind away from the pond into a thick-forested landscape carpeted throughout the spring and summer with numerous wildflowers, lichens, and mosses.

In 0.2 mile, turn right onto the French Trail. Meander over a rolling landscape of exposed ledges and boulders. In 0.3 mile, swing left onto the Northwest Trail. Follow this path 0.5 mile north. Near the halfway point, a trail diverges 0.1 mile right to Split Rock, an enormous boulder that is hard to miss. After passing a large forested wetland on the left, reach a three-way intersection.

Turn right on the Ridge Trail. After crossing a small stream, it climbs gradually and in 0.5 mile leads to a four-way intersection. The Bay Circuit Trail route continues straight along the Quarry Loop Trail. Bear right and remain on the Ridge Trail. The path proceeds with little elevation change. At a large boulder in 0.5 mile, veer abruptly south onto a narrower corridor and descend quickly to the Granite Hills Trail.

Stay left and descend 0.2 mile into a grassy field. Ahead, find a gate and views of Upper Leach Pond. The shortest route back to the visitor center, a little more than 1 mile, is to the right along the wide dirt road that eventually connects with the Pond Walk. To extend the adventure, turn left and walk to Mountain Street. Follow the pavement southeast 0.1 mile to a gate on the right. Join this route as it leads through a tall stand of

Scrambling up Bay Circuit Trail

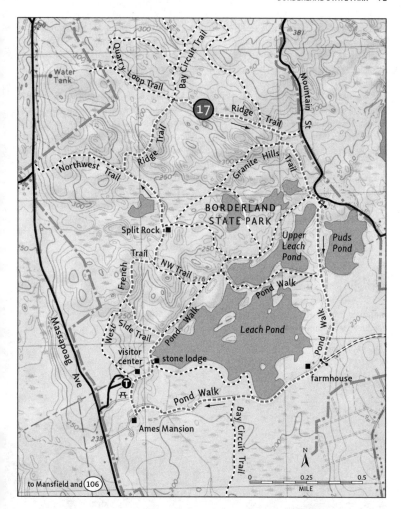

white pines and across an open field. In 0.2 mile, the trail crosses a small dam at the outlet of Puds Pond. Continue 0.1 mile, then enter the southern half of the Pond Walk.

The route leads 0.3 mile south through fields that have been maintained for more than 300 years. Hike around a gate and begin the final mile of the circuit. Turning right, the trail passes an old farmhouse and then approaches Leach Pond's southern shore. The Bay Circuit Trail enters from the left and merges with the Pond Walk. Together, the two routes continue 0.4 mile to the Ames Mansion. Turn right and pass through the picnic area to reach the trailhead.

EXTENDING YOUR HIKE

The Ames mansion is open for tours the third Sunday of the month from spring to fall. This immense stone structure was built in 1910 for botanist Oakes Ames and his wife Blanche, an artist and suffragist. What today is Borderland State Park was their estate throughout much of the 1900s. Their land and its many trails became a state park in 1971.

18 Noanet Woodlands

RATING/ DIFFICULTY	LOOP	ELEV GAIN/ HIGH POINT	SEASON
***/2	5 miles	450 feet/ 387 feet	Year-round

Map: USGS Medfield; **Contact:** The Trustees of Reservations; **Notes:** Dogs must be on leash or under control at all times. The reservation is open daily from sunrise to sunset; **GPS:** 42.228470, -71.256745

 For more than a century, The Trustees of Reservations and its members have conserved more than a hundred special places throughout Massachusetts. Noanet Woodlands Reservation, a 620-acre oasis in the Greater Boston area, is one such place. Hikers of all abilities will enjoy this reservation's peaceful trails that reveal history, natural beauty, and plentiful wildlife.

GETTING THERE

From Interstate 95 and Route 128 in Dedham, take exit 16B. Drive 0.9 mile west on Route 109 and then turn right onto Dover Street. Continue 2.3 miles to the parking area on the right (Dover Street becomes Powissett Street at the Westwood–Dover town line).

Upper Mill Pond

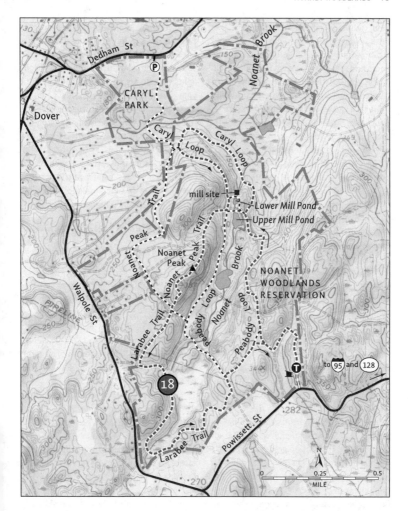

ON THE TRAIL

The reservation has numerous paths, official and unofficial, but its four primary trails are all well marked, especially at intersections. This described hike follows portions of each of the four trails and no other routes.

The hike begins at the northern end of the parking area, just beyond a small ranger station. Follow the trail over a wooden bridge and then stay left in 0.1 mile. Hike another 0.1 mile before turning right. The path soon arrives at a fork in the trail.

Bear right and immediately intersect the Peabody Loop.

Stay right on the blue-blazed Peabody Loop and enjoy a relaxing 0.6-mile stroll to the edge of Upper Mill Pond. The well-marked route winds over the rolling terrain through a dense oak forest lined with rock walls. After crossing a stone bridge near the shore of Upper Mill Pond, arrive at a junction with the red-blazed Caryl Loop.

Turn right and descend 0.1 mile to a flat boulder that resembles a sacrificial altar. The route veers left and continues easily 0.6 mile to the loop's northwestern corner. Here, a portion of the Caryl Loop Trail leaves right and makes its way to an alternative parking area at Caryl Park in Dover. Stay left on the well-used western branch of the Caryl Loop. It proceeds 0.4 mile, with little elevation change, to a more intimate view of Lower Mill and Upper Mill ponds. Once the home of an iron works, this former mill site has many steep drop-offs that are potentially dangerous. Please use caution while exploring this spot with young children. The ponds that remain are ideal places to spot resident wildlife such as eastern kingbirds feasting on flying insects.

Stay right and hike along the western shore of Lower Mill Pond. At a four-way intersection, turn right onto the yellow-blazed Noanet Peak Trail. Rising gradually 0.2 mile, the route then turns sharply left and heads up a steeper incline. However, the 0.2-mile final climb to the top of 387-foot Noanet Peak is over before you know it. From the rocky pinnacle, enjoy 180-degree views, including Boston's skyline to the north.

The Noanet Peak Trail continues south 0.3 mile. After swinging around a second summit, descend a narrow ridge to a junction. Stay left on the orange-blazed Larabee

Trail. In a few dozen feet, this path splits in two. Follow the more obvious route right. For the next 1.5 miles the trail explores the southern corner of the reservation. Highlights include a sprawling marsh and thick pine forests. Follow the blazes carefully; there are many turns and unmarked side trails along the way. After bearing sharply left onto an old road, ramble north 0.1 mile to a three-way intersection.

Stay right on the eastern branch of the Peabody Loop. This inviting path leads to an intersection in 0.2 mile. Turn right and follow the trail back to the parking area.

19 Middlesex Fells

RATING/ DIFFICULTY	LOOP	ELEV GAIN/ HIGH POINT	SEASON
***/3–4	4.6 miles	500 feet/ 285 feet	Year-round

Map: USGS Boston North; **Contact:** Massachusetts Department of Conservation and Recreation; **Note:** Map on state website shows all trails and allowed uses; **GPS:** 42.444471, -71.094776

Lying less than 5 miles from New England's largest city, the Middlesex Fells Reservation is a 2575-acre enclave of conservation land bisected by more than 100 miles of trails. This challenging hike in the park's eastern section offers stunning views of Boston's skyline and provides a great introduction to the area.

GETTING THERE
From the junction of Pond Street and Woodland Road in Stoneham, drive 1.1 miles south on Woodland Road. Turn right and use the parking area for the Flynn Rink in Medford.

The Boston skyline from Pinnacle Rock

ON THE TRAIL

Take your time crossing Woodland Road and pick up the blue-blazed Cross Fells Trail on the opposite side of the busy roadway. After a brief climb, the path levels off and reaches the start of the loop in 0.2 mile. Turn right onto the Rock Circuit Trail and you will quickly understand how it was named. Throughout, the route traverses a rolling landscape and demands care while crossing extensive rocky terrain—especially true along the loop's southern half. The Rock Circuit Trail intersects and parallels many wider paths and roads. Pay close attention to the prolific white blazes and small signs that lead the way.

Ascending a small rise, the route swings right and in 0.2 mile makes its way to the first of many vistas, a view looking west across the reservation. Proceed east and in 0.6 mile reach the remains of MIT's Middlesex Fells Geodetic Observatory, a stone structure built in the late 1800s. A few hundred feet beyond, the orange-blazed Rock Circuit Connector Trail veers left at an unmarked junction. Continue on the Rock Circuit Trail 0.1 mile to the scenic summit of Boojum Rock. At 275 feet, this outcrop provides expansive views of Boston, surrounding communities, and the Blue Hills to the south.

After hiking 0.4 mile to the east over rolling terrain, intersect the Cross Fells Trail near a gate. Both routes head across Fellsway East; use caution to avoid the fast-moving vehicles on this busy highway. Once across the pavement, the trails split once again. Stay right on the Rock Circuit Trail. Ascend a short, steep slope, then immediately descend. At the base, pay close attention to the signage, as the route passes an unmarked spur that leads south 0.1 mile up to the pointy and scenic summit of Pinnacle Rock. Explore this destination before continuing the loop.

For the next 1.2 miles, the Rock Circuit Trail wraps like a roller coaster up and over a series of named and unnamed rocky knolls, offering excellent views from Black Rock, Melrose Rock, and White Rock. The path also passes the top of a steep cascade. Beyond White Rock, descend to and recross Fellsway East.

The final 1.4 miles of the loop head across more gradual terrain, over fewer rocks, and under more impressive stands of trees. At an exposed ledge in 0.5 mile, a path diverges right toward a nearby hospital. Stay left and remain on the Rock Circuit Trail. In 0.4 mile, approach the northwestern shore of Fells

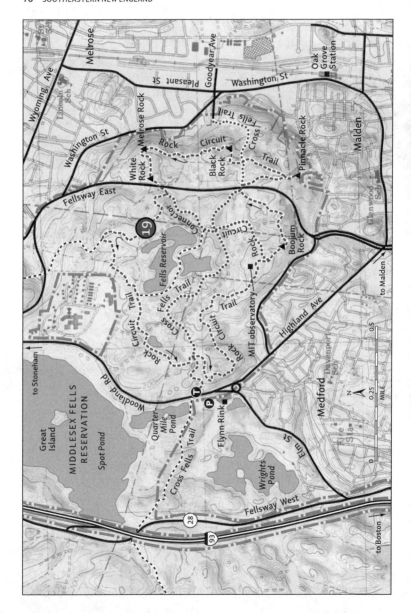

Reservoir, near a gap in the metal fence that surrounds the water body. Through the gap, a trail leads left and soon affords views of the reservoir. To complete the hike, remain outside the fenced-in area. On the left side of the dirt road that departs west from the reservoir, pick up the trail as it enters the forest. After swinging by a handful of small wetlands, reach a dirt road and follow it briefly to the right. Bear left once again. The Rock Circuit loop soon ends at a junction with the Cross Fells Trail. Turn right to return to the trailhead.

OTHER OPTIONS

Public transportation is available to an alternative trailhead. Take MBTA's Orange Line (subway) to Oak Grove Station. Walk 0.5 mile north on Washington Street and then turn left to reach the trailhead at the end of Goodyear Avenue. Follow the Cross Fells Trail to an intersection with the Rock Circuit Trail just south of Black Rock. From here, complete the loop in a clockwise direction to hike the toughest section first. Other shorter options are also available. Combine a portion of the Rock Circuit Trail with either the Cross Fells Trail or the Rock Circuit Connector to complete less challenging excursions.

20 Great Brook Farm

RATING/ DIFFICULTY	LOOP	ELEV GAIN/ HIGH POINT	SEASON
**/1	4.1 miles	50 feet/ 185 feet	Year-round

Map: USGS Billerica; **Contact:** Massachusetts Department of Conservation and Recreation; **Note:** Fee; **GPS:** 42.557471, -71.348637

This 1000-acre state park features more than 20 miles of trails for hikers and cross-country skiers of all ages. The mostly level landscape includes sacred Native American sites, artifacts from colonial settlers, quiet forest locales, and photogenic wetlands. A seasonal ice cream shop at the active Holstein farm offers cool treats to cap off a warm summer's day.

GETTING THERE

From Carlisle Center, drive 1.8 miles north on Lowell Street and then turn right onto North Road. Continue 0.3 mile before turning left into the parking area.

Meadow Pond's placid water

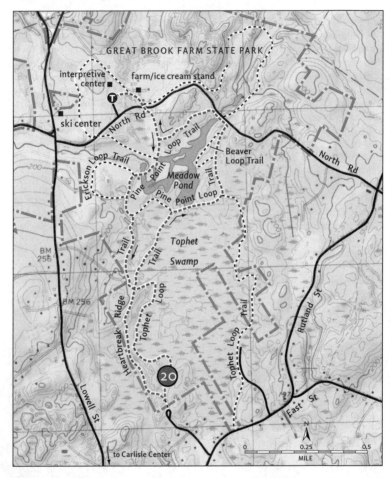

ON THE TRAIL

Starting at the interpretive center at the northern end of the parking area, follow the signs leading to the ice cream stand. In a few hundred feet, at a large kiosk, swing right. Between a small pond and the barn, hike 0.1 mile to North Road. Head straight across the pavement and pick up the path on the other side that leads into an open field. Proceed 0.1 mile ahead in the direction of Meadow Pond and an unmarked intersection with the Pine Point Loop Trail.

Stay right and follow the Pine Point Loop Trail south. This wide and easy-to-follow trail completes a 2-mile loop around Meadow Pond. Meander 0.4 mile past marshy coves and active pastures to the start of the Heartbreak Ridge Trail. Veer right onto this 0.8-mile route. It rises gently before passing a small wetland. Beyond a collection of large boulders, approach the Tophet Loop Trail. Stay right and descend gently 0.5 mile to the trail's end.

Pick up the Tophet Loop Trail by turning sharply left. Paralleling the Heartbreak Ridge Trail, this path takes a more circuitous course, weaving around and through the dense Tophet Swamp. At a junction in 0.7 mile, stay right. One last 0.4-mile stretch through the fertile swamp leads to an intersection with the Pine Point Loop Trail.

Bear right, rejoining the trek around Meadow Pond, and you soon encounter intimate views of the wildlife-rich waters. Swinging through a dark pine forest, the route continues 0.4 mile across level terrain to a parking lot on North Road. Consider exploring the Beaver Loop Trail as an alternative; it diverges left at a signed junction and parallels the main trail closer to the scenic pond. Stay alert for bird activity, including the graceful flight of great blue herons.

Remaining on the south side of North Road, the Pine Point Loop Trail bends left and crosses a large wooden bridge. In 0.2 mile veer left and hike through a small field. Continue 0.3 mile to complete the loop. Turn right to return to the trailhead.

OTHER OPTIONS

There are countless opportunities to shorten or extend the described hike. Be sure to pick up a detailed map at the interpretive center near the trailhead. In the winter, begin your travels at the Hart Barn and Ski Center on Lowell Street.

21 Bradley Palmer State Park

RATING/ DIFFICULTY	LOOP	ELEV GAIN/ HIGH POINT	SEASON
**/2	3.7 miles	300 feet/ 190 feet	Year-round

Map: USGS Ipswich; **Contact:** Massachusetts Department of Conservation and Recreation; **Note:** Most of the park trails are unnamed, but all intersections are numbered; **GPS:** 42.651019, -70.906956

The former 721-acre estate of an attorney whose resume included the Teapot Dome Scandal and the peace settlement ending World War I, Bradley Palmer State Park is crisscrossed by miles of trails with options suitable for hikers of all abilities. Connected to neighboring conservation areas via the Discover Hamilton and Bay Circuit trails, it is an ideal starting point for longer Essex County excursions.

GETTING THERE

From US Route 1 in Topsfield, follow Ipswich Road east 1.2 miles and then turn right onto Asbury Street. Continue 0.2 mile, then turn left into the park. Follow the main entrance road 0.3 mile (staying right at two intersections) to a large parking area on the left.

ON THE TRAIL

From the parking area follow the wide trail that enters the forest left of the gated park road and a small pond. Heading southeast, the unmarked but easy-to-follow trail skirts the pond's eastern shore and rises gently 0.4 mile to a granite post and major intersection (marker 54). Veer left onto the Discover

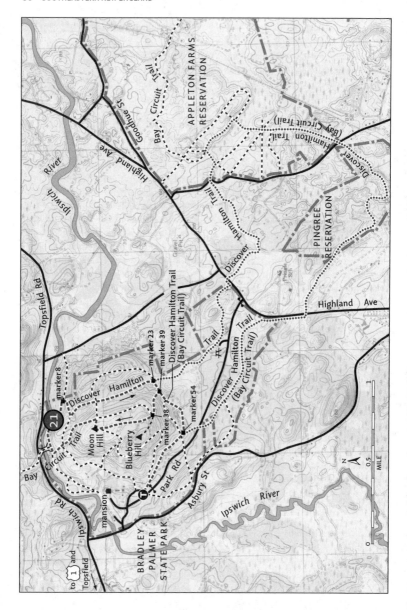

Heading across Moon Hill

Hamilton and Bay Circuit trails. Follow this well-marked route the next 1.2 miles.

In 0.4 mile, reach the start of the loop (marker 39). Stay left and gradually ascend the south side of Blueberry Hill. In a little more than 0.1 mile, arrive at another significant intersection (marker 38). Continue straight. Across rolling terrain, the route leads 0.2 mile to a large field atop Moon Hill. Head through the center of the open expanse. While views are limited, there is something liberating about walking across the grassy meadow.

A signpost awaits near the high point. Swing sharply right and depart the field in a few hundred feet. Winding north down the hillside, the wide path leads 0.4 mile to a large bridge that spans the slow, meandering Ipswich River. Approach the water quietly and survey the surrounding habitat for waterfowl, kingfishers, and other wildlife. The Bay Circuit Trail crosses the Ipswich River en route to nearby Willowdale State

Forest. To continue the day's trek, turn right and remain on the water's south side. Follow the Discover Hamilton Trail as it leads east, paralleling the river downstream.

In 0.1 mile, the path climbs away from the water, and shortly thereafter it turns sharply right at an obvious junction (marker 8). For three-quarters of a mile, the Discover Hamilton Trail heads across an increasingly wide corridor as it rises up and over a gentle slope. As the route descends, enter another expansive field. At an intersection (marker 23) where the Discover Hamilton Trail continues straight, turn right and in 0.1 mile reach the end of the day's loop. Stay left to retrace your steps back to the trailhead.

EXTENDING YOUR HIKE

Hike the entire Discover Hamilton Trail by following the trail east from Bradley Palmer to conservation land owned by the Essex County Trail Association and The Trustees of Reservations. The entire loop is nearly 10 miles.

22 Great Bay

RATING/ DIFFICULTY	ROUND-TRIP	ELEV GAIN/ HIGH POINT	SEASON
**/1–2	4.5 miles	200 feet/ 120 feet	Year-round

Map: USGS Newmarket; **Contact:** The Nature Conservancy, New Hampshire Chapter; **GPS:** 43.100382, -70.904567

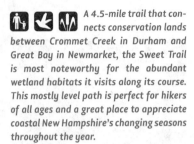

A 4.5-mile trail that connects conservation lands between Crommet Creek in Durham and Great Bay in Newmarket, the Sweet Trail is most noteworthy for the abundant wetland habitats it visits along its course. This mostly level path is perfect for hikers of all ages and a great place to appreciate coastal New Hampshire's changing seasons throughout the year.

Spotting wildlife on the Sweet Trail

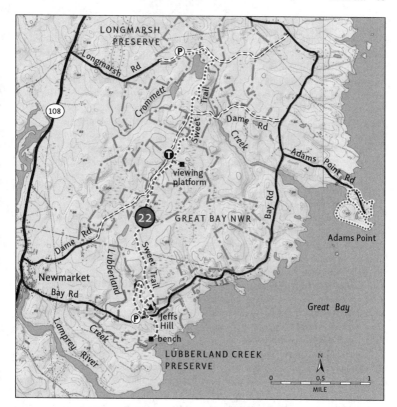

LONGMARSH PRESERVE

Longmarsh Rd

Crommett

Sweet Trail

Dame Rd

Creek

Adams Point Rd

108

viewing platform

T

22 GREAT BAY NWR

Bay Rd

Adams Point

Dame Rd

Lubberland

Sweet Trail

Newmarket Bay Rd

Lamprey River

Creek

P

Jeffs Hill

bench

LUBBERLAND CREEK PRESERVE

Great Bay

N

0 0.5 1
MILE

GETTING THERE

From downtown Newmarket, follow Route 108 north. In 0.2 mile turn right onto Dame Road. Drive 2 miles and then turn right into the parking area.

ON THE TRAIL

The Sweet Trail has three access points. Parking can be limited at both the northern and southern ends. Beginning in the middle helps to address that issue and provides hikers with more flexibility in terms of designing an itinerary. The described

5.6-mile trek explores the trail's southern half. If time and energy allow, visit the northern segment as well.

Before beginning your trek, check out the many displays at the Dame Road parking area. They describe some of the natural features and conservation history of the area. Bear right and hike south along the Sweet Trail. Immediately, a spur leaves left and heads a few hundred feet to a viewing platform on the edge of a secluded pond; the views are a good introduction of things to come. The main path continues south 0.3

mile to the edge of Dame Road. Bear left and follow the dirt road 0.2 mile before reentering the forest to the left.

Now traveling on an old farm road, the Sweet Trail leads straight through an attractive hardwood forest on private property that has been protected with a conservation easement. Slowly the corridor narrows as beaver-filled wetlands surround the trail. Swing across a narrow strip of land and ledge, 0.3 mile from Dame Road, and enjoy intimate views of the marshy water. Approach quietly and perhaps a turtle or hooded merganser will await discovery.

Straightening out again, the Sweet Trail meanders easily for almost a mile. Travel through a forested landscape dotted with small ponds and lined with rock walls. Soon, the trail enters The Nature Conservancy's Lubberland Creek Preserve, a 400-acre conservation area once proposed as the site of an oil refinery. A grassroots campaign emerged to ward off the industrial development. Today, this threat is simply a faded memory.

Remain on the Sweet Trail as it swings right at a junction where another path leads straight to the wooded summit of Jeffs Hill. The Sweet Trail takes a circuitous route down the hill's steep slopes and approaches the shore of another small pond. After leveling off, arrive at a four-way intersection.

Stay straight on the Sweet Trail, as the route right leads quickly to the southern parking area. Cross over Bay Road and continue 0.3 mile to a well-deserved bench on the scenic shores of Great Bay. Over the past decade, millions of dollars have been invested to protect this special coastal gem in southeastern New Hampshire.

Return along the same route, with one small diversion. After recrossing Bay Road and arriving at the four-way intersection, bear right and follow the path to the top of Jeffs Hill. Steep at first, the path bends sharply right and moderates. Continue up and over the wooded high point. Upon reaching the intersection with the Sweet Trail, proceed straight to reach the Dame Road parking lot.

EXTENDING YOUR HIKE

Follow the Sweet Trail north from the parking area. It leads nearly 2 miles to the northern trailhead on Longmarsh Road. The path swings through a town-owned preserve of shady forests, rocky ridges, and small secluded ponds. If you complete the entire trail, the hike is 9 miles. Also consider visiting nearby Adams Point in Durham. A state wildlife management area, Adams Point offers easy trails with stunning views of Great Bay.

Chauncey Peak ridge, Giuffrida Park (Hike 24)

monadnock-metacomet-mattabesett

Paralleling the Connecticut River valley, the Monadnock-Metacomet-Mattabesett landscape is noteworthy for its isolated mountain peaks (monadnocks), long trap-rock ridges, and bucolic countryside. Along the region's river valleys, mill towns and large cities serve as regional hubs and cultural centers for numerous rural communities.

A handful of long-distance trails link the region's patchwork of public and private conserved lands. For more than 200 miles, the Sunapee-Ragged-Kearsarge Greenway, the Monadnock-Sunapee Greenway, and the Monadnock-Metacomet-Mattabesett (now called the New England Trail) connect central New Hampshire with southern Connecticut. Similarly, the Wapack and Midstate trails join to form a shorter 115-mile north–south corridor to the east. Offering rewarding four-season hiking, the region is especially attractive in spring and late fall, when its northern destinations are engulfed in wintry conditions.

23 Sleeping Giant

RATING/ DIFFICULTY	LOOP	ELEV GAIN/ HIGH POINT	SEASON
****/4	5.8 miles	1400 feet/ 739 feet	Year-round

Map: USGS Mount Carmel; **Contact:** Connecticut Department of Energy and Environmental Protection; **GPS:** 41.421201, -72.898946

In one of Connecticut's most popular state parks, towering cliffs, many peaks, and thick for-ested slopes resemble a sleeping giant from a distance. While most visitors choose the well-manicured Tower Trail, opt for this less traveled and more rugged loop for a hike that poses more challenges than one would expect from a 739-foot mountain.

GETTING THERE

From the junction of Routes 10 and 40 in Hamden, drive 1.4 miles north on Route 10 and then turn right onto Mount Carmel Avenue. Continue 0.3 mile to the state park entrance and parking area on the left (across from Quinnipiac University).

ON THE TRAIL

Sleeping Giant State Park features a well-marked labyrinth of hiking trails. With the exception of the first 0.1 mile, this recom-mended circuit remains on two distinct paths: the Quinnipiac Trail and the Yellow Trail. Depart to the west from the main parking area and parallel Mount Carmel Avenue along the Violet Trail. It descends 0.1 mile to the banks of the Mill River, where it intersects the blue-blazed Quinnipiac Trail.

Stay right and follow the path as the two trails coincide upstream. In 0.1 mile, after passing a trail that diverges right and crossing a small tributary, arrive at a four-way intersection. Veer slightly right to begin a 3.4-mile roller coaster–like journey on the Quinnipiac Trail. Along the way, there are countless intersections. Stay alert for the route's blue blazes and enjoy the ride.

Ascend rapidly 0.1 mile to the top of a small knoll and the first views of the day: scenes of rocky slopes rising above a quarry. After a brief, steep drop, climb the most difficult section of the hike. Up the rugged, ledge-covered slope, the path ascends 0.3 mile to the top of a second distinct peak. To the south rises New Haven's skyline above the shores of Long Island Sound. The trail eases and skirts along the edge

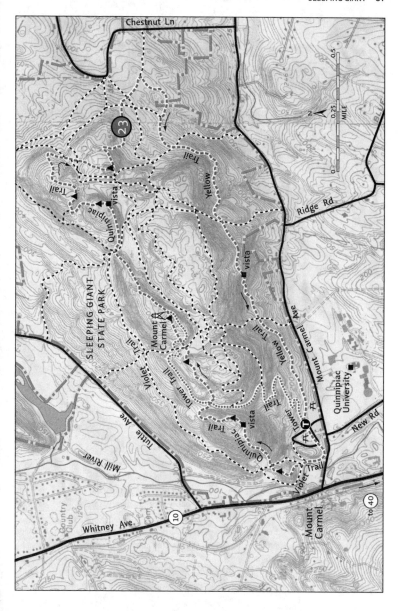

Quinnipiac Trail near the summit of Mount Carmel

of a precipitous cliff featuring views to the south and east; watch your step. A difficult 0.1-mile descent soon follows, just before an intersection with the Tower Trail.

Now, 1 mile from the start, proceed straight across the more popular route. Remain on the Quinnipiac Trail as it heads up and over a third rocky peak, a summit shaded by the surrounding forest. In 0.3 mile, cross the Tower Trail a second time. A final 0.2-mile climb leads to a historic stone structure atop 739-foot Mount Carmel. From its top floor, marvel at 360-degree views of southern Connecticut, but be prepared for a lot of company.

Time to leave the crowds behind. Rejoin the Quinnipiac Trail as it departs the tower to the northeast. After passing a handful of short spurs that lead right to precarious vistas, the trail drops rapidly into a scree-filled

saddle. Swing right and scramble 0.2 mile up the day's fifth distinct peak. From this quieter ridgetop locale, find secluded rock perches that lie beneath the soaring wings of hawks, vultures, and falcons.

Another 0.2-mile descent is followed by a rise of a similar length to the journey's sixth summit. Shrouded in boulders and a jagged ledge, this peak offers few views, but much solitude. The hike rambles 0.7 mile to the seventh and final bump on the ridge. Continue another 0.6 mile on the Quinnipiac Trail as it drops to flatter ground and leads easily to a junction with the Yellow Trail on the right.

Although the parking area is still 2.2 miles away, the most difficult terrain has passed. Over less pronounced ups and downs, the Yellow Trail ventures through a tranquil forested landscape offering countless opportunities to listen for resident songbirds or marvel at colorful wildflowers. In 1 mile, the path rises to a scenic vista with views south over the neighboring university. Shortly after, descend two wooden staircases. The final mile provides a relaxing conclusion to one of the most rigorous hikes one can find in southern New England.

SHORTENING YOUR HIKE

For a shorter trek, follow the Quinnipiac Trail to the top of Mount Carmel and return via the Tower Trail. This 3-mile loop visits the park's most dramatic natural features. Those seeking less adventure should stick to the Tower Trail both ways; it is appropriate for hikers of all ages. For the most serenity, avoid the tower area altogether. Visit the state park website for a detailed map of the many trails available for exploration.

24 Chauncey and Lamentation

RATING/ DIFFICULTY	LOOP	ELEV GAIN/ HIGH POINT	SEASON
****/3–4	4.2 miles	850 feet/ 720 feet	Year-round

Map: USGS Meriden; **Contact:** Meriden Land Trust; **Note:** Begins at a municipal park; **GPS:** 41.556523, -72.763975

Mesmerizing views highlight this dramatic cliff-top adventure in the heart of the Constitution State. While there are options available for the faint of heart or those seeking gentler terrain, complete this challenging loop over Chauncey Peak and Mount Lamentation to enjoy some of Connecticut's most breathtaking scenery.

Crescent Lake from Mattabesett Trail vista (Photo by Anthony Romano)

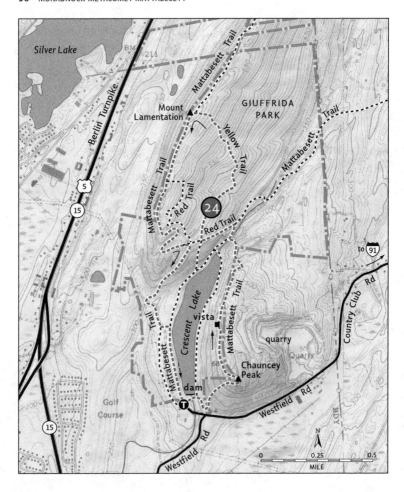

GETTING THERE

From Interstate 91, take exit 20 and head west on Country Club Road. Drive 2.6 miles (Country Club Road becomes Westfield Road after entering Meriden) and turn right into Giuffrida Park. Continue 0.1 mile to the parking area.

ON THE TRAIL

Begin on the blue-blazed Mattabesett Trail as it heads beneath the base of the dam forming Crescent Lake. Turn right and enter the forest. In 0.1 mile swing sharply left and begin an increasingly rocky and difficult ascent toward the summit of Chauncey

Peak. Though challenging, the 0.3-mile climb soon rises to the ridgeline. Turn right to reach an open outcrop with expansive views south and west.

The Mattabesett Trail proceeds more moderately 0.7 mile north along and then down the Chauncey Peak ridge. Remain on the blue-blazed trail as it passes numerous dramatic vistas of Crescent Lake, which lies far below. There are also occasional shots of the mountain's enormous quarry. Before the ridge's halfway point, arrive at the day's most spectacular perch, but watch your step near its precipitous edge. Eventually, a rocky descent leads to a seasonal stream and narrow gorge. Cross the bridge to a junction.

To the left, an unmarked path heads to Crescent Lake. This is a shortcut back to the trailhead. To continue the loop, turn right and ascend a small incline. In 0.1 mile, arrive at an intersection where the Mattabesett Trail stays straight. Turn left onto a red-blazed trail and rise gently 0.1 mile to another intersection. Follow the yellow-blazed trail right; it ascends moderately 0.8 mile to Mount Lamentation's 720-foot high point. The easy-to-follow route ends in a large grassy area and an unsigned junction with a different section of the Mattabesett Trail. Continue a few dozen feet ahead to a summit ledge with impressive views west and north, including some of Hartford's skyline.

Join the blue-blazed Mattabesett Trail left and begin the 2.1-mile journey south to the trailhead. Remaining high on the ridge, the trail meanders by one scenic cliff top after another. In 0.2 mile, pass a junction where a red-blazed trail departs left, providing an alternative route back; continue straight. Wind over a few more perches and then

descend off the ridge. Reach a second intersection with the red-blazed path in 0.5 mile and turn sharply right, remaining on the Mattabesett Trail.

The rocky corridor is level at first, but one final steep drop ensues. At the base, the footing becomes easier as the route leads to and then briefly follows a power line. Join a wide dirt road that ambles south back to the parking area. In 0.1 mile, at an unmarked intersection that can be easily overlooked, the Mattabesett Trail exits the dirt road left and marches 0.1 mile east to Crescent Lake. Once near the water's edge, swing right and hike 0.3 mile along this picturesque and popular stretch of trail.

25 Falls Brook Trail

RATING/ DIFFICULTY	LOOP	ELEV GAIN/ HIGH POINT	SEASON
*/2	1.8 miles	400 feet/ 1170 feet	Year-round

Map: USGS West Granville; **Contact:** Connecticut Department of Energy and Environmental Protection; **GPS:** 42.021439, -72.952290

Falls Brook Falls is a hidden gem in Connecticut's 9152-acre Tunxis State Forest. Appropriate for hikers of all ages, this pleasant loop walks beneath towering trees and around moss-covered boulders en route to a series of charming cascades.

GETTING THERE

From the junction of Routes 20 and 179 in East Hartland, drive 5.3 miles west on Route 20 to the trailhead on the left. Park along the left (southwest) side of the road.

ON THE TRAIL

The Falls Brook Trail leaves the southwest side of Route 20. Follow the blue-blazed route as it descends gradually toward Falls Brook. In 0.3 mile reach a junction and the start of a loop.

Stay left and parallel the cascading brook. The trail continues with minor elevation change before turning abruptly right in 0.3 mile. Continue a few dozen feet to the side of the brook and stand atop its highest waterfall. A large rock serves as an inviting picnic spot. Also, take some time and explore the unofficial paths that descend to the base of the falls and beyond to the top of another cascade. Watch your footing; the rocks can be slippery.

From the waterfall, the trail turns right and begins to follow the brook upstream. Immediately reach a crossing that can be difficult during high water. Use caution and take your time. Once on the other side, remain close to the inviting brook and rise to a reflective pool in 0.1 mile. Ahead, the route becomes a bit rougher. Make your way across the rocky landscape to the confluence of the brook's east and west branches.

Alongside a small cascade, ascend a ridge between the two branches of Falls Brook. For 0.2 mile, the path hugs the side of the more scenic western branch. After snapping a few photos of the last waterfall, swing right and hike 0.3 mile to the banks of the eastern branch. Briefly walk downstream to where a

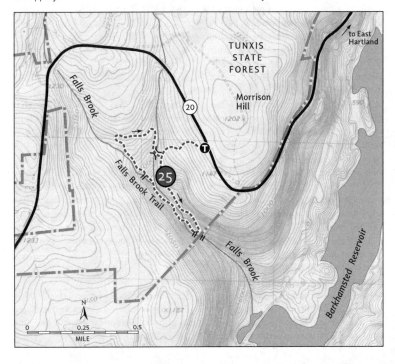

Falls Brook Falls

wooden bridge leads safely across the water. In 0.1 mile the loop ends. Turn left to return to the start.

26 Penwood State Park

RATING/ DIFFICULTY	LOOP	ELEV GAIN/ HIGH POINT	SEASON
***/2–3	4.2 miles	750 feet/ 730 feet	Year-round

Map: USGS Avon; **Contact:** Connecticut Department of Energy and Environmental Protection; **GPS:** 41.838680, -72.784836

In 1944, industrialist, inventor, outdoorsman, and hiker Curtis H. Veeder donated to the people of Connecticut nearly 800 acres atop a scenic traprock ridge draped in maturing hardwood forests and carpeted in wildflowers. As the donor intended, today Penwood State Park is "kept in a natural state so that those who love nature may enjoy this property as [he] enjoyed it."

GETTING THERE

From the junction of Routes 185 and 178 in Bloomfield, follow Route 185 1 mile west and turn right. Continue 0.1 mile to the parking area on the right. Alternatively, from the junction of Route 185 and US Route 202 and Route 10 in Simsbury, drive 1.6 miles east on Route 185. Turn left to enter the park.

ON THE TRAIL

Head north along the Metacomet Trail as it follows the park road paralleling the western shore of Gale Pond. In 0.1 mile, leave the pavement and turn left at a signpost. Begin a short but aggressive climb. The blue-blazed path soon levels off and for 1.5 miles winds atop the rolling ridgeline. Along the way, there are minor ups and downs, an artistic collection of cairns, and the remains of a stone pedestal. Descending to a paved trail not open to motorized vehicles, this section ends near the shores of Lake Louise. Named in honor of Curtis's wife, the peaceful water body has a viewing platform that is an ideal spot to scan the surrounding vegetation for birds and other wildlife.

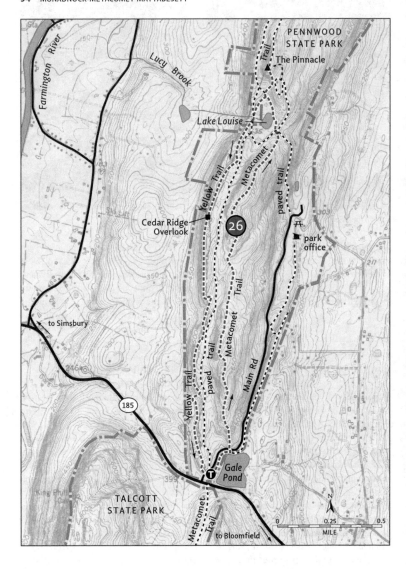

Exploring the Metacomet Trail

Remain on the Metacomet Trail as it treks north between the pond's eastern shore and an impressive talus slope. In 0.2 mile, stay straight at an unmarked junction where a path diverges left and then immediately arrive at a wooden signpost. Turn right as the blue blazes rise steeply up a stone staircase. The brief 0.1-mile climb soon plateaus. Veering left, the Metacomet Trail rises 0.1 mile farther before emerging atop The Pinnacle. From this open ledge, enjoy impressive views south toward Hueblein Tower and west across the Farmington River valley. With natural beauty in all directions, only the occasional disturbance of jet engines serves as a reminder of Hartford's proximity.

Retrace your steps down the stone staircase, past the wooden sign, and back to the unmarked junction. Follow the wide trail right. Intermittently blazed in white, the path leads 0.2 mile around the western shore of Lake Louise. Cross a wooden bridge that heads over a small stream and look for a yellow-blazed trail departing right.

Follow this meandering 1.8-mile route to conclude the day's hike. In 0.5 mile, it rises modestly to Cedar Ridge Overlook, a vista that offers impressive western views. Reenter the forest and enjoy a relaxing grade for 0.4 mile before descending left. Approach a paved trail, but turn sharply right before reaching it. The trail remains high above a deep ravine and proceeds south. The final stretch back to the parking area descends moderately for 0.9 mile, the slope occasionally interrupted by a short incline. Enjoy the many towering trees along the way.

27 Chester–Blandford State Forest

RATING/ DIFFICULTY	LOOP	ELEV GAIN/ HIGH POINT	SEASON
**/3	4.5 miles	1100 feet/ 1450 feet	Year-round

Maps: USGS Blandford and USGS Chester; **Contact:** Massachusetts Department of Conservation and Recreation; **GPS:** 42.255757, -72.947021

Sanderson Brook Falls

🔲 🔳 *During the Great Depression, young men in the Civilian Conservation Corps (CCC) spent long hours battling the heat of summer and the icy cold winds of winter developing trails and bridges in the 2308-acre Chester–Blandford State Forest. Nearly a century later, these now-rustic paths remain, leading hikers to dense wildflower-filled forests, impressive cascading brooks, and scenic views of the Westfield River.*

GETTING THERE

From Huntington, follow US Route 20 west. Reach the Huntington–Chester town line in 1.7 miles and continue another 2.4 miles to the Sanderson Brook parking area on the left.

ON THE TRAIL

Head up Sanderson Brook Road. Closed to motorized vehicles, the route passes through a gate and crosses over Sanderson Brook. In 0.1 mile, near a sign describing the forest's history, look for the H. Newman Marsh Trail (Marsh Trail) on the left.

Join the narrower footpath and begin the day's most difficult task. Named for a local outdoorsman, the blue-blazed Marsh Trail wastes little time ascending a steep slope of mossy ledges under shady hemlocks. The route soon rises into a forest of maturing yellow birch and maple. Parallel a notch on the left and then cross the seasonal stream that flows through it. Beyond a second sign pointing back to Sanderson Brook Road, arrive at an unsigned intersection, 0.6 mile from the start. Here the Marsh Trail forms a 0.5-mile loop.

Turn sharply left onto the loop's western portion. With the bulk of the hike's ascent complete, enjoy the less challenging terrain. After a small rise, descend through a tunnel of mountain laurel to an open ledge with pleasant views of the Westfield River valley. Swinging to the south, climb gradually past a less open eastern vista and catch a glimpse of Mount Tom in the distance. The path soon reaches another intersection. To the right, the Marsh Trail leads back to the parking area—a good option to complete a 1.8-mile hike. To tackle the longer circuit, continue

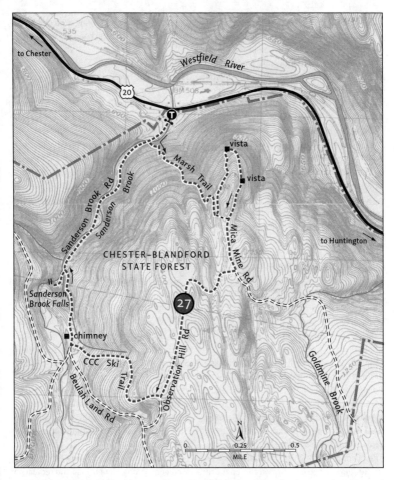

straight by following the blue markers a short distance to Mica Mine Road.

Hike southeast along the wide woods road. In 0.2 mile, reach an unmarked but obvious junction with Observation Hill Road. Turn right and follow this route 0.9 mile. It descends at first, then climbs to the forested high point of the day's journey. Meandering along the rolling landscape, the dirt road is easy to follow. Just before it begins to drop more steadily left, turn right onto the unsigned CCC Ski Trail.

Descend gradually at first. The 0.6-mile route quickly swings north to the banks of a small stream and then drops more aggressively. After leveling off, the path ends at a major intersection of woods roads. Straight ahead, atop a low bank, find an old chimney that sits high above Sanderson Brook.

Turn right onto Sanderson Brook Road. In 0.5 mile, just beyond a viewpoint of the tumbling brook, arrive at a signed junction on the left. Follow this spur 0.1 mile for intimate shots of Sanderson Brook Falls. This photogenic cascade carves its way down a steep, rocky slope. However, be sure to watch your footing at the base of the falls, because there are many slippery rocks and downed trees to navigate.

Rejoin Sanderson Brook Road for a relaxing 0.8-mile conclusion to a delightful exploration of this hidden forest in western Massachusetts.

28 Mount Holyoke

RATING/ DIFFICULTY	LOOP	ELEV GAIN/ HIGH POINT	SEASON
***/3	3.2 miles	900 feet/ 931 feet	Year-round

Map: USGS Mount Holyoke; **Contact:** Massachusetts Department of Conservation and Recreation; **GPS:** 42.295552, -72.597586

On the western flank of a long ridge of peaks, Mount Holyoke rises abruptly from the fertile banks of the Connecticut River. The mountain's rocky summit and ledge-covered slopes are surrounded by more than 3000 acres of state park land and crisscrossed by miles of enticing hiking trails.

GETTING THERE
From the intersection of Routes 47 and 9 in Hadley, drive south 4.2 miles on Route 47 and then turn left onto Old Mountain Road.

Continue 0.4 mile to parking area on the left (just before the summit road diverges left).

ON THE TRAIL
Head up the Two Forest Trail. This yellow-blazed route ascends gradually to the northeast, just to the left of the summit road it parallels throughout. In 0.4 mile, reach an imposing boulder on the left, the so-called Devils Football. Following both yellow and blue blazes, continue straight another 0.2 mile to the summit road. The loop proceeds straight across the road onto the Halfway House Trail; however, before beginning the final climb, check out the Halfway House area to the left. The remains of a summit tram offer a glimpse of a bygone era, when the nation's tourism industry was in its infancy.

The blue-blazed Halfway House Trail climbs very steeply 0.2 mile to an intersection with the Metacomet-Monadnock Trail. Stay left and wind 0.2 mile to Mount Holyoke's summit. There are numerous ledges and picnic spots that surround the historic Summit House, an impressive building whose origin goes back to the 1820s. The views over the Connecticut River north to Vermont and west to Mount Greylock are breathtaking. To the south, the skylines of Hartford and Springfield stand out amid the hilly landscape.

Retrace your steps 0.2 mile west along the Metacomet-Monadnock Trail and remain on it past the junction with the Halfway House Trail. The white-blazed path winds down the ridge, rising to one stunning promontory after another. In 0.3 mile, the green-blazed Hang Glider Trail diverges right to a scenic vista. Near the midway point ascend to the top of a long, picturesque ledge. Watch your footing while descending and stay alert for

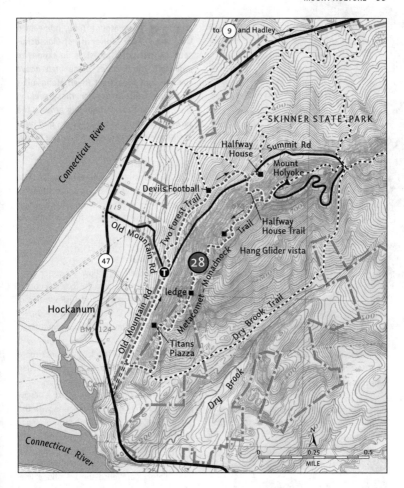

colorful songbirds including the very vocal great-crested flycatcher. A final bump offers a glimpse of nearby Mount Tom. Soon after, the trail descends rapidly under a power line. Bear sharply right at an intersection with the Dry Brook Trail and hike 0.1 mile to Old Mountain Road.

Turn right to conclude the loop and hike 0.5 mile along Old Mountain Road. This lightly used dirt road borders the park on one side and private land on the other. In a quarter mile, look for a sign on the right indicating Titans Piazza. Here a spur leads a hundred feet up a loose-rock slope to the

The Metacomet-Monadnock Trail features numerous viewpoints.

base of an overhanging ledge. Coming down is much more difficult, but it is still worth investigating.

29 Mount Toby

RATING/ DIFFICULTY	LOOP	ELEV GAIN/ HIGH POINT	SEASON
***/2–3	4.5 miles	1000 feet/ 1266 feet	Year-round

Map: USGS Williamsburg; **Contact:** University of Massachusetts, Amherst; **GPS:** 42.503720, -72.530477

Mount Toby, home to a University of Massachusetts experimental forest, is an expansive mountain that stands alone high above the nearby Connecticut River. Many miles of hiking trails await for those seeking the quiet solitude of babbling brooks, the serene beauty of towering pines, and panoramic views from atop a scenic fire tower.

GETTING THERE
From the junction of Routes 47 and 116 in Sunderland, drive 3.8 miles north on Route 47 and then turn right onto Reservation Road. Continue 0.6 mile to the parking area on the right.

ON THE TRAIL
From the large sign, follow a wooded path a few hundred feet straight to a junction of Tower Road (hiking trail) and the Robert Frost Trail. This is the start of the day's 4.5-mile loop. Stay right and join the orange-blazed Robert Frost Trail. Today's journey will traverse 2.6 miles of this long-distance route that travels 47 miles, connecting conservation areas from South Hadley to Wendell.

The ascent of Mount Toby begins gradually. Hike 1 mile to a junction with the Telephone Line Trail. Here, the route swings sharply right and coincides for 0.7 mile with this most direct path to the summit. The steep climb remains either underneath or immediately parallel to the telephone line. With increased elevation come occasional views north to distant rolling hills. Take your time; while the footing is not challenging, the incline is.

Before long, arrive at the 1266-foot summit and its tall fire tower. Not a great destination for those afraid of heights, the sturdy structure rewards those willing to scale its many

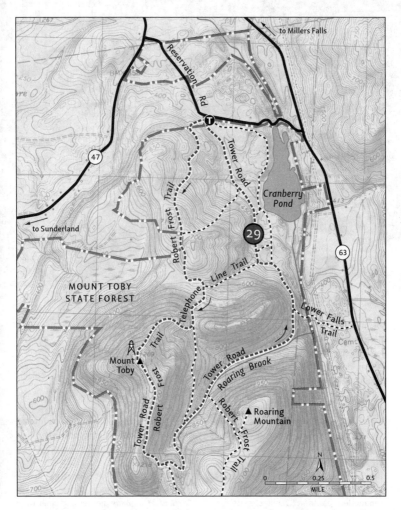

staircases. Views abound of the Pioneer Valley in the foreground as well as Mount Monadnock, the Holyoke Range, the Berkshires, and the Green Mountains in the distance.

The 2.8-mile descent follows the wide and easy-to-follow Tower Road. For the first 0.9 mile, the Tower Road and Robert Frost Trail combine. Proceeding easily at first, the route remains high along the ridge. In 0.5 mile begin a steady, rocky descent into a saddle and swing left. Paralleling the upper portions of Roaring Brook, the path

The Robert Frost Trail weaves past ledges.

continues to drop rapidly, but the terrain is more forgiving. Soon, the Robert Frost Trail veers off sharply to the right.

Continue straight on Tower Road 0.7 mile along the banks of the brook, occasionally crossing from one side to the other. The bubbling stream slowly grows larger with each step you take into the deep forested basin. As the brook drops precipitously to the right, the path bears left and levels considerably. Soon after, the very steep Lower Falls Trail departs right. Stay straight on the main route as it meanders another 1.2 miles to its conclusion. Near the base of the Telephone Line Trail, a number of paths leave right to Cranberry Pond. Consider exploring these alternative routes if time permits. They are not well signed, but they are also not far from civilization.

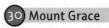

30 Mount Grace

RATING/ DIFFICULTY	LOOP	ELEV GAIN/ HIGH POINT	SEASON
**/2	3.4 miles	950 feet/ 1611 feet	Year-round

Map: USGS Mount Grace; **Contact:** Massachusetts Department of Conservation and Recreation; **GPS:** 42.689228, -72.340906

Mount Grace's modern history dates back to 1676, when a young mother and child were captured during King Philip's War. Named for the captured infant who was buried at the foot of the mountain, the peak is surrounded by a 1458-acre state forest where trails ramble to small ledges and a fire tower features sweeping views of three states.

GETTING THERE

From the junction of Routes 78, 10, and 119 in Winchester, New Hampshire, drive south on Route 78. In 3.5 miles, cross into Massachusetts. Continue 2.8 miles to a large parking area on the right.

ON THE TRAIL

From the parking area there are four possible routes to the summit of the third-highest peak in Massachusetts east of the Connecticut River. This recommended route follows the two shortest and most straightforward options.

Follow the sign pointing left toward the Tower and Around the Mountain trails. The trail swings south of a large field and picnic area before reaching a junction and the start of the loop in 0.2 mile.

Continue straight ahead on the blue-blazed Around the Mountain Trail. Winding steadily up the forested slope, the wide path ascends 0.4 mile to a dirt road. Bear left into a saddle to an intersection with the Metacomet-Monadnock Trail (MM). Here, the Around the Mountain Trail diverges sharply left and descends the dirt road.

Veer slightly left onto the MM Trail. It rises gradually over a small forested bump and then, in 0.2 mile, drops into a low spot. Hike another 0.3 mile to the top of Little Mount Grace. Draped with ledges, the diminutive peak showcases quaint views south and west over the lightly developed countryside.

Retrace your steps to the previous intersection. This time follow the MM Trail steeply up near a utility corridor. The 0.5-mile climb swings into the forest and then back into the open before ending at the base of the Mount Grace summit fire tower. Ascend the staircases for exceptional views west to Vermont's Green Mountains, east across New

Mount Monadnock dominates Mount Grace's eastern skyline.

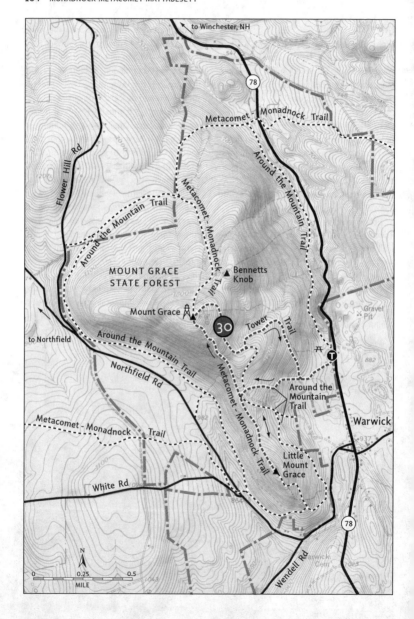

Hampshire's Monadnock region, and south toward Massachusetts's Quabbin Reservoir.

The 1.2-mile descent begins on the MM Trail, but this white-blazed route departs left in a few dozen feet. Continue straight on the Tower Trail, which proceeds along a wide dirt road. Dropping quickly at first, the route veers abruptly left at a trail sign in 0.4 mile. Meandering through more pleasant forested surroundings, the narrower but still easy-to-follow path winds 0.7 mile to the end of the loop. Turn left to reach the parking area.

EXTENDING YOUR HIKE

Consider descending north along the MM Trail rather than following the Tower Trail. This quiet route drops gradually a little more than 1 mile to the west side of Route 78. Turn right and follow the Around the Mountain Trail 1.5 miles back to the parking area. It passes easily beneath an abandoned ski area at first, but be prepared: the final stretch climbs a bit and is slightly overgrown in places.

31 Pisgah State Park

RATING/ DIFFICULTY	LOOP	ELEV GAIN/ HIGH POINT	SEASON
***/3–4	8 miles	1600 feet/ 1329 feet	Year-round

Map: USGS Hinsdale; **Contact:** New Hampshire Division of Parks and Recreation; **GPS:** 42.841685, -72.483332

Pisgah State Park, 13,500 acres of rolling hills and sprawling wetlands, is a perfect destination for spring bird-watchers, summer wildflower enthusiasts, autumn leaf peepers, and winter wildlife trackers. Once the domain of local paper mill owners and rural farmers, today the park is a permanently protected preserve where hikers of all abilities can find beauty and rejuvenation on more than 50 miles of trails.

Cairns adorn Pisgah Mountain Vista.

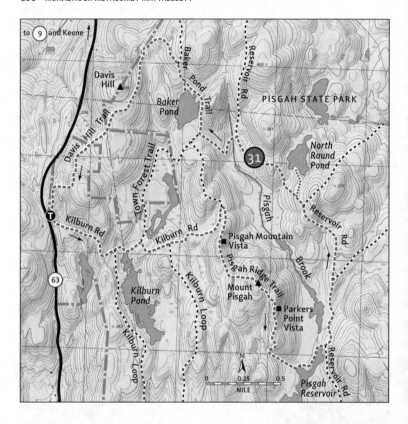

GETTING THERE

From the junction of Routes 9 and 101 in Keene, follow Route 9 west for 9 miles and then turn left onto Route 63. Continue straight 4.5 miles until you reach the Kilburn Road parking area on the left.

ON THE TRAIL

One of the park's more scenic and quiet loops begins on Kilburn Road, a wide footpath that meanders over easy grades 0.6 mile to the north shore of Kilburn Pond. Here the

western branch of the popular 5-mile Kilburn Loop leads right along the pond's shore. Stay left on Kilburn Road. After a sharp right turn at a junction with the Town Forest Trail, the path narrows and crosses a small stream before gradually climbing up a hemlock-covered hillside. At an intersection with the Kilburn Loop's east branch, veer left. Reach the Pisgah Ridge Trail 1.5 miles from the start.

Turn right and begin the steady climb south along the narrowing ridgeline. Soon the trail reaches Pisgah Mountain Vista, an open ledge where views of Mount Monadnock dominate the eastern skyline. There are also views west to the rolling hills of southern Vermont. The trail drops into a small saddle and then quickly ascends to Mount Pisgah's 1329-foot wooded summit. Continue down to Parkers Point Vista, the finest viewpoint of the day. Here, a spur trail leaves left to the top of a steep ledge. This is a great spot to enjoy the park's tranquil scenery, scenery that has changed greatly over the past 150 years. In fact, the area's most famous descendant, Harlan Fiske Stone, would not recognize the thick forests that now grow in the farmland he knew in the late nineteenth century. A lifelong Republican, Stone was appointed the twelfth chief justice of the US Supreme Court by President Franklin Roosevelt.

Beyond the ledge, the trail passes a large rock, enters a small notch, and follows the gradual slope to the shore of Pisgah Reservoir. Approach the water quietly and you may encounter waterfowl feeding in the cool waters. After hugging the shoreline, the path crosses a small bridge and ends at Reservoir Road, a multiuse trail also enjoyed by snowmobilers and mountain bikers. Turn left and follow the wide route 1.8 miles up and over a number of low ridges, past numerous small wetlands and a handful of well-signed side trails. The 0.2-mile spur to North Round Pond is a nice diversion to a quiet corner of the park.

Upon reaching the Baker Pond Trail, turn left, cross Pisgah Brook, and travel 0.5 mile to the path's namesake pond. The route winds around the water from a distance but soon reaches a short spur that departs left to the serene shoreline. Continue on the main trail 0.1 mile to a three-way intersection and bear left on the 1.7-mile Davis Hill Trail.

Follow this route over a series of old roads that weave up the wooded landscape and through the abundant mountain laurel. Over the final stretch, the trail passes two town boundaries and briefly leaves state land. Climb up a few small inclines before descending one last time. Swing left to return to the parking area.

32 Pack Monadnock

RATING/ DIFFICULTY	ROUND-TRIP	ELEV GAIN/ HIGH POINT	SEASON
***/3–4	8 miles	2000 feet/ 2290 feet	Year-round

Maps: USGS Peterborough South, USGS Peterborough North, USGS Greenville, and USGS Greenfield; **Contact:** New Hampshire Division of Parks and Recreation; **Note:** Fee; **GPS:** 42.850111, -71.886886

Two loops in one, a relaxing trek across an attractive ridge, and views stretching from New England's highest point to its largest city highlight this adventure in southwestern New Hampshire. The hike takes place within nearly 3000 acres of contiguous conservation land pieced together through public-private partnerships at the local, state, and federal levels. Together, these protected lands provide valuable habitat for moose, deer, fishers, and countless songbirds.

GETTING THERE

From the junction of US Route 202 and Route 101 in Peterborough, follow Route 101 east 3.9 miles and turn left into the Miller State Park entrance. Use the large parking area at the base of Miller Park Road.

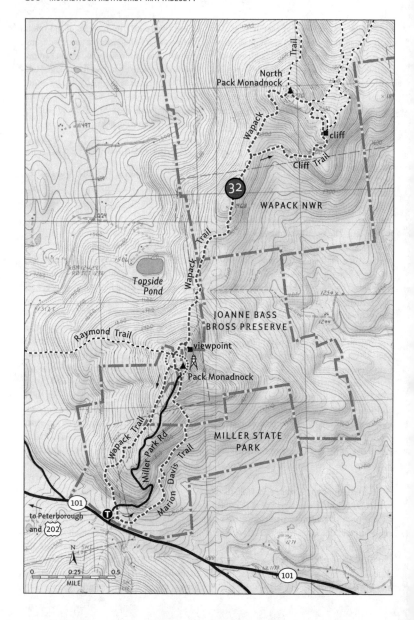

ON THE TRAIL

Named to honor a War of 1812 hero, Miller State Park was established in 1891 as New Hampshire's first state park. Its centerpiece, which now encompasses 550 acres of land, is 2290-foot Pack Monadnock. While many reach the summit via the 1.3-mile auto road, hiking up remains the most pleasurable option.

Two footpaths leave the eastern side of the parking area. Leading left is the Wapack Trail, a 21-mile route established in 1923 running from Mount Watatic in Massachusetts to North Pack Monadnock. You will be joining this trail later. Turn right onto the 1.4-mile trail named in honor of Wapack Trail cofounder Marion Davis.

The Davis Trail gradually winds through a rock-shrouded forest. Just before arriving at the Pack Monadnock summit, pass through a portion of The Nature Conservancy's 500-acre Joanne Bass Bross Preserve. Reenter the state park as you arrive at the top of the auto road. Straight ahead, find picnic tables at the base of the mountain's lookout tower. The mostly wooded peak offers expansive views from this manmade structure and along a short 0.4-mile loop trail, blazed in red, that passes a number of vistas while circling the summit.

When you are ready for a quieter destination, hike north along the Wapack Trail. Head across an open ledge. The trail enters the forest and swings right where a short spur leads east to a viewpoint. Beyond, a steady descent through the dark evergreen forest winds to the low point of the ridge, carpets of ferns, and a large sign that more formally welcomes you to the Joanne Bass Bross Preserve.

Continue along the gentle ridge and enter the Wapack National Wildlife Refuge at a kiosk. This 1672-acre refuge, which encompasses much of North Pack Monadnock, is managed primarily for the protection of nesting songbirds, upland mammals, and migrating hawks.

The trail ascends a wooded knoll on the ridge and reaches a junction with the Cliff Trail 1.7 miles from Pack Monadnock. Turn right and follow this 1.2-mile path to the most scenic spot on the mountain. First descend to a small stream. Quickly, the route climbs aggressively to the base of a talus slope. Swing right, then left. Scramble through the woods to the top of

Cliff Trail panorama

the cliff, where expansive views of Mount Monadnock, Mount Wachusett, and the Boston skyline await. This quiet spot is a great location to scan the sky for circling raptors.

Remain on the Cliff Trail as it passes through woods and gently ascends open ledges before reaching the summit of North Pack Monadnock in 0.6 mile. It stands slightly lower than its southern neighbor, and growing trees have slowly restricted its views. However, there are still plenty of places to enjoy the surrounding scenery.

The 3.7-mile return trek follows the Wapack Trail exclusively. Beginning at a large cairn, the path gradually descends south through the forest. Stay right at the Cliff Trail intersection and remain on the ridge. Climb back to the top of Pack Monadnock. From the summit parking area, the Wapack Trail begins its descent at a western viewpoint of Mount Monadnock. Joined by the red-blazed summit loop at first, the path soon veers sharply left. Dropping steadily over rocky terrain, the trail becomes steeper and more rugged as you drop farther down the mountain. A series of switchbacks leads to numerous ledges, some with views. Descend to and then cross the auto road. Hike a few hundred yards to the trail's end.

SHORTENING YOUR HIKE

If 8 miles sounds too long, limit the loop to Pack Monadnock. The Wapack and Marion Davis trails easily combine for a 2.8-mile hike.

33 Willard Pond

RATING/ DIFFICULTY	LOOP	ELEV GAIN/ HIGH POINT	SEASON
***/3	3.5 miles	900 feet/ 2021 feet	Year-round

Map: USGS Stoddard; **Contact:** New Hampshire Audubon; **Note:** Open during daylight hours only; **GPS:** 43.016461, -72.021006

 New Hampshire Audubon's largest sanctuary, Willard Pond is surrounded by nearly 1700 acres of wetlands, rocky hillsides, and scenic ledges. This sanctuary, a good first stop in the region, is adjacent to many nearby preserves, including the Harris Center, that together form a more than 10,000-acre complex of conservation lands. Hiking opportunities in this region are seemingly endless.

GETTING THERE

From the southern junction of Routes 9 and 123 in Stoddard, follow Route 123 south 3.3 miles and then turn left onto Willard Pond Road. In 0.5 mile, stay straight on the main road. In 0.3 mile, continue left. Drive 0.9 mile to the parking area on the left.

ON THE TRAIL

Follow the Tamposi Trail as it leads west from the parking area. The yellow-blazed path rises quickly up a boulder-covered ridge. After a brief descent, resume the steady climb, past stone walls and additional large rocks. In 0.7 mile, reach a fork where the trail forms a loop. To the right, one can reach the sanctuary's most scenic ledges in 0.3 mile. However, stay left and enjoy the more circuitous route.

Through a young forest and thick carpets of fern, the western branch of the Tamposi Trail continues an aggressive ascent for 0.3 mile before arriving at a junction. Departing left is the blue-blazed Spur Trail, a diversion of more than a mile that leads to the sanctuary's quietest corner. Remain right on the Tamposi

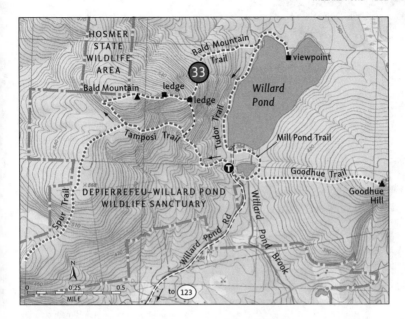

Trail. It rises rapidly into an evergreen forest. Weave 0.2 mile around moss-covered ledges and up the day's last incline to the wooded summit of Bald Mountain.

Beyond the cairn that marks the high point, the Tamposi Trail coincides with the red-blazed Bald Mountain Trail. The two routes soon descend to open ledges and the first of many breathtaking vistas. Enjoy views of Pack Monadnock to the east, Mount Monadnock to the south, and Willard Pond far below. Reenter the forest and its inviting rocky landscape. The path continues to a second panoramic perch with even more intimate views of Willard Pond. Here the Tamposi and Bald Mountain trails split.

Stay left on the Bald Mountain Trail and drop swiftly 0.6 mile to an intersection with the Tudor Trail. Turn left and follow the yellow blazes 0.3 mile to the tip of a peninsula

that provides stunning shots of Willard Pond and the surrounding hills. En route, the easy-to-follow path passes a small cascade and traverses a forest of large white pines and massive boulders.

Retrace your steps back along the Tudor Trail and remain on it as it follows the pond's western shoreline 0.6 mile farther. Take advantage of the many viewpoints along the way. In addition, you will find a number of lichen-draped stones to admire and photograph.

Turn right upon reaching Willard Pond Road, then immediately left to join the 0.5-mile Mill Pond Trail. It loops easily to the shores of a small wetland that provides an ideal backdrop for observing wildlife. Stay right at the start of the 1-mile Goodhue Trail and soon after return to Willard Pond Road. Turn right to reach the parking area.

Willard Pond from Bald Mountain ledges

EXTENDING YOUR HIKE

The Goodhue Trail and the lightly used Spur Trail are possible additions to this 3.6-mile loop. Both offer additional scenic viewpoints and diverse forest habitats to explore. Each would add at least 2 miles to the described hike and 4.5 miles together.

34 Mount Sunapee

RATING/ DIFFICULTY	LOOP	ELEV GAIN/ HIGH POINT	SEASON
***/3	6.2 miles	1800 feet/ 2745 feet	April–Nov

Map: USGS Sunapee Lake South; **Contact:** New Hampshire Division of Parks and Recreation; **Note:** Ski trails are closed to hikers during ski season; **GPS:** 43.331313, -72.080658

More famous as a winter ski destination, Mount Sunapee State Park is also an attractive hiking location. This moderately difficult loop visits scenic promontories showcasing views north to the White Mountains, west into Vermont, and south across the Monadnock region. Along the journey, be alert for resident wildlife at a secluded pond and within the mountain's acres of rich forestland.

GETTING THERE

From the junction of Routes 103 and 103B in Mount Sunapee, take the southern exit out of the rotary toward Mount Sunapee Ski Area. Drive 0.6 mile and park in the ski area's Lot 1, near the Sunapee Lodge.

ON THE TRAIL

The trailhead is behind the Sunapee Lodge. To the right of the mountain's main chairlift, find a sign for the Summit Trail. The route heads right, crosses a wooden bridge, and then proceeds over a ski trail. Reentering the woods, the red-blazed path leaves civilization behind for the next 2 miles.

Rising quickly through a maze of tall trees, the Summit Trail reaches a large boulder and an intersection with the Sunapee-Ragged-Kearsarge Greenway 0.5 mile from the start. This 75-mile loop, maintained by a nonprofit organization with the same name, provides many day-hiking opportunities in the region. Today's journey will cover 4 miles of this enticing circuit.

To the right, the greenway coincides with the Province Trail. Turn left onto the long-distance path as it joins the Summit Trail. The easy-to-follow route winds gently through changing forests. After dropping to and crossing a small stream, swing right

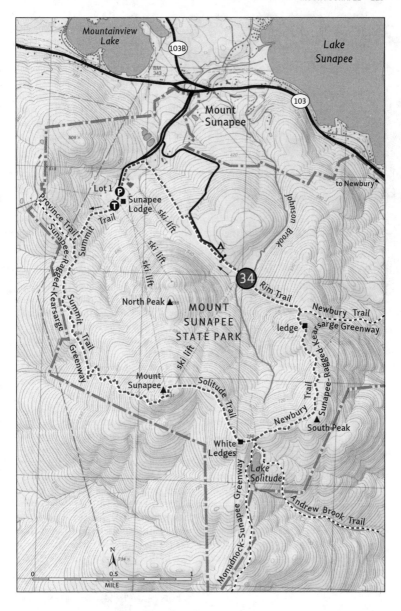

Lake Solitude's serene shoreline

and ascend more modestly. Eventually, the trail bends sharply left and enters a series of small switchbacks. Accompanying the change in elevation is an increase in conifers and rocky terrain. One last pitch and the 2.4-mile ascent ends atop the 2745-foot summit.

From various locations, different ski trail openings provide a wide array of views, including the blue waters of nearby Lake Sunapee. The scenery continues along the 1-mile Solitude Trail. Follow this route as it descends north, then east, down a ski slope. Head back into the forest to the right, a little more than 0.1 mile from the high point.

The white-blazed Solitude Trail continues through a picturesque evergreen forest. Proceed over roots and around boulders to the top of White Ledges. Here an unmarked spur descends right a few hundred feet to a breathtaking vista over Lake Solitude to the hills and valleys beyond. This is the mountain's most beautiful spot and an ideal location to enjoy lunch or a midday nap.

From White Ledges, descend swiftly 0.1 mile to Jack and June Junction. The loop turns left on the Newbury Trail. Before venturing down the Newbury Trail, drop 0.1 mile right to the shores of Lake Solitude. The best views can be found on the eastern shore along the Andrew Brook Trail. Partly covered with numerous lily pads, the lake also reflects the white cliffs above.

Return to the Newbury Trail, the most lightly used section of the day's hike, and turn right. Down the rolling terrain and through dense forests, the path leads 1.2 miles to an open ledge with intimate views of Lake Sunapee. From the ledge, drop quickly to an intersection. The Newbury Trail, and with it the Sunapee-Ragged-Kearsarge Greenway, bends sharply right and continues east to a different trailhead.

Turn left onto the Rim Trail. Blazed in yellow, this route wastes little time descending. In 0.4 mile, cross Johnson Brook and then reach the trail's end in an open area. Follow the road straight uphill 0.2 mile to a gate. Hike around the gate and pass the park's campground on the right. Remain on the park road 0.3 mile. As the pavement swings sharply right, turn left and follow an unmarked path that leads to a chairlift. Head straight down the ski slope; it descends directly to Lot 2. Turn left and walk 0.1 mile to reach Lot 1.

Lions Head (Hike 39) offers pleasant views.

berkshires

With the highest elevations in Massachusetts and Connecticut, the Berkshire region forms a western barrier between New England and New York's Hudson River valley. Running in a north–south direction, the region includes some of the oldest mountain ridges in New England. The Berkshires are also home to an abundance of quintessential New England villages and inns.

While largely forested, the Berkshires are noteworthy for their steep slopes, scenic cascades, and a scattering of prominent rock outcroppings. Many of these dramatic features occur along or near the Appalachian Trail as it leads north into Vermont. This excellent year-round destination is the perfect location to warm up for more challenging excursions in northern New England.

35 Kettletown State Park

RATING/ DIFFICULTY	LOOP	ELEV GAIN/ HIGH POINT	SEASON
**/3	6.5 miles	1150 feet/ 521 feet	Year-round

Map: USGS Southbury; **Contact:** Connecticut Department of Energy and Environmental Protection; **Note:** Fee in season; **GPS:** 41.425758, -73.207193

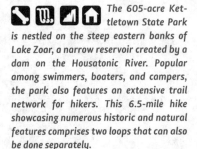 *The 605-acre Kettletown State Park is nestled on the steep eastern banks of Lake Zoar, a narrow reservoir created by a dam on the Housatonic River. Popular among swimmers, boaters, and campers, the park also features an extensive trail network for hikers. This 6.5-mile hike showcasing numerous historic and natural features comprises two loops that can also be done separately.*

GETTING THERE

From the junction of Kettletown Road and US Route 6 in Southbury, drive 3.2 miles south on Kettletown Road. Continue straight 0.2 mile on Maple Tree Hill Road and then turn right onto Georges Hill Road. Drive 0.8 mile to the state park entrance on the left. Follow the main park road straight toward the beach. In 0.4 mile, there are parking spaces on the left and right, just beyond the picnic area turnoff.

ON THE TRAIL

From the parking area, follow the paved road down the hill toward the beach. Just before the bottom of the slope, the road intersects the Brook Trail. This path, blazed in blue and yellow, connects the two separate loop hikes along the day's journey. Veer right onto the Brook Trail to reach the first circuit. The path climbs easily 0.1 mile into a picnic area. Straight ahead, on the other side of the road, find a gate at the start of the Miller Trail.

Head up the wide path a few dozen feet to an intersection. Here the blue-blazed Miller Trail forms a 1.8-mile loop. Stay right to complete the journey in a counterclockwise direction. The well-blazed route meanders across a rolling landscape past numerous impressive rocks and ledges. Near the halfway point, two trails diverge left, offering shorter alternatives.

After completing 1.5 miles of the loop, arrive at the site of an old charcoal hearth. Here a blue- and orange-blazed path leads right 0.1 mile before splitting in two. Both branches end quickly at mostly overgrown overlooks providing limited views. Beyond the overlook spur, the main trail descends steeply down a rocky slope before returning to the picnic area.

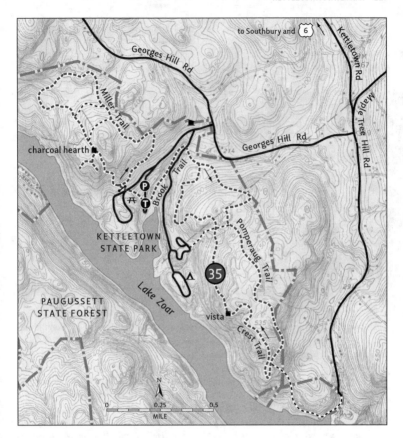

Follow the Brook Trail back toward the start and then beyond, to the mouth of Kettletown Brook. The trail swings sharply left, crosses a wooden bridge, and then parallels the cascading brook for 0.3 mile as it cuts through a scenic narrow gorge seemingly far removed from civilization. The path ends at the park's campground road. Hike straight across to reach the Pomperaug Trail.

Blue blazes lead 0.2 mile to a junction with the Crest Trail. Begin the day's second loop, a 3.2-mile circuit, by remaining left on the Pomperaug Trail. Past stone walls, the path rises steeply to the top of a wooded hill only to descend rapidly down the other side. In 0.5 mile, stay left at a junction where a connector trail departs right. The main path winds up, over, and down a series of rocky ridges and has alluring geologic features and

Lake Zoar from Crest Trail vista

thick mazes of mountain laurel. Descend aggressively to reach the southern end of the Crest Trail just before the loop's halfway point.

Turn right onto the blue- and white-blazed Crest Trail. It leads 0.1 mile ahead to the top of a steep, forested ravine before completely reversing direction. Ascend the rocky hillside 0.2 mile to an overgrown vista with limited views. The trail briefly swings away from the edge before reaching a more prominent outcrop and the hike's best views. Marvel at the lake far below and a large waterfall tumbling into the distant shore.

The Crest Trail continues north another 1.1 miles. While not flat, the terrain is not difficult, either. Stay straight where a path departs left to the campground. The Crest Trail swings past a large boulder before approaching the campground. Swing sharply right and rise easily to the trail's end. Turn left onto the Pomperaug Trail to retrace your steps back to the trailhead.

SHORTENING YOUR HIKE

Either loop can be done individually from the same trailhead. The Miller loop on its own is 2.1 miles, and the Pomperaug/Crest loop is 4.4 miles.

36 Mattatuck Trail

RATING/ DIFFICULTY	LOOP	ELEV GAIN/ HIGH POINT	SEASON
***/3	5.2 miles	950 feet/ 780 feet	Year-round

Map: USGS Thomaston; **Contact:** Connecticut Department of Energy and Environmental Protection; **Notes:** Fee in season, parking is also available on Bidwell Hill Road; **GPS:** 41.653793, -73.097866

Walking in the footsteps of Connecticut's legendary Leatherman, standing atop panoramic ledges, and tunneling under a canopy of towering trees, hikers can enjoy this attractive 5.2-mile loop in the heart of Connecticut's Naugatuck River valley. In summer months, complete your adventure by cooling off in Black Rock Pond, then spend the night camping under the stars.

GETTING THERE

From the junction of US Route 6 and Route 109 in Thomaston, follow US Route 6 west 0.4 mile to the Black Rock State Park entrance. Turn right and drive 0.1 mile to the large parking area.

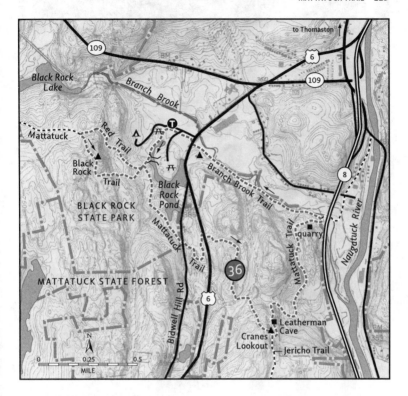

ON THE TRAIL

The trail begins in the picnic area on the south side of the parking lot. Follow the grassy path 0.1 mile past a small wetland to the shores of the larger Black Rock Pond. To the left, a metal bridge leads to a swimming area. Stay straight and in a few hundred feet intersect the blue-blazed Mattatuck Trail, a 36-mile route connecting the Naugatuck River valley with the Litchfield Hills. This journey traverses 3.2 miles of this long-distance path, completing two loops along the way.

Stay right to begin the first loop, a 1-mile circuit over Black Rock. Reaching a junction in 0.1 mile, turn right onto the 0.4-mile Red Trail. This route rises steadily while passing numerous rocks and exposed ledges. After heading under a power line, the path follows a woods road left and ends at a junction with the Mattatuck Trail.

Turn left and head up a small incline. After passing under the power lines again, the blue blazes swing left into the darker forest. As the descent begins, look for a spur that departs left to the top of Black Rock

Winding through the most well-known Leatherman Cave

and impressive views. While it is easy to stay at a safe distance, watch your step near the edge of this precipitous cliff. Rejoin the Mattatuck Trail. It drops steadily for 0.3 mile, occasionally over loose soil, and leads back to the shores of Black Rock Pond.

The much longer 3.8-mile loop to Leatherman Cave begins right. Remain on the Mattatuck Trail and wind south of the pond's shore. Cross three small streams and in 0.4 mile reach Bidwell Hill Road. Head straight across the pavement and around a gate. Continue 0.3 mile to US Route 6. Use caution heading across this busier thoroughfare before rejoining the trail.

Climbing rapidly, the path weaves through stands of mountain laurel, scrambles up a series of ledges, and passes a number of dramatic cliff tops. Descend into a small saddle before resuming the ascent up the slightly eroded trail. Ignore the many unmarked paths. In 0.8 mile from Route 6, the blue blazes lead to expansive views from the open summit of Cranes Lookout.

The Mattatuck Trail continues south at first. Stay left at a signed junction where the Jericho Trail departs right. In 0.1 mile, descend north through the state's most famous Leatherman Cave. According to legend, this is one of many locales between the Connecticut and Hudson rivers that a leather-wearing tramp regularly visited along a 34-day, 365-mile loop that he completed repeatedly for three decades in the late 1800s. More an overhang than a cave, this imposing geologic feature is a fun place to explore.

Proceed north 1 mile as the Mattatuck Trail leads across increasingly gradual terrain. In places, the path becomes less obvious. Take your time; the blazes are there. Make your way past a rock quarry and, just before Route 8, turn sharply left onto the Branch Brook Trail. Level throughout, this old road is blazed in blue with a yellow dot. It follows the small stream 1.1 miles to US Route 6, at a point directly across from the Black Rock State Park entrance. Carefully cross the pavement to complete your journey.

37 Pine Knob Loop

RATING/ DIFFICULTY	LOOP	ELEV GAIN/ HIGH POINT	SEASON
***/2–3	2.5 miles	725 feet/ 1160 feet	Year-round

Map: USGS Ellsworth; **Contact:** Connecticut Department of Energy and Environmental Protection; **GPS:** 41.833066, -73.383509

While steep in places, the 2.5-mile Pine Knob Loop fills hikers of all ages with a sense of accomplishment and offers many rewards. Venturing to perches high above the winding banks of the Housatonic River, the trail visits pleasant cascades, passes under the shadows of towering pine trees, and meanders around moss-draped remnants of the most recent ice age.

GETTING THERE
From the junction of Route 4 and US Route 7 in Cornwall Bridge, follow US Route 7 north 1.1 miles to a parking area on the left.

ON THE TRAIL
Leaving the north side of the parking lot, the trail quickly crosses Hatch Brook with the aid of large, flat boulders. Up a small rise, pass through a gap in a rock wall and reach the start of the loop.

Continue straight and begin a modest ascent up the Pine Knob Loop's 0.6-mile

Appalachian Trail viewpoint

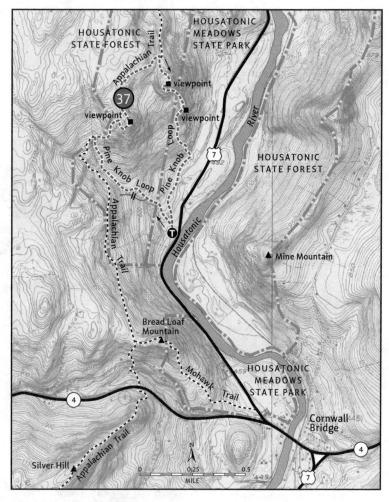

southern branch. Nearing the banks of Hatch Brook again, though well above it, the path is shaded by tall evergreen trees. As the trail levels off, approach the running water near a series of small cascades. The gentle grade continues upstream while the path weaves between two large boulders. Swing right and join an old woods road for a final climb to a junction with the Appalachian Trail (AT).

Turn right at the intersection. For the next 0.7 mile, the blue-blazed Pine Knob Loop and white-blazed AT coincide. Switchbacks ease the ascent up the modestly steep slope. Soon after, the vegetation transitions from conifers to oaks. Arrive at the hike's high point and splendid views across the Housatonic Valley. The trail continues north. Remain high atop the ridge with minor elevation changes, until a short descent leads to a cairn at a well-signed intersection.

Turn right onto the Pine Knob Loop's northern branch. A brief scramble up a ledge requires some attention. Atop the knob, the forest canopy slowly opens. Follow the path as it drops and quickly emerges onto a wide-open ledge 0.2 mile from the intersection. Enjoy the day's best panorama over the steep, rocky slopes. Watch your footing here, especially if the trail is wet or icy.

The first half of the hike's final 0.8 mile is demanding. Back into the forest, the trail descends steadily, occasionally over loose soil. At the bottom of the descent, stay right at a sign pointing to the parking area. Here, the terrain moderates significantly. Enjoy the final stretch through pine forests and past stone walls—signs of a bygone era when this wooded landscape was pastureland.

38 Hang Glider View

RATING/ DIFFICULTY	ROUND-TRIP	ELEV GAIN/ HIGH POINT	SEASON
**/3	5.2 miles	1250 feet/ 1360 feet	Year-round

Maps: USGS South Canaan and USGS Sharon; **Contact:** Appalachian National Scenic Trail; **GPS:** 41.932555, -73.363455

A hemlock forest slope along the Appalachian Trail

This quiet excursion begins along the banks of the Housatonic River, traverses an enticing forested landscape, and ends with a vista of Connecticut's highest summits. Be sure to pack your binoculars and field guides; who knows which songbird or wildflower awaits beyond the next bend in the trail?

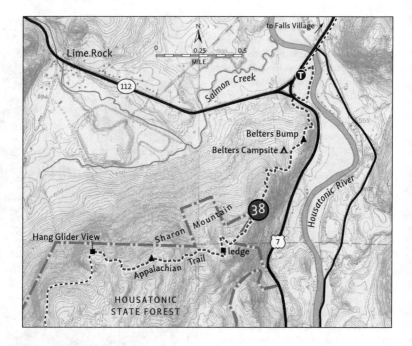

GETTING THERE

From the junction of US Route 7 and Route 112, south of Falls Village, follow US Route 7 north 0.1 mile to a large parking area on the right (just before the road crosses the Housatonic River).

ON THE TRAIL

Follow the white-blazed Appalachian Trail (AT) south as it parallels the gently flowing Housatonic River on one side and a cornfield on the other. The farmland is managed by the National Park Service to preserve the trail's pastoral setting. Please remain on the footpath to protect this historic landscape. After reaching US Route 7 in 0.1 mile, use extreme caution while crossing. Once on the other side, the trail begins a short, steady

ascent to Belters Bump. This small knoll, once surrounded by pastureland, today provides limited views from atop its rocky, forested high point. A little less than 0.5 mile from the start, it is a good place to grab a snack before the next climb.

Drop 0.1 mile to a spur leading right to a campsite. Continue straight, passing numerous stone walls blanketed with invasive plants. Native vegetation becomes more obvious as the trail rises up an increasingly steep slope. Under the shade of oaks and eastern hemlocks, wind past large rocks and gnarly ledges. The AT levels atop a high ridgeline and begins a relaxing stretch with minimal elevation change. Swing sharply right and then left to a long ledge just beyond the hike's halfway point. Through the expanding oak leaves, catch a glimpse of New York State in the distance.

After a brief descent, follow the white blazes as they lead around the north side of a wooded peak. Cross an overgrown woods road and begin a short, aggressive climb up the rocky slope. The route eases as it leads to the left of a small bump and then over a second one—the highest point of the hike.

Before retracing your steps to the start, continue 0.4 mile west along the AT. Under tall pines and down a steep ledge, the trail makes one last drop before reaching Hang Glider View. High above the Lime Rock Park racetrack, this former launching area provides an attractive vista north toward Bear Mountain, Mount Frissell, and Mount Everett.

39 Lions Head

RATING/ DIFFICULTY	ROUND-TRIP	ELEV GAIN/ HIGH POINT	SEASON
***/3	4.8 miles	1200 feet/ 1732 feet	Year-round

Map: USGS Sharon; **Contact:** Appalachian National Scenic Trail; **Note:** Outhouse at trailhead; **GPS:** 41.994094, -73.426521

  A welcoming excursion for hikers of all ages, this trek along the Connecticut section of the Appalachian Trail (AT) ends atop a rocky ledge with inviting views of a pastoral New England landscape. Along the journey, while serenaded by a chorus of towhees

Heading to Lions Head on a sunny spring day

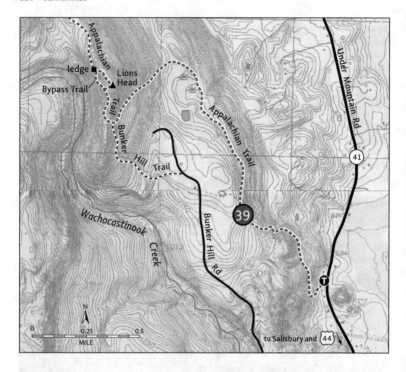

and thrushes, enjoy the carpets of wildflowers below, and marvel at the maturing
trees offering shade from high above.

GETTING THERE

From the junction of Route 41 and US Route
44 in Salisbury, drive 0.8 mile north on Route
41 (Under Mountain Road). Turn left into the
small AT parking area.

ON THE TRAIL

A large kiosk marks the start of the hike.
Beyond, the AT quickly winds up the hillside
as the sound from the busy road slowly
fades in the distance. Scaling the steepening
slope, approach the edge of a large field.

Remaining in the forest, the trail soon
descends briefly before rising to a large rock
1 mile from the start.

For the next 0.6 mile, enjoy a relatively
flat section of trail lined with stone walls;
both are occasionally interrupted by small
streams. The third and largest stream emp-
ties from an expansive forested wetland on
the left. Rise over a small bump to the right
of the wetland and stay alert for resident
songbirds flitting in the understory. One last
level stretch above the wetland follows, as
rock steps lead across the moist landscape.

Upon arriving at the base of the mountain's steep slopes, begin a demanding
0.5-mile climb. Be alert for the trail markings

as the trodden path makes a couple of abrupt turns before arriving at a well-marked junction. The Bunker Hill Trail departs left. This is a much shorter and more popular alternative route to the summit.

Bear sharply right, remaining on the AT, and rise up the rocky terrain through a canopy of mountain laurel. In 0.2 mile, reach a junction with the Bypass Trail, a short path that provides AT hikers with an option to avoid the high point of Lions Head during bad weather. Stay right and scramble 0.1 mile up the ledge-covered slope to the 1732-foot summit. To the right, a short spur ends atop an open perch with impressive views south and east over the lakes and rolling hills of northwestern Connecticut.

Before heading back, continue 0.1 mile north along the AT to the upper junction of the Bypass Trail. Just north of this intersection, find a ledge that features views of Bear Mountain and points beyond. Follow the Bypass Trail south to rejoin the AT for the 2.3-mile journey back to the start.

40 Jug End

RATING/ DIFFICULTY	ROUND-TRIP	ELEV GAIN/ HIGH POINT	SEASON
***/3	4.4 miles	1350 feet/ 1911 feet	Year-round

Map: USGS Egremont; **Contact:** Massachusetts Department of Conservation and Recreation; **GPS:** 42.144462, -73.431495

This out-and-back excursion along the Appalachian Trail (AT) rises steeply to Jug End, a rocky knoll with breathtaking views of the surrounding summits, valleys, and rolling countryside. Once atop the ridge, the hike

A turkey vulture soars above Jug End.

rambles more leisurely for nearly 1.5 miles up and over a series of scenic peaks and promontories.

GETTING THERE

From the junction of Routes 41 and 23 in Egremont, drive 2.3 miles south on Route 41 and then turn right onto Guilder Hollow Road. Drive 1.6 miles to where the AT crosses the road. Parallel parking is available along the left (south) side of the road.

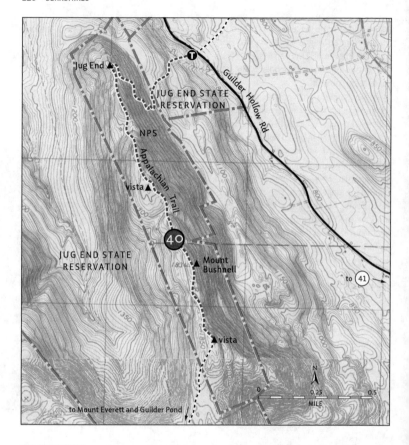

ON THE TRAIL

Follow the AT south. The white-blazed path climbs up a steep incline away from the road. Quickly leveling off, continue 0.3 mile to an immense boulder at the base of a more imposing slope. Catch your breath before beginning the day's most challenging ascent.

For 0.5 mile, the AT rises steadily while weaving through a rocky landscape covered in moss and lichen. Beneath the forest canopy, wildflowers add splashes of color. Take your time as your hard work will soon be rewarded with a more dramatic backdrop. One last pitch leads across an open ledge to the 1750-foot summit of Jug End. This rocky, pine-covered pinnacle offers extensive views north to Mount Greylock, west into New York, and east across the Housatonic River. It is the perfect spot for an afternoon picnic or to gaze upon an early morning sunrise.

Continue along the AT another 1.4 miles as it remains high atop a narrow ridge. While mostly gradual, this alluring section is occasionally interrupted by a short, demanding climb. Along the way, the easy-to-follow trail ascends three distinct, partially wooded peaks. Each summit features scenic vistas of points both near and far. Located 1 mile from Jug End, 1834-foot Mount Bushnell offers the most extensive scenery of the three. An unnamed 1911-foot pine-covered summit is the final stop of the journey. Retrace your steps 2.2 miles from here to return to the trailhead.

EXTENDING YOUR HIKE

Follow the AT south a little more than 2 miles from the unnamed 1911-foot summit past scenic Guilder Pond to the top of Mount Everett. Enjoy views from the highest peak in the southern Berkshires along the way.

41 Pine Cobble

RATING/ DIFFICULTY	LOOP	ELEV GAIN/ HIGH POINT	SEASON
***/3	5 miles	1500 feet/ 2110 feet	Year-round

Map: USGS Williamstown; **Contact:** Williamstown Rural Lands Foundation; **Note:** Trailhead parking is limited; **GPS:** 42.716149, -73.185154

Pine Cobble's rocky quartzite pinnacle is surrounded by 400 acres of conservation land in the Pine Cobble Preserve bordering thousands more in the northwest corner of Massachusetts. Along trails maintained by the Williams College Outing Club, this rugged loop weaves through quiet forests and rewards visitors with sweeping views of mountain ridges in three states.

GETTING THERE

From Route 2 in Williamstown, drive 0.8 mile north on Cole Avenue and then turn right onto North Hoosac Road (after crossing the Hoosic River). Continue 0.4 mile before turning left onto Pine Cobble Road. Drive 0.1 mile to the small parking area on the left (parking is not allowed on the road).

ON THE TRAIL

From the parking area, follow the pavement uphill a few hundred feet to the trailhead on the right. After entering the forest near a big sign, the route heads southeast. Enjoy the easy start. The path eventually bends left and ascends a steeper slope, aided by switchbacks and well-designed steps. After plateauing, swing right and proceed to an intersection with the Class of '98 Trail. This is the start of the loop, 0.9 mile from the trailhead.

Remain straight on the Pine Cobble Trail. The route climbs steadily, and the footing becomes increasingly rocky as you enter the heart of the Pine Cobble Preserve. This protected land is owned by Williamstown Rural Lands Foundation, a membership-based land trust focused on conserving open spaces and farmland in the surrounding communities. The trail continues to rise through a dense oak forest. At 0.7 mile from the junction, reach a small saddle where a spur leads right 0.1 mile to Pine Cobble's 1894-foot summit. There are two vistas near the high point: one south toward Mount Greylock's imposing slopes and the other, a more bucolic shot, west to the Taconic's long ridgeline.

Return to the main trail and stay right. The final 0.5-mile stretch along the Pine Cobble Trail is level at first but soon climbs more aggressively past a number of modest

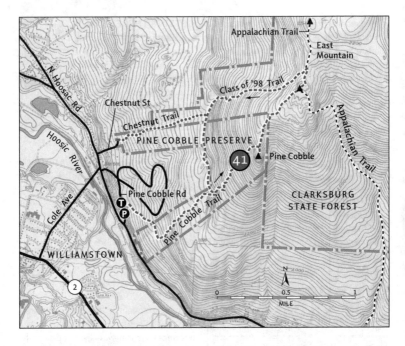

viewpoints. The footing across the white-rock landscape is rough in places, as the blue-blazed path ends at an intersection with the Appalachian Trail (AT). Turn left onto the AT and hike 0.1 mile into a low spot on the ridge. Pick up the Class of '98 Trail as it leaves left. Meanwhile, the AT proceeds 1 mile straight over East Mountain's wooded summit to the Vermont border and the start of that state's 272-mile Long Trail.

Gradual to start, the descent along the Class of '98 Trail becomes more challenging as the path swings right and drops steeply into a boulder-filled bowl. Lined with mountain laurel, the steep drop is short, and numerous steps ease the way. Veering left, the route more gently follows an old road to a junction with the Chestnut Trail, 1.1 miles

from the AT. This path offers an alternative access point to Pine Cobble but does not provide parking at its trailhead.

As you continue straight to complete the final 0.6-mile section of the Class of '98 Trail, look left through the trees to an impressive cliff. Remain well below this rugged terrain. After one brief climb, follow the trail to its conclusion. Turn right on the Pine Cobble Trail to wrap up the day's journey.

OTHER OPTIONS

Parking is limited at the trailhead, but the Pine Cobble and Chestnut trails are also accessible from the center of Williamstown. While this starting point will add 2 to 3 miles round-trip to your trek, this charming village is an ideal starting and ending point.

Pine Cobble summit ledges

42 Mount Greylock

RATING/ DIFFICULTY	LOOP	ELEV GAIN/ HIGH POINT	SEASON
****/4	7.6 miles	2400 feet/ 3491 feet	Year-round

Maps: USGS Williamstown and USGS Cheshire; **Contact:** Massachusetts Department of Conservation and Recreation; **GPS:** 42.625830, -73.137553

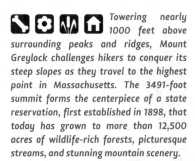

Towering nearly 1000 feet above surrounding peaks and ridges, Mount Greylock challenges hikers to conquer its steep slopes as they travel to the highest point in Massachusetts. The 3491-foot summit forms the centerpiece of a state reservation, first established in 1898, that today has grown to more than 12,500 acres of wildlife-rich forests, picturesque streams, and stunning mountain scenery.

GETTING THERE
From Route 8 in downtown Adams, follow Maple Street west 0.4 mile. Turn left onto West Road. Drive 0.4 mile and then turn right onto Gould Road. Continue 0.3 mile and turn left, remaining on Gould Road. Parking is available immediately on the right.

ON THE TRAIL
Pick up the trail under power lines and follow the first of many signs pointing to Bellows Pipe. The route leads 0.2 mile past a scenic pond to a picnic area and a larger pond with intimate views of Mount Greylock. This is the start of the loop.

Near the pond's southwestern edge, follow a grassy path into the forest. In 0.1 mile, turn right. The route, sometimes labeled Bellows South, briefly parallels a property line and in 0.3 mile rises to a four-way intersection. To the right, signs point to the Bucket Trail and Thiel Road. Stay left and begin a steadier climb toward Bellows Pipe.

The wide route, open to mountain bikes, passes a small waterfall on the left. Remain on the main path and ascend to a junction with the Thunderbolt Trail. Designed for downhill skiing, the Thunderbolt was once a

First view from the trail of Mount Greylock

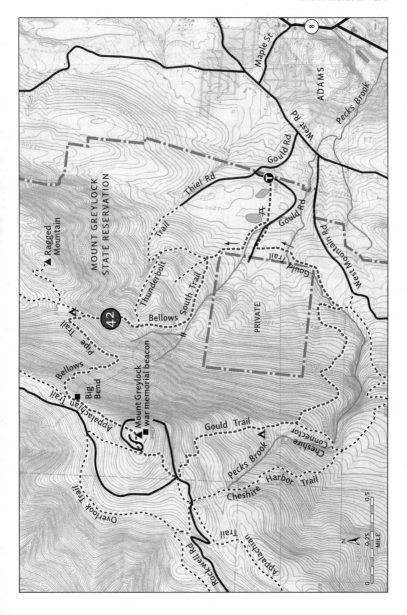

shorter but steeper alternative route to the summit. Portions of the trail are now closed to hikers. Follow the Bellows South Trail straight. After it crosses a small stream, two switchbacks lead to a three-way intersection, 1.8 miles from the start.

Still 1.6 miles from the summit, turn left on the Bellows Pipe Trail. Immediately rise past a shelter that is available for overnight use. The trail climbs steadily at first but soon swings south and proceeds with minor elevation gain. Turning abruptly right, begin an extremely demanding 0.5-mile ascent. Fortunately, the footing is good. The climb ends at a junction with the Appalachian Trail (AT). To the left an unmarked path leads a few dozen feet to the Thunderbolt Trail and excellent views from atop the Big Bend, a sharp turn along the historic ski slope.

Follow the AT south along a wide corridor that soon coincides with the Thunderbolt Trail. Rise steadily 0.4 mile to a parking area. One last incline leads to the high point and an impressive lighthouse-shaped monument commemorating soldiers who died in World War I. There are 360-degree views from the top of the monument when it is open (it was closed for repairs at the time of this writing). In addition, enjoy expansive scenes east and north from a nearby walkway.

The 4.2-mile descent starts south on the AT. Once through the summit area, reenter the mountain's boreal forest. Wind down the rocky trail 0.4 mile to a three-way intersection of summit roads. Follow Rockwell Road straight and quickly reach a small parking area on the left. Join the Gould Trail and drop steadily for 1 mile.

After passing a spur that leads to Peck Shelter, the footing improves and the route descends more moderately 0.5 mile through a lush hardwood forest. At a junction with the Cheshire Connector, stay left on the Gould Trail. The path gradually weaves 1.1 miles down the slope and, after swinging sharply right, reaches Peck Brook. Take the bridge across the brook.

Now, with a little more than a mile to the trailhead, turn left onto more level terrain. Paralleling the running water, the route passes a number of rock walls and old woods roads. Remain on the well-marked Gould Trail. After crossing Peck Brook one last time, climb to the edge of a large field. Continue straight to Gould Road. Follow the pavement right and, in 0.1 mile, head left back into the picnic area and the end of the day's circuit.

Little Rock Pond reflection (Hike 49)

vermont

The 270-mile Long Trail is the hiking centerpiece of Vermont. Dubbed the "footpath in the wilderness," the Long Trail was developed between 1910 and 1930. Running the length of the state from Massachusetts to Quebec, it is the nation's oldest long-distance trail and the inspiration for the much longer Appalachian Trail (the two coincide for about 100 miles). Famous as a backpacking destination, it joins with more than 175 miles of connecting trails and offers countless day hikes as well.

Vermont, New England's least populated state, is also home to the 385,000-acre Green Mountain National Forest and numerous state-owned lands. A wonderful year-round destination for hikers of all skill levels, the Green Mountain State's topography is most alluring in autumn when its prolific maple forests are aglow in bright reds and oranges.

Hardwood forest en route to Harmon Hill

43 Harmon Hill

RATING/ DIFFICULTY	ROUND-TRIP	ELEV GAIN/ HIGH POINT	SEASON
**/3	3.6 miles	2800 feet/ 2325 feet	Year-round

Maps: USGS Woodford, Bennington, and Pownal; **Contact:** Green Mountain National Forest; **GPS:** 42.885041, -73.115858

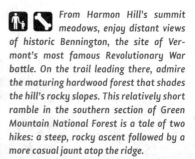 *From Harmon Hill's summit meadows, enjoy distant views of historic Bennington, the site of Vermont's most famous Revolutionary War battle. On the trail leading there, admire the maturing hardwood forest that shades the hill's rocky slopes. This relatively short ramble in the southern section of Green Mountain National Forest is a tale of two hikes: a steep, rocky ascent followed by a more casual jaunt atop the ridge.*

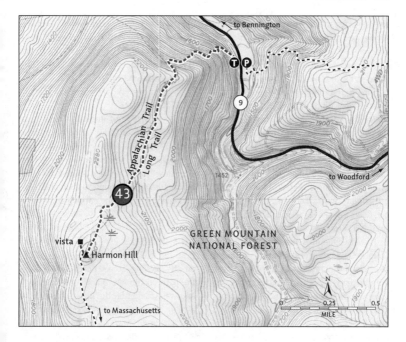

GETTING THERE

From the junction of Route 9 and US Route 7 in Bennington, follow Route 9 east 4.9 miles to the parking area on the left.

ON THE TRAIL

The trek to Harmon Hill begins on the other side of Route 9. Use extreme caution in crossing this busy, winding road; traffic moves rapidly. Once safely across, proceed to a sign marking the Appalachian and Long trails (AT/LT), two routes that coincide for a little more than 100 miles in southern Vermont. This hike, a well-trodden path that is clearly marked with white blazes, remains on the AT/LT throughout.

Wasting little time leaving Route 9, the trail climbs steeply up the boulder-filled landscape. Numerous steps aid the ascent, but the grade is very challenging. Take your time; there are many natural features to enjoy. Towering above are impressive hardwood trees including sugar maples, white ash, and yellow birch. Along the forest floor, shrouded in moss and ferns, are gnarly ledges and large rocks. As the sound of the busy highway fades in the distance, listen for boisterous red-eyed vireo calls emanating throughout the canopy.

Before long, the trail rises to the top of the slope and moderates significantly. The remaining 1.2-mile section that leads to the summit is much more relaxing. Over rolling terrain, the path heads through changing habitat. While the trees are not as stately, the forest surroundings form a nice backdrop with colorful wildflowers emerging in the spring and vibrant leaves appearing in autumn.

The path weaves through a forested wetland on a series of boardwalks before beginning the final, gradual ascent. The forest slowly thins as the summit nears. Notice the views open on the right, across the widening meadow. At a wooden sign marking the high point, a spur leads right to an open vista looking north and west to the Bennington Monument and beyond. Maintained by the US Forest Service through prescribed burns, Harmon Hill's historic meadows remain a scenic picnic spot in southern Vermont.

The AT continues south, reaching the Bay State in 12.5 miles and Georgia's Springer Mountain in more than 1500 miles. If you are not ready to retrace your steps to the start, venture farther toward the Massachusetts border across forested hillsides and past babbling brooks. While there are no noteworthy natural features for miles, the Congdon Shelter is 2.5 miles to the south.

44 Mount Equinox

RATING/ DIFFICULTY	ROUND-TRIP	ELEV GAIN/ HIGH POINT	SEASON
***/4	6.2 miles	2750 feet/ 3840 feet	Year-round

Map: USGS Manchester; **Contact:** Equinox Preservation Trust; **Notes:** Route traverses private land; **GPS:** 43.162757, -73.082440

The highest peak in the Taconic Range, Mount Equinox is the centerpiece of a 914-acre preserve showcasing 11 miles of hiking trails that traverse wildlife-rich and ecologically diverse habitats. This challenging adventure leads to the 3840-foot summit and a nearby promontory. Each location offers a scenic panorama of mountains, ridges, and valleys both near and far.

GETTING THERE

From the junction of Routes 7A and 30 in Manchester Center, drive 1.2 miles south on Route 7A into Manchester Village and then turn right onto Seminary Avenue (which becomes Prospect Street). Drive 0.3 mile before turning right onto West Union Street. Continue 0.2 mile to the parking area on the right.

ON THE TRAIL

Grab the Red Gate Trail near a large kiosk on the parking area's north side. Follow the path up the hill. Quickly intersect with and stay straight on the Blue Summit Trail, a route that also descends right past Burr and Burton Academy to the Equinox Resort & Spa in 0.3 mile. Today's hike will traverse the 914-acre Equinox Preserve on land the resort owns.

Take advantage of the easy beginning; it will not last long. Remain on the Blue Summit Trail as it passes a number of well-marked junctions, including one at which the Red Gate Trail departs left. After briefly entering private property, the route reaches the Maidenhair Trail, 0.6 mile from the start. This is the final intersection for a while.

The Blue Summit Trail begins an aggressive 1-mile ascent up the increasingly steep slope. While the terrain is physically demanding, the footing is not. After the trail swings sharply left, the incline slightly moderates. Hike under a canopy of young birch trees to a wooden bench. At a little more than halfway to the summit, this is a

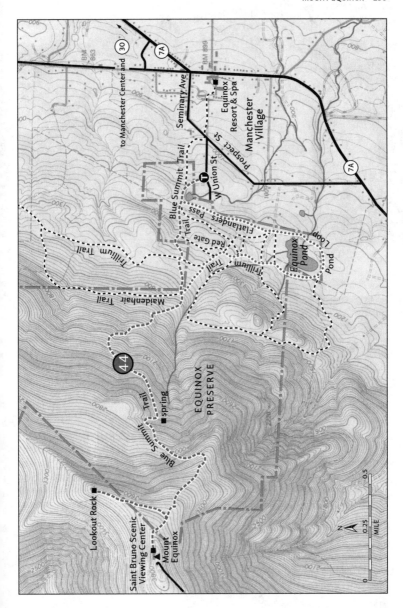

Scenic view from Equinox Pond

good location to fuel up for the remaining 1.2-mile climb. To the left, a spur leads to a spring.

Turn right at the bench onto the narrower and rougher trail. Still rising steadily, swing left into a forest dominated by birch trees and hobblebush. A little more than a half mile from the spring, ascend to a ridge crest. The path bends right and enters an inviting evergreen forest, lush with a green mossy carpet. Follow the more welcoming pitch 0.6 mile to a junction with the Lookout Rock Trail.

Turn right and follow the mostly level path. It leads 0.4 mile across a narrowing ridgeline to a series of viewpoints east across Manchester Village. The final stop, Lookout Rock, offers a bench for sitting and enjoying the Green Mountain scenery. Retrace your steps back to the Blue Summit Trail. Turn right and climb 0.1 mile past a communications tower to Mount Equinox's 3840-foot summit.

Not part of the Equinox Preserve, the summit area (accessible via an auto road) is home to the Saint Bruno Scenic Viewing Center and additional short hiking paths. The center offers very limited services; please respect its posted rules. From the high point, there are views of mountains in four states. Marvel at the surrounding beauty before following the Blue Summit Trail back to your car.

EXTENDING YOUR HIKE

Consider adding 1.9 miles to your hike on the descent by turning right onto the Maidenhair Trail. Continue south along the Trillium Trail and Pond Loop to the scenic shore of Equinox Pond. Follow the Red Gate and Flatlanders Pass trails back to the parking area. These and other nearby paths in the Equinox Preserve also provide shorter, less challenging alternatives to the described hike. In addition, Equinox Preserve trails are ideal for snowshoeing and cross-country skiing.

45 Mount Olga

RATING/ DIFFICULTY	LOOP	ELEV GAIN/ HIGH POINT	SEASON
**/2	1.9 miles	525 feet/ 2418 feet	Year-round

Map: USGS Jacksonville; **Contact:** Vermont Department of Forests, Parks, and Recreation; **Note:** Fee; **GPS:** 42.852414, -72.814920

The centerpiece of Molly Stark State Park, this picturesque loop aptly honors the wife of Revolutionary War general John Stark. Together this couple left a lasting impact on the formation of the country, helping to secure a key victory against the British in nearby Bennington. Today, hikers of all ages can appreciate these sacrifices by enjoying the panoramic view from the park and scenic highway that bear Molly Stark's name.

GETTING THERE

From the junction of Routes 9 and 100 in Wilmington, drive 3.3 miles east on Route 9. Turn right onto the Molly Stark State Park entrance road. Drive 0.1 mile to the park office and parking area.

ON THE TRAIL

Head up the northern branch of the Mount Olga Trail as it enters the forest just east of the park office building. Descend quickly to a small mountain stream and then cross a wooden bridge. Rising gradually at first, the well-marked trail leads over a stone wall before beginning a steadier ascent under birch and spruce. Continue up the winding trail to an intersection 0.7 mile from the start.

Turn left up the steep slope. In 0.1 mile, the path enters an open area atop the 2418-foot

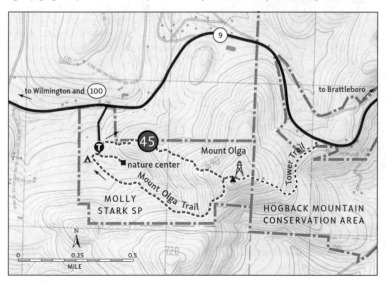

summit of Mount Olga. Blocked by tall trees, views are hard to find. Fortunately, a sturdy fire tower awaits. Five staircases lead to a small cabin and extensive views. To the north lie higher summits including Stratton Mountain. To the southwest, rolling hills lead to Mount Greylock and the Berkshires. Scenes east include New Hampshire's Monadnock and Sunapee regions.

Head back to the Mount Olga Trail. Turn left and descend the trail's 0.8-mile southern branch. Meandering past a prominent ledge and a collection of small boulders, the path swings right. With few obstacles remaining, the trail provides a perfect opportunity to scan the dense forests for resident flora and fauna. Listen for the diminutive ovenbird, whose raucous call often reverberates in New England's hardwood forests. After paralleling a rock wall, the path leads to the state park campground.

Before concluding the day's hike, turn right onto the 0.1 mile Nature Trail. It swings around a few campsites before ending at a former Civilian Conservation Corps bathroom facility that today serves as a modest nature center. Check out the displays describing the area's natural and human history. Once back to the campground, follow the road downhill to the day-use parking area.

EXTENDING YOUR HIKE

Molly Stark State Park borders the Hogback Mountain Conservation Area. This town-owned forest offers numerous hiking paths, some lightly maintained. Consider descending the Tower Trail from Mount Olga's summit. It offers modest views from former ski trails as it drops to Route 9. On the opposite side of the busy road, additional trails form loops on the slopes of Hogback Mountain.

Mount Olga summit tower

46 Jamaica State Park

RATING/ DIFFICULTY	ROUND-TRIP	ELEV GAIN/ HIGH POINT	SEASON
**/3	7 miles	1150 feet/ 1370 feet	Year-round

Map: USGS Jamaica; **Contact:** Vermont Department of Forests, Parks, and Recreation; **Note:** Fee; **GPS:** 43.109073, -72.775092

An excursion through 1122-acre Jamaica State Park, this 7-mile hike features picturesque Hamilton Falls, a scenic stretch of the West River, and quaint views from ledges atop Little Ball Mountain. This is now a hidden gem in south-central Vermont, but evidence suggests native Abenaki lived here for thousands of years and once used the region as a commerce center along a major transportation corridor._

GETTING THERE

From Route 30 in Jamaica, drive 0.5 mile north on Depot Street. After crossing the West River, turn left and drive 0.1 mile to the state park entrance. Continue 0.2 mile straight to the Salmon Hole parking area.

ON THE TRAIL

Walk through the playground to pick up the West River Trail, sometimes referred to as the Railroad Bed Trail. This wide, inviting path parallels the river for more than 2.5 miles to the Ball Mountain Dam. Today's hike will traverse the first 1.9 miles.

The West River Trail rises very gently and includes numerous signs describing the park's natural features and human history. Beneath the steep slopes of Little Ball Mountain on one side, the old rail bed passes numerous viewpoints of the rushing river on the opposite side. One unique feature is The Dumplings, a group of large glacial erratics. These boulders, deposited by glaciers long ago, are popular obstacles for white-water enthusiasts. At 0.8 mile reach the base of the Overlook Trail on the right. You will follow this route later. For now, continue straight on the West River Trail.

Soon, swinging left, the trail follows a bend in the river. Continue to parallel the

Hamilton Falls

water, but from a greater distance. Under the shady hardwood forest, reach the well-signed start of the Hamilton Falls Trail. Follow this path right. Leading 1 mile to the impressive cascades, it never strays far from Cobb Brook. Ascend steadily over rocky terrain. The brook sinks farther below at first, but eventually runs closer to the path. Enjoy less challenging terrain while approaching a spur that drops left 0.1 mile to the base of the cascading falls.

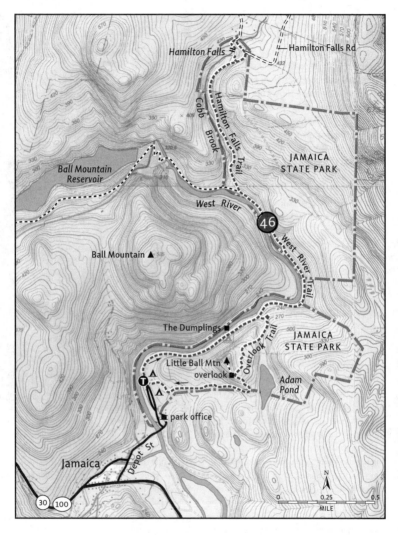

Beyond the spur, the main trail quickly reaches Hamilton Falls Road. Follow the road left 0.1 mile to an unmarked path that ends at the top of the falls. Watch your step near the edge. Note: Swimming is prohibited in this area. The terrain at the top of the falls is very dangerous.

Retrace your steps back down the Hamilton Falls Trail and then turn left on the West River Trail. Make your way to the Overlook

Trail and bear left. Leading 0.6 mile to a scenic ledge atop Little Ball Mountain, this moderately difficult route includes a few short climbs. The pine-covered overlook provides tranquil scenes of Jamaica Village and surrounding hills. To the right, an unmarked path leads to the summit of Little Ball Mountain and additional vistas.

Remain on the Overlook Trail as it descends to the campground. It drops 0.3 mile to a small stream and then veers sharply right onto an old woods road. Enjoy the relaxing 0.6-mile conclusion to the day's adventure. The Overlook Trail ends in the state park campground near the Hackberry Lean-to. Follow the camp road right to return to the parking area.

47 Mount Ascutney

RATING/ DIFFICULTY	LOOP	ELEV GAIN/ HIGH POINT	SEASON
****/3–4	7.3 miles	2800 feet/ 3150 feet	Year-round

Map: USGS Windsor; **Contact:** Vermont Department of Forests, Parks, and Recreation; **GPS:** 43.457016, -72.422068

Brownsville Rock provides impressive western views.

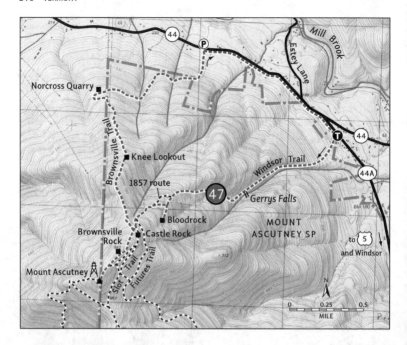

Mount Ascutney rises high above the nearby banks of the Connecticut River in southeastern Vermont. Its steep slopes feature cascading brooks and scenic rocky promontories. This demanding loop, which includes a road walk, visits numerous natural features and showcases breathtaking views from the 3150-foot summit's observation tower.

GETTING THERE

From the junction of US Route 5 and Route 44A in Windsor, follow Route 44A northwest. Drive 2.5 miles and turn left into the parking area for the Windsor Trail. To reach the Brownsville Trail, continue 0.2 mile north on Route 44A and turn left onto Route 44. Drive 1 mile to the trailhead on the left.

ON THE TRAIL

The Windsor Trail heads across a wide-open meadow with views of Mount Ascutney's imposing slopes. Enter the forest and begin a steady ascent. The path parallels a cascading mountain stream and, in 0.8 mile, arrives at Gerrys Falls, a picturesque cascade.

Continue the aggressive climb, now in a little more circuitous fashion, and reach a trail junction near Halfway Spring in 0.8 mile. Here, the route splits, providing two options: the 1857 route and the 1903 route. Stay left and follow the 1903 route 0.2 mile to a spur on the left that leads 0.1 mile to Bloodrock, an impressive ledge with a vista.

The Windsor Trail swings right and quickly reconnects with the 1857 route, now only 0.8 mile from the summit.

Head up the final leg of the climb and enjoy the less demanding terrain. Weaving along ledge and rock through an inviting evergreen forest, the path passes two junctions where the Futures Trail and the Slot Trail diverge left. Consider adding a brief diversion on the Slot Trail, which leads 0.1 mile to Castle Rock and pleasant eastern views. Shortly after, rise to an intersection with the Brownsville Trail. Turn left; the routes coincide for 0.3 mile to the summit.

Before reaching the summit, pass the former site of a stone hut built in 1858. Nearby, a spur right leads to Brownsville Rock and expansive western views of the Killington Range and surrounding Green Mountain ridges. At the summit, there are two peaks. The first is slightly lower but houses an observation tower with incredible scenery in all directions. A second, less attractive peak a few hundred feet away is the mountain's high point.

The 3.2-mile descent follows the Brownsville Trail exclusively. Head back to the intersection with the Windsor Trail and bear left. Dropping steadily, the path heads down a long ridge, passing a number of scenic vistas. In 0.6 mile hike over the mountain's north peak, and 0.3 mile farther enjoy views from Knee Lookout.

The journey becomes more challenging over the next 0.8 mile. Take your time and make your way to a vista above the Norcross Quarry. The trail drops rapidly, levels off, and then swings right through the remains of the quarry. The final mile begins fairly easily, but soon the terrain becomes steeper. Wind down the slope to reach Route 44 and the end of the Brownsville Trail. To return to

your car, carefully follow the pavement right 1 mile. Stay right on Route 44A and continue 0.2 mile to the start of the Windsor Trail.

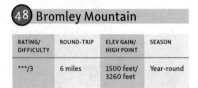

48 Bromley Mountain

RATING/ DIFFICULTY	ROUND-TRIP	ELEV GAIN/ HIGH POINT	SEASON
***/3	6 miles	1500 feet/ 3260 feet	Year-round

Map: USGS Peru; **Contact:** Green Mountain National Forest; **GPS:** 43.207140, -72.969924

Bromley Mountain sits in the heart of Vermont's southern Green Mountains and provides an ideal perspective from which to enjoy this scenic part of the state. The 3-mile hike to its summit is a moderate trek, carving through a tunnel of hardwood forests teeming with wildflowers and ringing with the calls of countless songbirds.

GETTING THERE

From the junction of Route 11/30 and US Route 7 in Manchester, drive 4.4 miles east on Route 11/30 and turn left into the Appalachian Trail/Long Trail (AT/LT) parking area. If you are traveling from the east, the parking area is on the right, 0.6 mile west of the junction of Routes 11 and 30 in Winhall.

ON THE TRAIL

Follow the AT/LT as it leaves the eastern side of the parking area on an old road. The route almost immediately turns left. Cross a small stream and head under the power lines. In 0.1 mile, enter the maturing hardwood forest. Rising gradually at first, the trail provides ample time to loosen up. Wind over the

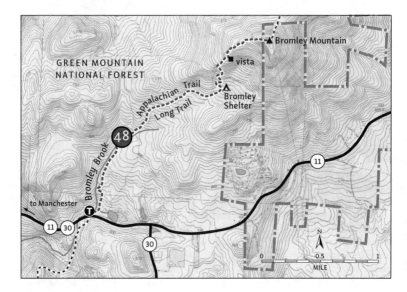

somewhat rocky landscape to a pair of size-able boulders. The trail's white blazes weave through the giant obstacles and soon lead to Bromley Brook, 0.7 mile from the start.

Take advantage of the sturdy wooden bridge leading to the other side. The modest ascent continues another 1.3 miles, initially across boardwalks near the slow-moving Bromley Brook. Proceed to an intersection with a bike trail. The AT/LT continues straight at first but quickly swings left. Meandering along a rolling landscape lined with tall maples and yellow birch, the route slowly gains elevation. Occasionally, the terrain is rough, but the well-used trail is easy to navigate. As the forest canopy thickens with beech trees, reach an intersection. The path right leads to the Bromley Shelter, a lean-to used by backpackers.

Now with only 1 mile to the summit, more than 700 feet remain to climb. The hike continues left and rises up a newer section

of trail. Thanks to a series of short switch-backs, the steep slope is somewhat easier to tackle. Reach a short spur that drops right to a rocky vista and scenes south, including Stratton Mountain. Beyond, the trail ascends rock and wooden steps before flattening. Ahead, at a large rock, emerge onto a grassy ski slope.

Swing left; the well-trodden path leads 0.2 mile up the wider corridor. While the trail is fairly steep at the end, with each step more of the surrounding mountains and valleys come into view. Ascend to the high point amid a collection of ski lifts and buildings. The 3260-foot summit of Bromley Mountain was once the site of an observation tower, later found to be unsafe. A campaign began in 2012 to replace it. With or without a tower, there are views in all directions and welcoming grassy spots to enjoy a picnic lunch. Return along the same route to complete the day's journey.

The AT/LT path cuts through boulders near Bromley Brook.

49 Little Rock Pond and Green Mountain

RATING/ DIFFICULTY	LOOP	ELEV GAIN/ HIGH POINT	SEASON
****/3	7.3 miles	1500 feet/ 2509 feet	May–Nov

Map: USGS Wallingford; **Contact:** Green Mountain National Forest; **GPS:** 43.372687, -72.962677

Little Rock Pond on a fall day

Tucked away and far removed from civilization, Little Rock Pond's waters reflect Green Mountain's ledge-covered slopes. This pleasant jaunt visits both the pond and the mountain to complete a journey lined with spring wildflowers, serenaded by summer songbirds, or dazzled with fall foliage. It is one of the most picturesque locations along the Appalachian Trail's journey through Vermont.

GETTING THERE
From US Route 7 in Danby, drive east on Mount Tabor Road. Drive 1 mile (the road beyond here is not maintained in the winter) and then cross Big Branch. Continue 2.3 miles up Forest Road 10 to the parking area on the right.

ON THE TRAIL
Follow the Appalachian Trail/Long Trail (AT/LT) north. Well-used by backpackers and day hikers alike, the trek's first 2 miles are easy to follow. With less than 400 feet of elevation gain between the trailhead and the pond, there is also more than enough time to warm up before the modest ascent of Green Mountain. Cross Little Black Branch, a small stream, in 0.6 mile, and then cross it a second time shortly after. The white-blazed trail utilizes numerous boardwalks throughout. Just beyond a spur trail that leads right to the Lula Tye Shelter, a lean-to offering overnight shelter for backpackers, complete the journey to Little Rock Pond's southern shore.

At the edge of the expansive pond, you face the day's only dilemma. To the left, the Little Rock Pond Loop leads 0.4 mile along the western shore to the Green Mountain Trail. Heading right, the AT/LT traverses 0.3

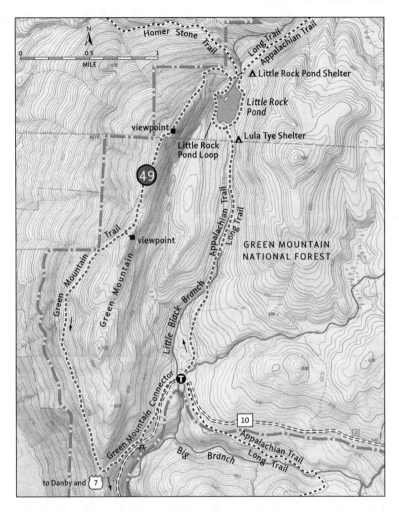

mile along the eastern shore to the Green Mountain Trail. The western shore is quieter and more rugged, while the eastern offers more rewarding views. If you have the time, complete the entire circuit (this will require hiking one section twice).

At either junction with the 4-mile Green Mountain Trail, near the northern shore of Little Rock Pond, turn left and begin a steady climb up the mountain's northern ridge. In a little more than a half mile, rise through the deciduous forest and emerge atop a more rocky landscape of evergreens. Leading up the granite ledges, the trail displays numerous scenes, especially north toward Killington Peak. There are also two spur trails that depart left. The second spur leads to a perch with views of Little Rock Pond, now 2 miles away.

The trail's final 2-mile stretch is noteworthy for its changing forested landscape. Descend gradually and depart the spruce-covered summit area. Joining an old woods road, the route continues under the shade of maple and birch trees. Near the trail's conclusion, swing across a steep slope shrouded in hemlock. After passing a narrow western viewpoint, continue 0.2 mile to an intersection where the main trail departs right to a picnic area. Turn left and follow the Green Mountain Connector 0.6 mile to the parking area. This final leg of the journey, while unremarkable, is preferable to hiking along FR 10, which it parallels.

SHORTENING YOUR HIKE

Skip the excursion over Green Mountain and combine the AT/LT with the loop around the pond to complete a 4.7-mile adventure.

50 White Rocks

RATING/ DIFFICULTY	ROUND-TRIP	ELEV GAIN/ HIGH POINT	SEASON
**/3	5.4 miles	2000 feet/ 2400 feet	May–Nov

Map: USGS Wallingford; **Contact:** Green Mountain National Forest; **GPS:** 43.450949, -72.943364

The white quartzite cliff that forms the centerpiece of White Rocks National Recreational Area within *the Green Mountain National Forest is as fascinating to gaze upon as it is to stand atop. This half-day adventure combines both experiences, but be prepared to exert some energy on the steep mountain slopes.*

GETTING THERE

From Wallingford, follow Route 140 east 2.1 miles and then turn right onto Sugar Hill Road. Drive 0.1 mile and turn right onto Forest Road 52. Follow this dirt road 0.5 mile to the large parking area.

ON THE TRAIL

This hike includes two separate excursions that leave from two trailheads at the same parking area. Head first to the top of White Rocks Cliff by joining the blue-blazed Keewaydin Trail as it departs east. Level only initially, this 0.4-mile route rises high above the banks of Bully Brook to an intersection with the Appalachian Trail/Long Trail (AT/ LT). For a quick diversion, turn left and drop a few hundred feet to the cascading brook.

The journey to White Rocks Cliff continues right on the AT/LT. Climbing steadily for 0.7 mile, the trail winds through a picturesque northern hardwood forest. At a junction where a spur departs left to Greenwall Shelter, catch your breath. The remaining 0.5 mile along the AT/LT rises much less aggressively. Soon, the trail heads in a westerly direction. While less steep, the path becomes rockier. After entering an evergreen forest, swing south to an intersection covered with a wild assortment of cairns.

Turn right onto the blue-blazed White Rocks Cliff Trail. Watch your footing; the route is rough in places and steep. Fortunately, the 0.2-mile trail levels off rapidly. A short ascent leads to an outlook atop

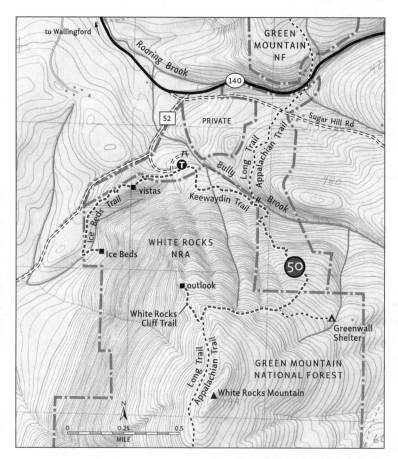

a narrow, rocky promontory that affords excellent views south down the valley and west to the Taconic Range. Well above the cliff's steepest parts, resist the temptation to explore below.

After retracing your steps back to the trailhead, look for the start of the Ice Beds Trail on the southern side of the parking area. This trek also begins easily but, like the previous trail, the easy beginning is followed by a challenging climb. Pay close attention to the blue blazes; there are many unofficial paths that lead to the top of a small knoll. The main trail rises up the north side, away from the edge. In 0.2 mile, reach the first of a series of vistas that provide exceptional views of the dramatic White Rocks Cliff.

White Rocks Cliff from Ice Beds Trail

The Ice Beds Trail continues another 0.7 mile. Swing down the knoll's southwest side under a thick canopy of evergreens. Level off briefly before dropping left to a small stream. The path crosses a wooden bridge to the other side and then leads upstream to the base of an immense talus slope. Deep within the maze of rocks, ice and snow linger for much of the year. Even when they are out of sight, their presence can be felt in the cool breezes emanating from the rocky crevasses. Return to the trailhead along the same route.

SHORTENING YOUR HIKE
The White Rocks Cliff adventure is 3.6 miles round-trip, and the Ice Beds Trail is 1.8 miles. Both hikes are worthy of exploration.

51 Glen Lake

RATING/ DIFFICULTY	ROUND-TRIP	ELEV GAIN/ HIGH POINT	SEASON
**/2	4.4 miles	600 feet/ 650 feet	Year-round

Map: USGS Bomoseen; **Contact:** Vermont Department of Forests, Parks, and Recreation; **GPS:** 43.660122, -73.232042

The reflective blue waters of Glen Lake provide a scenic backdrop to this pleasant hike near Vermont's western border. Tall trees, secluded wildlife-rich coves, and attractive picnic spots are some of its highlights.

GETTING THERE
From the junction of Routes 4A and 22A in Fair Haven, drive 0.4 mile north on Route 4A. Veer left onto Dutton Avenue. In 0.5 mile pass under US Route 4. Continue straight 4 miles on Scotch Hill Road/West Castleton Road. Turn left onto Moscow Road and drive 0.2 mile to the parking area on the right.

ON THE TRAIL
The Glen Lake Trail begins on the opposite side of the road. Enter the forest to the right of the dam and immediately reach the shore of the mostly undeveloped lake. Follow the blue-blazed path right as it remains close to the shoreline, offering occasional views. In 0.2 mile, swing right and begin a short, steady climb. Before long, the route veers

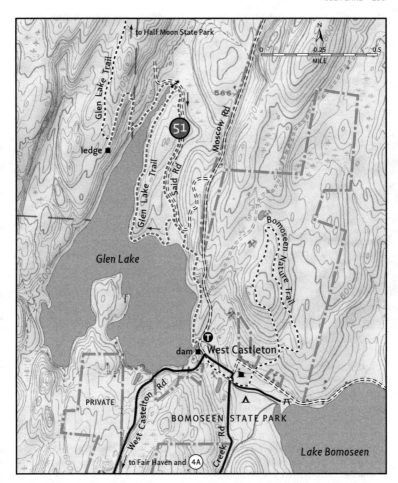

left and descends back to the water's edge. Turn right and hike to a junction with Said Road, 0.5 mile from the start.

The Glen Lake Trail follows the lightly used dirt road left for 0.1 mile. After crossing a small stream, look for the route reentering the forest sharply left. Under a tall canopy of white pines, meander 0.1 mile across the level terrain to a rocky point jutting into the lake. Hike 0.2 mile west along the Glen Lake Trail as it parallels the shore to the tip of a more prominent peninsula. The route bends right and provides intimate views of a narrow cove for the next 0.7 mile. Proceed quietly; this area is frequented by great blue herons, waterfowl, and other critters.

Finding solitude along the Glen Lake Trail

Once again, the trail intersects Said Road. Turn left, hike around a gate, and cross a large culvert that separates the cove from a marshy wetland. Just before the road climbs right, stay left on the Glen Lake Trail. Now following the cove's western shore, the journey is easy at first. However, it quickly bends right and rises gradually up the rocky hillside. Follow the blazes carefully; there are numerous turns, but the trail is well marked. Upon leveling off, head straight through a semi-open forested area. In 0.1 mile, the Glen Lake Trail veers sharply right, and its 3-mile course north to Half Moon State Park becomes less obvious. Here, follow an unmarked spur left leading a few hundred feet to the top of a ledge with sweeping views of the lake below and mountains on the horizon.

From the ledge, retrace your steps 0.7 mile back to Said Road and turn right. Beyond the gate, avoid the peninsula on the return trip. Instead, hike 0.6 mile east along Said Road. Turn right to rejoin the Glen Lake Trail and follow it 0.5 mile back to the start.

EXTENDING YOUR HIKE

Nearby Bomoseen State Park, popular with swimmers and campers, features a 1.5-mile nature trail. It winds under diverse forest canopies, through open fields, and by hidden wetlands. The loop, steep in places, is a good way to end your day in this quiet corner of Vermont.

52 Snake Mountain

RATING/ DIFFICULTY	LOOP	ELEV GAIN/ HIGH POINT	SEASON
***/2	3.8 miles	1000 feet/ 1270 feet	Year-round

Map: USGS Port Henry; **Contact:** Vermont Fish and Wildlife Department; **Note:** The route crosses a preserve owned by The Nature Conservancy; **GPS:** 44.049078, -73.291916

  Once the site of a summit hotel, Snake Mountain in the lower Champlain Valley showcases one of the finest views of New York's Adirondack Mountains. Surrounded by a 1215-acre state wildlife management area, as well as privately owned conservation land, the relatively diminutive peak is very popular with hikers of all ages and abilities.

GETTING THERE

From the junction of Routes 22A and 17 in Addison, drive 2.9 miles south on Route 22A and turn left onto Wilmarth Road. Travel 0.6 mile before turning left onto Mountain Road. Drive 0.1 mile to the large parking area on the left.

ON THE TRAIL

The trailhead is located 0.1 mile south of the parking lot, near the intersection of Mountain and Wilmarth roads. Enter the forest on the left and follow an old woods road beyond a red gate. Quickly arrive at a sign for Wilmarth Woods, a preserve owned by the Vermont chapter of The Nature Conservancy. The hike begins in this 81-acre site noted for its high concentration of mature trees, one of the largest low-elevation stands in the Champlain Valley.

While not well marked, this and other paths on Snake Mountain are obvious and

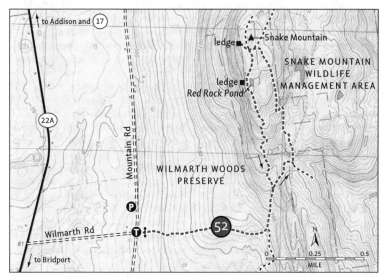

The Adirondacks rise above Champlain Valley.

easy to follow. Remain on the main trail as it leads gently over rolling terrain 0.6 mile to a three-way intersection. Turn left and begin a steadier climb. In 0.2 mile reach an unsigned fork in the trail that marks the beginning of the day's loop.

Stay right and continue the ascent up the more obvious footpath. The forest, composed mostly of hardwood trees, provides welcoming habitat for a great diversity of warblers and other songbirds. Winding up the valley, the trail veers right and rises rapidly to another three-way intersection 1.2 miles from the start.

Follow the trail left to reach Snake Mountain, now only 0.7 mile away. The route drops into a small saddle, but a moderate climb quickly ensues. Rising higher up the mountain, the trail eventually levels off before descending to an unmarked four-way intersection. Continue straight and immediately reach the summit ledge, just west of the mountain's high point. The former site of the Grand View Hotel, the ledge is no longer an overnight destination, but the view remains as grand. Standing prominently over pastoral scenes of the Champlain Valley, the high peaks of the Adirondacks dominate the western skyline.

To descend, return to the four-way intersection in 0.1 mile and turn right. This narrower path heads over a small bump on the ridge and then drops to a slightly less scenic, but quieter, ledge. Follow the exposed rock along the western edge of Red Rock Pond and then veer sharply left into the forest for good. Remain on this path as it descends steadily 0.6 mile. Under an increasingly tall stand of trees, the path returns to Snake Mountain's main trail. Continue straight 0.2 mile and then right to retrace your steps back to Mountain Road.

53 Killington Peak

RATING/ DIFFICULTY	ROUND-TRIP	ELEV GAIN/ HIGH POINT	SEASON
***/4	7.6 miles	2500 feet/ 4235 feet	Year-round (see note)

Map: USGS Killington Peak; **Contact:** Vermont Department of Forests, Parks, and Recreation; **Note:** Trails closed in spring before Memorial Day; **GPS:** 43.619243, -72.876912

While more famous for its alpine ski slopes, Vermont's second-highest peak is equally alluring to hikers in search of breathtaking views in the heart of the Green Mountains. This challenging trek through the diverse habitats of Vermont's 16,166-acre Coolidge State Forest provides subtle beauty from late spring through winter.

GETTING THERE

From the junction of US Routes 4 and 7 in Rutland, follow US Route 4 for 5 miles east into Mendon. Turn right onto Wheelerville Road and drive 4 miles south to a large parking area on the left.

ON THE TRAIL

The 3.4-mile Bucklin Trail begins under a stand of tall white pines. Leading over level ground, it is immediately joined from the right by the Catamount Trail, a cross-country ski route. The route proceeds to a large kiosk in 0.1 mile and, beyond, to a bridge that spans Brewers Brook. Once across, swing right. The Catamount Trail quickly departs left. Remain on the Bucklin Trail up the valley, and in 0.2 mile it turns sharply left away from the brook. Over gently rolling terrain, the route parallels the water, but now from a distance. Follow the blue blazes closely, as a number of old woods

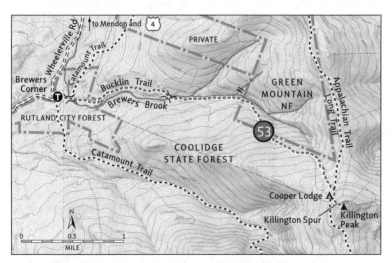

View of Pico Peak from Killington Peak

roads depart left. Eventually, the trail bends right and descends rapidly to Brewers Brook, 1.2 miles from the start.

Cross the bridge and turn left. The Bucklin Trail follows the brook 0.8 mile with minimal elevation change, but the footing becomes a bit rougher. As the valley narrows, look left through the trees and spot a tributary cascading into the main waterway. Shortly after, the Bucklin Trail veers sharply right and begins an aggressive 1.3-mile climb to the ridgeline. The ascent combines steady grades with occasional moderation. While difficult, the terrain is straightforward and easy to navigate. Higher up the slope, the hardwood forest slowly transitions to evergreens. Before long, arrive at a wooden sign at a junction with the Appalachian Trail/ Long Trail (AT/LT).

Turn right and follow these two long-distance routes that coincide for more than 100 miles in southern Vermont. Marked with white blazes, the AT/LT rises moderately 0.2 mile to Cooper Lodge. Don't be fooled by the term "lodge"; this is a rustic building that provides bunks for backpackers and a nearby privy but no other services. It is a good location to catch your breath before the final stretch.

Just after Cooper Lodge, the AT/LT bears right. Stay straight at this intersection and join the Killington Spur. Only 0.2 mile long, this spur is the hike's most demanding section. Rising steeply, the route weaves up ledges and through the thinning forest. Soon the trail rewards that hard work as it emerges atop the open 4235-foot summit to nearly 360-degree views. Before retracing your steps back to the trailhead, enjoy a nice picnic lunch while gazing upon the mountains and ridges that include the Adirondacks to the west, the main spine of the Green Mountains to the north, and New Hampshire's White Mountains to the east.

54 Mount Tom and the Pogue

RATING/ DIFFICULTY	LOOP	ELEV GAIN/ HIGH POINT	SEASON
***/2	5.2 miles	800 feet/ 1300 feet	Year-round

Maps: USGS Woodstock North and USGS Woodstock South; **Contact:** Marsh-Billings-Rockefeller National Historical Park; **Note:** Portion of hike in municipal park; **GPS:** 43.631956, -72.516308

The lands surrounding Mount Tom and the Pogue (a large pond nestled high atop Woodstock's rolling hills) are crisscrossed with more than 20 miles of hiking paths and former carriage trails that originate from the 550-acre Marsh-Billings-Rockefeller National Historical Park. This living history museum is a fitting tribute to three pioneers of America's conservation movement.

GETTING THERE

From the junction of US Route 4 and Route 12 in Woodstock, drive west on Route 12 (Pleasant Street). In 0.2 mile, turn right onto Elm Street (Route 12). Drive 0.2 mile and stay right on River Road (Route 12). In 0.3 mile, turn right onto Old River Road and immediately arrive at the large parking area for the Billings Farm and Museum and the Marsh-Billings-Rockefeller National Historical Park on the right.

ON THE TRAIL

Head to the Billings Farm and Museum and then follow the crosswalk to the west side of Route 12. On the path leading toward the national historical park's mansion, the first building is the park's visitor center. Check out the displays and ask for a detailed hiking map. You can also sign up for a tour of the mansion, but reservations fill up quickly.

From the visitor center, walk down the hill and turn left onto Mountain Road. This wide dirt road (like other roads in the park) is

The Pogue

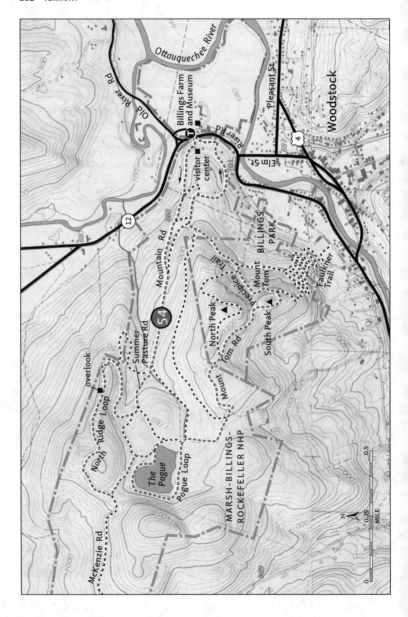

open only to foot traffic. It passes a number of exhibits early on, then gently ascends the modest slope. The maturing forest is quite impressive. You will quickly notice that, despite the high number of available trails, all junctions are well marked. Follow Mountain Road 1 mile and then turn right onto Summer Pasture Road

Wrap around the northern edge of a pasture. In 0.2 mile stay right and immediately intersect the North Ridge Loop. Veer right and join this path for a pleasant 1.3-mile trek. It rises gently, circuitously ascending a ridge. Near the halfway point, pass an overlook and small bench on the right. Ahead, witness evidence of forest management. This is a working landscape, in the spirit of the thoughtful stewards who carefully managed the property for years. Descend left at a junction with McKenzie Road and then bear right toward the Pogue.

Upon arriving at the Pogue, turn right onto the loop that circles its reflective waters. There are numerous views early and then late along the 0.7-mile circuit. In between, enjoy dense hardwood forests and scenes of an expansive field. The trail never strays too far from the shore.

After crossing the pond's outlet, turn right. The next stop is Mount Tom's South Peak, which lies 1 mile away. Follow Mount Tom Road. It winds across the rolling terrain past many side trails. Remain on the main route. After a sharp right bend, enter Billings Park. Owned by the town of Woodstock, this municipal park includes both of Mount Tom's summits. Continue 0.5 mile, rising easily to the mountain's 1250-foot South Peak. Although it is mostly wooded, through gaps in the trees, enjoy picturesque scenes of the valley below and distant mountains.

Two options depart from the same location on the summit's southeastern side: the Faulkner and Precipice trails. Stay left on the Precipice Trail. It snakes steeply down and around ledges, but fences help ensure a safe descent. In 0.1 mile, the terrain becomes less rugged. Continue on the Precipice Trail another 0.4 mile across the rocky landscape to a woods road. Follow the road downhill. Turn right in 0.1 mile on a wider corridor and hike 0.4 mile back to the visitor center.

EXTENDING YOUR HIKE

To avoid the Precipice Trail, take the Faulkner Trail from the South Peak. It winds down a seemingly endless series of switchbacks to Woodstock's Mountain Avenue. Turn left and then left again on River Street to complete the hike. While less steep, this far more popular option is also longer.

55 Brandon Gap

RATING/ DIFFICULTY	ROUND-TRIP	ELEV GAIN/ HIGH POINT	SEASON
**/3	6.8 miles	2200 feet/ 3366 feet	Year-round

Map: USGS Mount Carmel; **Contact:** Green Mountain National Forest; **Note:** Some years, the cliffs are closed during spring and early summer to protect nesting peregrine falcons; **GPS:** 43.839731, -72.968505

This suggested itinerary combines a popular excursion to the awe-inspiring edge of Mount Horrid's Great Cliff with a less dramatic journey across a quiet, forested stretch of Vermont's Long Trail. Both segments offer different rewards to enjoy throughout the year unless nesting peregrine falcons say otherwise.

GETTING THERE

From the junction of Routes 73 and 100 in Rochester, drive 10 miles west on Route 73 to the parking area on the left. From the intersection of Route 73 and US Route 7 in Brandon, follow Route 73 east for 7.8 miles to the parking area on the right.

ON THE TRAIL

Follow the short path north to Route 73 and carefully cross the pavement. Up a short incline, find a large kiosk and the Long Trail. Stay left and quickly enter the forest. The trail rises rapidly and in 0.1 mile enters the 12,333-acre Joseph Battell Wilderness. Battell was a conservationist who bequeathed much of the surrounding land to Middlebury College in 1915. The bulk of his donation was later sold to the US Forest Service and today forms the core of the Green Mountain National Forest's northern section.

The trail rises along switchbacks and climbs steadily. Winding past boulders and

under a canopy of birch trees, ascend to the base of a large ledge. Climb a rock staircase to a junction 0.7 mile from the start. Take the right spur that leads 0.1 mile to the top of Mount Horrid's Great Cliff. Perched high above Brandon Gap, this rocky promontory provides stunning 180-degree views.

The Long Trail north of the cliff remains open year-round whether or not falcons are present. What this stretch lacks in terms of spectacular scenery, it makes up for with remoteness. Leave the crowds behind and follow the white blazes as far as Gillespie Peak, 2.6 miles away.

From the Great Cliff spur junction, the Long Trail rises into an evergreen forest and in 0.6 mile reaches the wooded summit of Mount Horrid. After a brief descent, head across a saddle before steadily climbing to the top of Cape Lookoff Mountain. Here, find a small ledge with views over the Champlain Valley to the Adirondacks. The final 1.5-mile hike to Gillespie Peak remains high atop the

Great Cliff showcases impressive views.

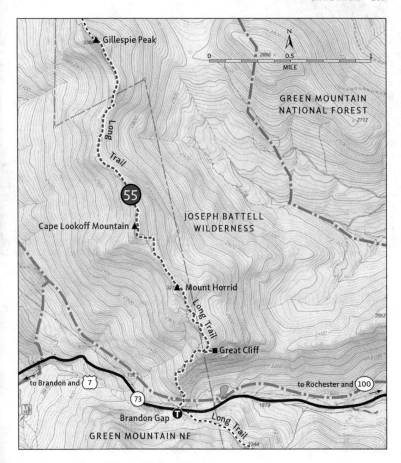

ridge over mostly gentle terrain, but there are a couple of short steep sections. The path leads past moss-covered boulders through a dark boreal forest. Take advantage of the tranquility; who knows what mushroom, wildflower, or amphibian lurks around the next corner? Gillespie Peak has two summits: the second is the high point and offers very limited views north to the

Breadloaf Wilderness. Retrace your steps south to return to the start.

SHORTENING YOUR HIKE

There are a number of options to shorten this hike. The round-trip to Mount Horrid's Great Cliff is only 1.6 miles. Turn around at Cape Lookoff Mountain to complete a 3.8-mile trek.

Below the ledge-covered high point of Camels Hump

56 Camels Hump

RATING/ DIFFICULTY	LOOP	ELEV GAIN/ HIGH POINT	SEASON
*****/4	5.8 miles	2600 feet/ 4083 feet	Year-round (see note)

Map: USGS Huntington; **Contact:** Vermont Department of Forests, Parks, and Recreation; **Note:** Trails closed in spring until Memorial Day weekend; **GPS:** 44.304889, -72.907887

Perhaps Vermont's most distinctly shaped mountain, Camels Hump towers above the Winooski River and is easily recognizable from as far away as the White Mountains. This popular loop visits numerous scenic outcrops before reaching the alpine summit, where sweeping views of three states await.

GETTING THERE

From Huntington Center, follow Camels Hump Road east. Stay right on Camels Hump Road at an intersection in 0.6 mile. Continue 2.8 miles to the end of the road and a large parking area.

ON THE TRAIL

Enter the forest to the east and proceed a few dozen feet to a trail intersection and the start of the day's loop. Turn right onto the 0.1-mile Forest City–Burrows Connector. The path drops quickly to Brush Brook and a large wooden bridge that spans a deep gorge. Bear left onto the Forest City Trail. This path rises gradually 1.4 miles under a shady hardwood forest, occasionally crossing small mountain streams.

At the junction with the Long Trail, turn left and follow the white blazes 0.2 mile into Wind Gap, a narrow pass on the ridge. Catch your breath; the next 1.7 miles are a lot more

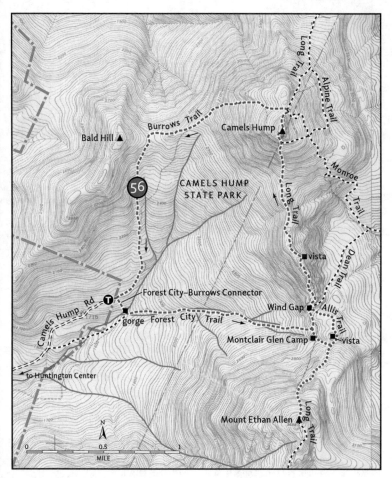

CAMELS HUMP
STATE PARK

56

Bald Hill ▲

Burrows Trail

Camels Hump ▲

Long Trail

Alpine Trail

Monroe Trail

■ vista

Dean Trail

Forest City–Burrows Connector

Wind Gap ■ Allis Trail

■ vista

gorge Forest City Trail

Montclair Glen Camp ■

Camels Hump Rd

Ⓣ

to Huntington Center

Mount Ethan Allen ▲

Long Trail

N

0   0.5   1
MILE

demanding. Stay left on the Long Trail as it heads north and winds up the steep slope to the first of many rocky outcrops. This first perch features views of Mount Ethan Allen. The path winds through a maze of rocks before ascending to a second knoll with more expansive scenery. Reenter the forest and climb steadily beneath an impressive

ledge. The route soon rises to another vista, and Camels Hump's imposing summit is visible for the first time.

The Long Trail returns to the forest and continues with minor elevation change for a bit. Eventually, the ascent becomes more aggressive and the terrain uneven. The hard work leads to an intersection with the Alpine

Trail, a bad-weather alternative that avoids the mountain's exposed summit.

With only 0.2 mile left to climb, remain on the Long Trail and swing left into the open, precariously under a steep rock face. Watch your footing and then make your way up a wide ledge. Veering right, one last push leads to the 4083-foot high point and incredible views in all directions. On a clear day, the panorama includes the Green Mountains from Killington to the Canadian border as well as the Adirondacks, Lake Champlain, and New Hampshire's White Mountains. While enjoying the scenery, remain on the summit's rocky surfaces and do your best to avoid trampling the fragile alpine flowers that thrive in this harsh environment.

Resume the loop by following the Long Trail 0.3 mile north to the Camels Hump Hut Clearing. At the clearing, formerly the site of a hotel, there is a major trail intersection. Turn left onto the 2.1-mile Burrows Trail. This path drops steadily through the boreal forest. Somewhat rough at first, the footing improves with each step. Swing left near the trail's halfway point, in a saddle that separates Camels Hump from Bald Hill. Complete the circuit under the shady limbs of maples, beech, and birch. The final stretch descends moderately to the parking area.

EXTENDING YOUR HIKE

There are two extensions to consider; both involve turning right onto the Long Trail at the Forest City Trail junction. Use the Allis Trail to reach Wind Gap and enjoy an unusual perspective of Camels Hump. This only adds 0.3 mile to the hike. For a longer adventure, scale Mount Ethan Allen. This quiet location with limited views honors Vermont's most famous Green Mountain Man. This option adds 1.6 miles.

57 Niquette Bay

RATING/ DIFFICULTY	LOOP	ELEV GAIN/ HIGH POINT	SEASON
***/2	3.5 miles	600 feet/ 410 feet	Year-round

Map: USGS Colchester; **Contact:** Vermont Department of Forests, Parks, and Recreation; **Notes:** Park charges a fee and has designated some trails as off-leash areas for dogs; **GPS:** 44.589569, -73.189795

A quaint state park only a few miles from Vermont's largest city, Niquette Bay invites hikers to explore its 553 acres on meandering trails that lead to scenic vistas, lakeshore promontories, and moss-filled forests. The park's fertile soil sustains tall trees that shade lush carpets of trilliums and ring with the melodious calls of thrushes.

GETTING THERE

From Interstate 89 north of Burlington, take exit 17 and head west on US Route 2. Drive 1 mile and then turn left onto Raymond Road (there is no sign for the state park). Continue 0.2 mile to the signed park entrance road on the left. Proceed 0.1 mile to the gate and then 0.1 mile to the parking area.

ON THE TRAIL

Find the trailhead at the southern edge of the park road's cul-de-sac. Enter the dark forest and immediately reach a four-way intersection. Turn left onto the aptly named Ledges Trail. This 0.9-mile path snakes its way around moss-covered rocks to the top of a forested ridge. Near this path's halfway point, arrive at the Bay View Vista

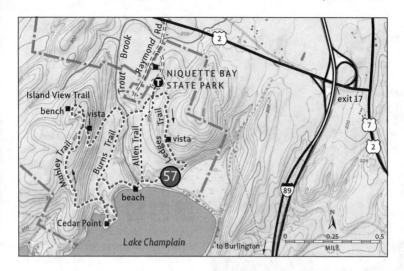

and enjoy distant views of Lake Champlain. Descending quickly, the trail approaches the shoreline and crosses a marshy wetland. Rise atop a pine-covered mound and proceed 0.2 mile to a junction with the Allen Trail.

Stay left and head over a short bridge that crosses Trout Brook. To the left, a spur leads a few dozen feet to a sandy beach on the shores of Lake Champlain. It is the perfect place to cool off on a hot summer day. Remain on the Allen Trail as it continues west and climbs steeply away from the water. Fortunately, the incline is short. Level off and enjoy the Allen Trail's final 0.3-mile stretch.

Turn left onto the Burns Trail. On this and nearby paths in the park's western half, dog owners may allow their pets to be off leash. While the dogs must remain under control, be prepared: many owners take advantage of this leash-free opportunity. Hike south 0.1 mile to a three-way intersection. The hike continues right on the Muhley Trail,

but first stay straight on the Burns Trail. The path leads quickly to the start of the 0.3-mile Cedar Point Bluff Loop. Follow this route as it circles up and around a scenic peninsula with excellent views of the lake and Camels Hump.

Upon looping back to the Muhley Trail, bear left. This 1.3-mile route gradually rises up wooded slopes past rocks and fallen trees. In 0.7 mile, stay left on the Island View Trail. Leading to a bench and scenes of Lake Champlain, this 0.4-mile spur climbs to and then loops over the hike's high point. Return to the Muhley Trail and then descend east to the appropriately named Mount Mansfield Vista. The path begins to drop quickly but eases atop a plateau. Parallel Trout Brook's slow-moving waters from above. After descending to the Burns Trail, turn left. The route follows a bridge across Trout Brook before climbing rapidly to the top of another plateau. The final 0.3 mile is easy—the perfect ending to this enticing jaunt.

Cedar Point Bluff vista

58 Missisquoi Wildlife Refuge

RATING/ DIFFICULTY	LOOP	ELEV GAIN/ HIGH POINT	SEASON
**/1	4.4 miles	30 feet/ 130 feet	Year-round

Map: USGS East Alburg; **Contact:** Missisquoi National Wildlife Refuge; **Notes:** Some refuge trails are seasonally closed, and some are susceptible to high water, especially in the spring; **GPS:** 44.954024, -73.205289

Established in 1945 to protect wetland habitat critical to migratory birds and other wildlife species, today Missisquoi National Wildlife Refuge consists of more than 6700 acres near the shores of Lake Champlain. The refuge boasts 7.5 miles of level trails past fields, ponds, rivers, and forests where as many as 200 species of birds have been observed.

GETTING THERE
From the intersection of US Route 7 and Route 78 in Swanton, drive northwest on Route 78 toward Alburg. In 5.5 miles, turn left onto Tabor Road. Continue 1.1 miles to the parking area on the left (0.9 mile south of the visitor center).

SHORTENING YOUR HIKE
The 0.5-mile Allen Trail is the shortest route to the water. This path and the parallel Burns Trail can be used as alternatives for completing shorter loops within the park. If time and energy permit, however, opt for the described hike. It visits all of the trail network's most alluring features.

ON THE TRAIL
Two trails depart the parking area, a 1.4-mile loop and a 3-mile round-trip trek down an abandoned rail bed. Together, they provide a good introduction to the refuge and a great opportunity to observe wildlife. Be prepared for potentially wet trail surfaces. Biting insects are also likely from late spring through summer. Other than that, grab your binoculars and field guides to enjoy the show.

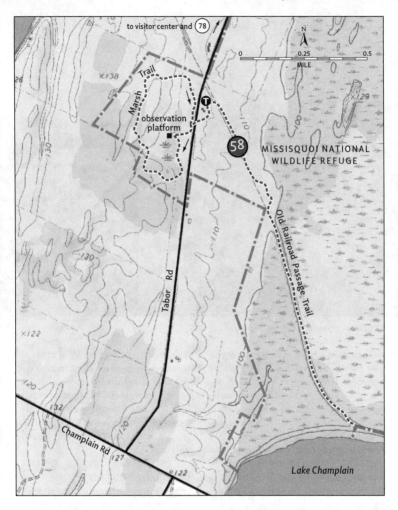

The first stop on the day's travels is the Stephen J. Young Marsh Trail, one of the refuge trails least likely to be inundated by water. The path heads south from the parking area, hugging the edge of a large field frequented by the fluttering flight of bobolinks. In 0.1 mile, cross Tabor Road to reach the start of the loop.

Turn left as the path leads gently to the edge of a pond in 0.1 mile. A short spur departs right to an observation platform beneath an osprey nest. Scan the narrow

Missisquoi's marshes teem with wildlife.

wetland for other signs of life including great blue herons, wood ducks, and red-winged blackbirds. The loop continues south and enters the forest in 0.2 mile. Swing sharply right and hike around the southern edge of the marsh. For 0.6 mile the circuit winds away from the water through an island of trees. After bearing right and heading over a boardwalk to the northern edge of the marsh, the trail emerges into the open once again. Walk 0.2 mile to complete the circuit before turning left to return to the parking area.

Upon reaching the trailhead, turn right and join the Old Railroad Passage Trail. This 1.5-mile one-way route ends within a few dozen feet of Lake Champlain. It is easy to follow throughout and very flat, but it can be quite wet toward the end if the lake level is high. Beginning along the edge of a field, the trail soon meanders through a forest. Rejoin the original rail line. It proceeds straight, with a modest curve. The path is surrounded by marsh and flowering plants, stay alert for American woodcock and other reclusive animals. At the trail's end, retrace your steps back to the start.

EXTENDING YOUR HIKE

Stop at the visitor center on Tabor Road for more information on nearby trails. From the visitor center enjoy a 1-mile loop into Maquam Bog. The refuge's longest option is the 5-mile round-trip Jeep Trail. Closed from April to August to protect nesting birds, when open it provides views of the Missisquoi River.

59 Mount Mansfield

RATING/ DIFFICULTY	LOOP	ELEV GAIN/ HIGH POINT	SEASON
*****/4	7 miles	3250 feet/ 4393 feet	Year-round (see note)

Map: USGS Mount Mansfield; **Contact:** Vermont Department of Forests, Parks, and Recreation; **Note:** Trails closed in spring before Memorial Day; **GPS:** 44.538037, -72.790956

The highest point in Vermont, Mount Mansfield offers the state's most spectacular stretch of alpine hiking, with scenes from the Adirondacks of New York to New Hampshire's White Mountains. While this challenging loop will take its toll on your body, it will delight the senses and create memories to last a lifetime.

GETTING THERE
From the junction of Routes 100 and 108 in Stowe, drive northwest on Route 108. In 8.1 miles, pass the trailhead on the left (after entering Smugglers Notch State Park). Continue a few hundred feet to the parking area on the road's left side.

ON THE TRAIL
From the parking area, follow Route 108 south a few hundred feet and then turn right onto the white-blazed Long Trail. Beyond the trail register, a moderate climb through a northern hardwood forest commences. In 0.8 mile, cross a small mountain stream. The steady ascent continues as the forest slowly transitions to spruce and fir. At mile 1.9, arrive at a junction. To the left, the Profanity Trail immediately swings past the

Taft Lodge and then proceeds to the Long Trail. This route avoids the summit of Mount Mansfield and serves as an alternative to the Long Trail if the weather is bad. Despite its name, the Taft Lodge does not offer services. Maintained by the Green Mountain Club, it is a rustic cabin used for overnight stays.

Stay straight on the Long Trail and rise through an open meadow with views of the rocky peak above. In 0.2 mile, two trails diverge right, including one that leads

Approaching Vermont's high point

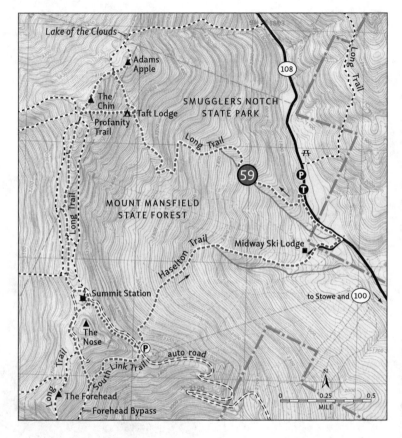

quickly to the open summit of the Adams Apple (many of Mount Mansfield's peaks are named for the facial features that they resemble from a distance). Consider adding this brief diversion. Otherwise, stay left on the Long Trail for the final 0.3-mile climb to the top of Vermont. Winding steeply up and around ledges, the trail reveals expanding views in all directions. From the Chin, Mount Mansfield's barren summit, the

scenes west over the Champlain Valley are especially mesmerizing. Be sure to remain on the trail to avoid trampling the fragile alpine plants.

The loop continues south along the Long Trail. For the next 1.2 miles, descend gradually across the mostly open landscape. The path occasionally drops into a forest of small trees, but more often the scenery is spectacular in all directions. Take your time and hike up and over a number of small knolls on the ridge. While numerous side trails depart in both directions, remain on the top of the ridge to complete the most straightforward trek to the Summit Station, a small visitor center which lies at the upper end of the auto road.

Continuing south, the Long Trail leads toward the steep, rocky face of the Nose and then bears right, wrapping around to its western side. After turning left on a service road and following it briefly, veer right into the dark forest to a junction with the Forehead Bypass. Stay left and follow this path 0.3 mile downhill to an intersection with the South Link Trail. Turn left onto this 0.5-mile path. Far removed from the mountain's most frequented spots, this route rises moderately through the high-elevation forest before ending at a parking area on the auto road.

Hike straight across the road and enjoy exquisite views north of the Chin and Smugglers Notch. Here, pick up the Haselton Trail. For the next 0.3 mile, it steeply descends ski slopes by heading straight, bearing right, winding left under a large ledge, and then dropping right once again. After the second sharp right turn, while descending, look for a sign on the left where the trail departs the ski slope and enters the forest.

Over the next 0.5 mile, the route begins rough but grows easier with each step. Cross a series of small brooks and one last ski slope. Soon, the trail bears sharply right and descends steeply. Rise easily to the top of an impressive spine, high above two parallel streams. Drop steadily 0.7 mile along the spine. The trail ends at the base of the ski area.

Continue straight to the Midway Ski Lodge and parking area. To return to your car, follow the entrance road to Route 108 and turn left.

Stay on the west side of the road and follow the de facto path that parallels the road 0.5 mile to the Long Trail parking area.

SHORTENING YOUR HIKE

There are numerous opportunities to shorten the described hike. Consider combining the Long and Profanity trails to complete a 5.1-mile hike that includes a small loop. Another option is to skip the southern portion of the loop. Follow the auto road from the Summit Station to the Haselton Trail. This would result in a 6.3-mile loop.

60 Jay Peak

RATING/ DIFFICULTY	LOOP	ELEV GAIN/ HIGH POINT	SEASON
***/3	3.4 miles	1700 feet/ 3858 feet	Year-round (see note)

Map: USGS Jay Peak; **Contact:** Vermont Department of Forest, Parks, and Recreation; **Note:** Trail closed in spring before Memorial Day; **GPS:** 44.912884, -72.504032

Jay Peak, the northernmost mountain along Vermont's Long Trail, honors John Jay, our nation's first chief justice of the Supreme Court. The panoramic views atop the summit crag are a fitting tribute to this American patriot whose legal expertise helped pave the way for Vermont to become the fourteenth state in the Union.

GETTING THERE

From the junction of Routes 242 and 101 in Troy, follow Route 242 as it climbs west 6.4 miles into Jay Pass. Parking is on the left side of the road.

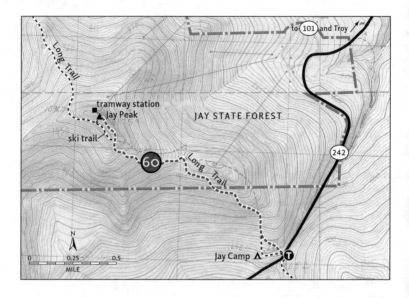

ON THE TRAIL

Carefully cross to the road's north side. Join the Long Trail as it enters the forest and quickly reaches the Atlas Valley Shelter, a small plywood-framed building not suitable for overnight use. In 0.1 mile, arrive at the lower branch of the Jay Loop. Descending left, this blue-blazed path leads 0.2 mile to Jay Camp, a small building that is used by backpackers.

Remain on the Long Trail as it swings right and climbs to the upper branch of the Jay Loop in 0.2 mile. Beyond, the path maintains a steady climb up the slope. While the ascent is somewhat demanding, the footing is not challenging. The trail weaves through a forest dominated by birch, beech, and maple, and the understory is carpeted with wildflowers and home to many colorful songbirds.

Just beyond the halfway point, the Long Trail rises to a saddle on the ridge. Briefly leveling off, the route carves through a dense patch of ferns, now under a canopy of conifers. Straight ahead lies the mountain's ski area, somewhat visible through the dense vegetation. Veer left and follow the white-blazed trail as it parallels an alpine ski slope en route to the summit.

Climbing more steeply now, take your time on the increasingly rocky terrain. The trail leads up stone steps and across granite ledges, occasionally offering glimpses of distant peaks and ridges. Eventually, the hard work leads to the edge of a ski trail. Use caution crossing over the snowmaking equipment, as the metal can be hot during the summer, and emerge onto the grassy slope.

Pick up the Long Trail on the far side and begin the final 0.2-mile trek to the summit.

Final stretch to Jay Peak

Up the steep, rocky landscape, the path leads across a mostly open ridgeline with views stretching in all directions: south to Mount Mansfield, east to the White Mountains, and north into the Eastern Townships of Quebec. The incline rapidly moderates as the final steps lead to the high point at the ski area's summit lodge and tramway station.

Retrace your steps to return to the parking area in 1.7 miles. For an easier start to the descent, follow the ski trail east from the summit. It parallels the Long Trail 0.2 mile. Turn right to continue the descent down the Long Trail. Be careful not to miss the intersection, because the base of the ski area and the trailhead are far apart.

61 Mount Hunger and White Rock

RATING/ DIFFICULTY	LOOP	ELEV GAIN/ HIGH POINT	SEASON
*****/4	6.4 miles	2100 feet/ 3539 feet	Late May– Nov

Map: USGS Stowe; **Contact:** Vermont Department of Forest, Parks, and Recreation; **GPS:** 44.372057, -72.639986

A challenging loop over two scenic summits in Vermont's rugged Hunger Range, this daylong adventure is as beautiful as it is demanding. Along the trek, scan the changing forests in search of songbirds in late spring, wildflowers throughout the summer, and brilliant foliage during the cool days of autumn.

Views from White Rock Mountain spur

GETTING THERE

From Route 12 near the Wrightsville Dam turn west onto Shady Rill Road and follow it 2.2 miles. Turn right onto Story Road and in 0.4 mile bear left onto Chase Road. In 0.2 mile, turn left onto North Bear Swamp Road. In 1.5 miles, veer sharply left as the road becomes narrower and rougher. The parking area is 0.4 mile on the right.

ON THE TRAIL

From the parking area follow the Middlesex Trail 0.1 mile and soon reach a woods road. The route turns left, joining the road. Slowly swinging right, ascend gradually. After crossing a small stream, 0.8 mile from the start, look for a small trail sign and cairn. Turn left off the road into a more inviting landscape. The trail soon crosses another stream and passes a Putnam State Forest sign that recognizes the efforts of The Nature Conservancy to protect the area's landscape. Continue the modest ascent; the footing is rocky but not difficult. Before long, reach a junction and the start of the day's loop, 1.6 miles from the trailhead.

Turn right and remain on the Middlesex Trail. Initially, the path rises gradually along a slope blanketed by an increasing number of small ledges. As the trail swings left, the incline steepens. Under a thinning canopy of birch trees, make your way up to a spur that leads right to an inviting eastern vista. The trail moderates as it weaves through a meadow of ferns to the base of a granite ledge. Now the fun begins.

The final ascent is short, yet extremely demanding. Aided at first by a rope, pull yourself up the steep rock wall. Very slowly, the terrain becomes easier to navigate, but

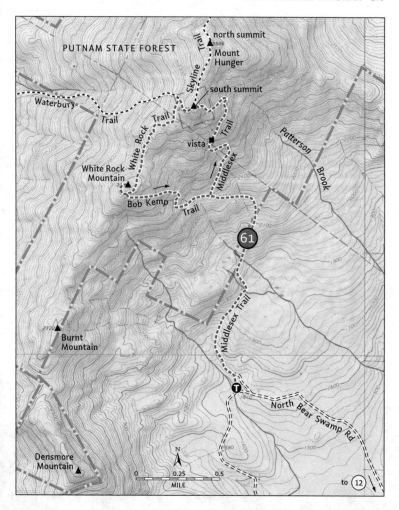

it remains challenging. Ascend the exposed rock—especially difficult if wet or icy—and enjoy the spectacular views east to the White Mountains. Hike through one last forested section before arriving at Mount Hunger's south summit and awe-inspiring views in all directions.

To the north, the Skyline Trail leads across mostly forested terrain to the Hunger Range's high point and beyond. Today's loop continues west down the Waterbury Trail. Descending in the open, with enticing views of Camels Hump and Mount Mansfield, the blue-blazed trail quickly drops into the boreal forest. Down the rocky trail, watch your step and take your time. In 0.2 mile, reach an intersection.

Turn left onto the White Rock Trail. This route continues to descend, but not as aggressively. However, the footing for the next 0.75 mile is rough in places. A short climb out of a saddle leads to an open ledge. Soon after, a spur leads right to the wide-open summit of White Rock Mountain. The 0.2-mile route begins easily, but ends with a scramble up the pointy peak. This short diversion is well worth the extra effort.

Back on the main route, turn right and head east along the White Rock Trail (sometimes referred to as the Bob Kemp Trail). Crossing one last scenic ledge, the path descends quickly into the forest. Hike 0.6 mile, occasionally over rough terrain, back to

the Middlesex Trail. Stay right and return to the parking area in 1.6 miles.

62 Elmore Mountain

RATING/ DIFFICULTY	LOOP	ELEV GAIN/ HIGH POINT	SEASON
***/2–3	4 miles	1300 feet/ 2608 feet	Year-round

Map: USGS Morrisville; **Contact:** Vermont Department of Forests, Parks, and Recreation; **Note:** Fee; **GPS:** 44.539801, -72.535889

The perfect choice for young hikers and families, Elmore Mountain features panoramic views that include Stowe Valley,

Stowe Valley panorama

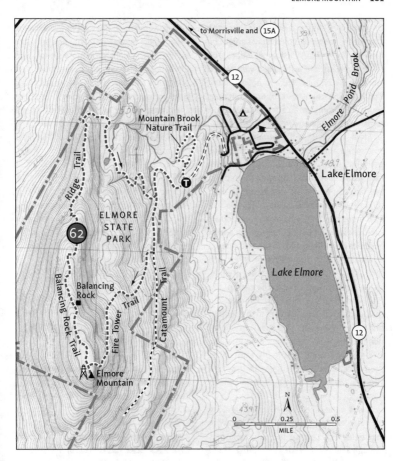

the Northeast Kingdom, and peaks along the Quebec border. After spending a day enjoying the scenery and exploring the area's many natural features, as an added bonus, cool off in the waters of Lake Elmore.

GETTING THERE

From the junction of Routes 15A and 12 in Morrisville, follow Route 12 southeast 4.2 miles to the park entrance on the right. Reach the park office in 0.1 mile and then continue straight ahead 0.3 mile. Follow the dirt road as it bears right before ending at the parking area in 0.3 mile.

ON THE TRAIL

Past a kiosk and around a gate, head up the wide trail. As it approaches a small wetland, the path veers left and quickly reaches the start of the loop in 0.3 mile. Stay straight on the Fire Tower Trail. Past small ledges, the route levels off and arrives at a well-signed junction in 0.2 mile. Here the Catamount Trail, a cross-country ski route, continues south. Turn right up a series of rock steps, remaining on the narrower Fire Tower Trail.

After swinging left, parallel a small streambed and begin a steadier climb. The trail gradually winds its way up the mountain. As boulders and ledges begin to cover the landscape, rise quickly to the site of the former fire warden's cabin. This spot, a little more than 1 mile from the start, offers excellent views of Lake Elmore below and of northern New Hampshire in the distance.

The final 0.2-mile climb is steep and rocky, but not long. Past a number of small vistas, the trail soon rises to the crest of the ridge and an intersection. Turn left on a spur that leads a few hundred feet to the summit fire tower. Ascend to the cabin for sensational views in all directions. There is also an unmarked route that leads south from the tower to an open ledge with excellent shots of Mount Mansfield and the Hunger Range.

Resume the hike by heading north along the ridge on the Balancing Rock Trail. With minor elevation change, the path meanders through a moss-covered boreal forest. There are a number of impressive ledges along the way, some of which provide excellent views. A half mile from the summit, reach the trail's namesake natural feature, a small boulder that has somehow failed to tumble down the ridge.

Continue north along the recently constructed Ridge Trail. It leads 1.7 miles back to the Fire Tower Trail. The upper section is very pleasant as it remains atop

a narrowing spine, flat sections alternating with an occasional descent. As the route swings sharply right, drop more steeply with the aid of wooden steps. The path levels off briefly in a small saddle and proceeds past a small forested wetland. Heading down once again, pass a large ledge on the left. After a number of small stream crossings, return to the Fire Tower Trail. Turn left to complete the journey.

EXTENDING YOUR HIKE

Explore the Mountain Brook Nature Trail that leaves west from the parking area. The 0.5-mile path loops past a cascading stream and provides basic information on the area's history, flora, and fauna.

63 Owls Head Mountain

RATING/ DIFFICULTY	ROUND-TRIP	ELEV GAIN/ HIGH POINT	SEASON
***/2	3.2 miles	500 feet/ 1958 feet	Year-round

Map: USGS Marshfield; **Contact:** Vermont Department of Forests, Parks, and Recreation; **Note:** Fee; **GPS:** 44.313836, -72.288756

Groton State Forest, one of Vermont's largest blocks of state-owned conservation land, is a hiker's paradise that features miles of trails to remote ponds and rocky summits. This moderate climb to the top of the area's signature natural feature is a great introduction.

GETTING THERE

From US Route 2 in Marshfield, drive 4.2 miles south on Route 232 and then turn left

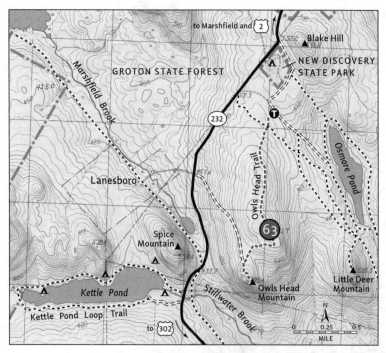

into the New Discovery State Park Campground. Stop at the gate and then continue 0.2 mile before turning right toward Osmore Pond. Drive 0.4 mile to the trailhead on the right. Park off the road. Winter parking is usually available near the campground entrance just off Route 232.

ON THE TRAIL

Follow the Owls Head Trail west along a wide woods road. In 0.1 mile, after passing a large boulder, arrive at a sign and register box. Turn left and wind through an area recently harvested for timber. The path proceeds with little elevation change. Follow the blue blazes to a four-way intersection in 0.2 mile, where a multiuse trail leads north

to Route 232 and south to Lake Groton. Continue straight on the Owls Head Trail, which rises gently.

Take your time and scan the surrounding forest of birch and maple for colorful wildflowers and resident fauna, from the majestic moose to the diminutive red-breasted nuthatch. Near the 1-mile mark, pass a small wetland on the right as the trail crosses a ledge. After a modest descent, head over a series of bog bridges near another forested wetland. The route quickly emerges onto the upper end of an auto road used by many to access Owls Head's summit more easily.

Turn left for the final 0.2-mile climb. The trail ascends a long rock staircase and then swings right. The stone steps continue into the evergreen forest as the trail winds carefully around a moss-covered ledge. A few more steps lead to the high point and a stone building—a charming reminder of the work completed here by the Civilian Conservation Corps in the 1930s. Beyond, find summit ledges that showcase a stunning view west over Kettle Pond. Camels Hump and other high peaks of the Green Mountains form the distant horizon.

Looking south from Owls Head summit ledge

Since Owls Head is easily accessible, you are likely to have a lot of company. Choose this hike midweek or off-season for greater solitude. Enjoy a nice snack or picnic lunch before retracing your steps.

EXTENDING YOUR HIKE

The 26,000-acre Groton State Forest features countless miles of additional trails that invite exploration. One option that complements Owls Head well is the 3-mile loop circling nearby Kettle Pond. The loop begins at a parking area on Route 232, 2.2 miles southwest of the New Discovery Campground. Paralleling the shoreline throughout, the loop provides excellent views of Owls Head and offers prime wildlife observation opportunities. It is also a great location for backcountry camping. While the trail is more challenging than the minimal elevation change would suggest, it is appropriate for hikers of all ages.

64 Mount Monadnock

RATING/ DIFFICULTY	ROUND-TRIP	ELEV GAIN/ HIGH POINT	SEASON
**/3	5 miles	2150 feet/ 3148 feet	Year-round

Map: USGS Monadnock Mountain; **Contact:** Vermont Department of Forest, Parks, and Recreation; **Note:** Trail is on private land; **GPS:** 44.900883, -71.507204

Rising on its own and dominating the skyline above the Connecticut River, Mount Monadnock in northern Vermont sees far less traffic than its namesake peak in southern New Hampshire. On the eastern edge of Vermont's Northeast Kingdom, this peaceful trek through quiet woods rises to a tower that features boundless views of three states and Canada.

GETTING THERE

From the northern junction of Route 26 and US Route 3 in Colebrook, New Hampshire, follow Route 26 west 0.6 mile. After crossing the Connecticut River into Vermont, turn right onto Route 102. Drive 0.2 mile north and then turn left onto a gravel pit entrance-way. Look for the parking area and trailhead on the far left.

ON THE TRAIL

Located on private land, Mount Monadnock is the centerpiece of a 1471-acre conservation easement that secured public access with funds from Vermont's Forest Legacy program. Begin on a dirt road closed to vehicles. Rising gently just south of a gravel pit, the route quickly reaches a kiosk and register. Turn left onto the narrower corridor. Head through a meadow and, soon after, enter an evergreen forest.

The trail drops briefly as it approaches the banks of a small stream. Climb gradually and pass to the left of an imposing ledge that towers over the trail. Beyond, descend once again to the stream, but this time cross to the other side.

The trail rises steadily to an old woods road, 0.7 mile from the trailhead. Pay close attention to this intersection marked by a small sign and a cairn. You do not want to miss it on the way down.

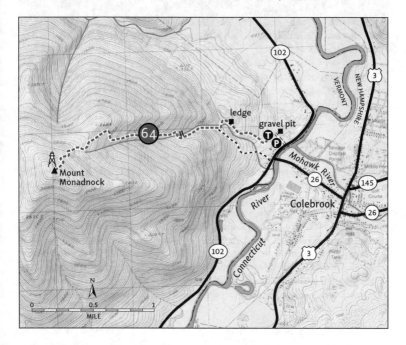

Hikers scale Mount Monadnock.

Swing right. Now on the original route to the summit, you parallel the bubbling stream, and the incline becomes more rigorous. Enjoy the serene hardwood forests and the many small cascades. After passing the most picturesque of the diminutive falls, the trail crosses a wooden bridge. While you are now almost halfway to the summit, the remaining stretch is the most demanding.

For the most part, the final 1.4-mile climb to the top is aggressive but straightforward. Winding through the forest, numerous rock steps and a well-drained path await. As you rise higher up the mountain, the vegetation slowly transitions to spruce and fir. Occasional level sections provide opportunities to catch your breath and scan the dense forest

for mushrooms, flowers, and wildlife. One last ascent leads to the wooded summit and the base of a tall fire tower.

Renovated recently, the tower includes six staircases and a small cabin on the top. Make your way up and above the tallest trees to marvel at 360-degree views that include northern Vermont, the White Mountains, and numerous hills and ridges in southern Quebec. Especially impressive is the scene south over the Connecticut River as it snakes through green fields surrounded by towering mountains. Before following the same trail back to your car, explore the summit area. Short, unmarked paths lead to a stone chimney and other remains of the fire warden's cabin that once stood here.

Boulder Loop clifftop (Hike 74)

northern new hampshire

Stretching from the Granite State's Lakes Region to its northernmost county, the centerpiece of northern New Hampshire is the White Mountains, New England's premier hiking destination. Featuring alpine summits, deep valleys, scenic waterfalls, and secluded ponds, this region offers a wide array of natural features to enjoy.

This must-visit destination is within a few hours of New England's largest cities and is crisscrossed by well over 1000 miles of trails. A popular destination twelve months a year, northern New Hampshire affords the widest variety of hiking opportunities in New England—from short nature walks to challenging ascents of the region's most rugged summits to everything in between.

and then turn right onto Hoyt Road. Drive 1.8 miles and turn right onto Belknap Mountain Road. Continue 0.6 mile, then turn left onto Carriage Road. Parking is available 0.3 mile on the left, just before the gate.

ON THE TRAIL
Follow Carriage Road and hike past the gate into Belknap Mountain State Forest. This 1300-acre expanse is surrounded by a growing collection of conservation lands, the focus of a land-protection effort spearheaded by the Belknap Range Conservation Coalition. Immediately reach the 1.1-mile Gunstock Mountain Trail on the left. Follow this orange-blazed trail (sometimes blazed in white) as it enters the forest and begins

65 Belknap Range

RATING/ DIFFICULTY	LOOP	ELEV GAIN/ HIGH POINT	SEASON
***/3	4.6 miles	1850 feet/ 2382 feet	Year-round

Map: USGS Laconia; **Contact:** Belknap Range Conservation Coalition; **Note:** Portion of hike crosses private property; **GPS:** 43.517701, -71.390498

While modest in elevation, the Belknap Range rises high above New Hampshire's Lakes Region and is prominently visible from miles away. This scenic loop scales some of the range's highest summits, traverses numerous ledge-covered ridges, and takes in scenery in all directions.

GETTING THERE
From the junction of Route 11A and US Route 3 in Gilford, follow Route 11A 1.6 miles east

Old Piper Trail

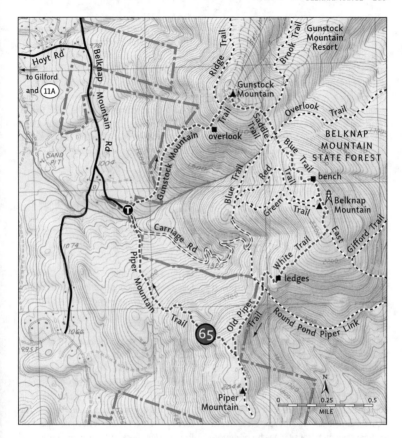

a modest ascent. After swinging sharply right, level off briefly. A short climb follows and leads right to an overlook with pleasant views 0.8 mile from the start.

From the overlook, head back in a westerly direction. The trail then veers right and rises up a ledge. Soon after, reach an intersection with the Ridge Trail, which coincides here with the Belknap Range Trail (BRT). The BRT is a nearly 12-mile route that connects Gunstock Mountain and Mount Major. Today's hike will follow this route for just over a mile. Stay right and hike 0.1 mile to Gunstock's summit.

From the top of the Gunstock Mountain Resort ski area, there are sweeping views north over Lake Winnipesaukee to the White Mountains. Continue the loop by joining the yellow-blazed Brook Trail. It heads east, paralleling ski trails at first, before descending 0.3 mile to a junction. Stay straight and follow the white-blazed Saddle Trail 0.1 mile to a four-way intersection. Pick up the Blue Trail by hiking straight.

A modest 0.5-mile ascent ensues. Just before the trail's end, pass an inviting bench with picturesque views of New Hampshire's Lakes Region. Atop Belknap Mountain a fire tower rises above the forested surroundings to encompass 360-degree views from the seacoast to New England's highest summits and over many natural features in between.

Four colored trails converge atop Belknap: blue, red, green, and white. Join the White Trail as it leads south around a communications tower. Beyond, emerge onto open ledges and an intersection where the BRT departs left using the East Gifford Trail. Stay right, remaining on the White Trail, and begin a steady descent. Through evergreen forests, the trail is mostly across exposed granite.

Entering a more open landscape, the path leads to a series of ledges with serene views of Round Pond and Mount Major. After the most prominent perch, swing northwest and then descend south into a small notch 1 mile from Belknap's summit. Turn left onto the 0.5-mile Old Piper Trail. After it veers right, continue straight where a trail exits left to Round Pond. Follow the orange-blazed path as it ascends numerous ledges before arriving atop a largely treeless summit, just north of Piper's forested high point. A chair made of stones provides an ideal vantage point to view the surrounding beauty.

From the stone chair, begin the final leg. Leading northwest, the red-blazed Piper Mountain Trail descends 1 mile, mostly across private land. The route drops aggressively at first; watch your footing on the ledges and uneven terrain. Eventually, the path levels off and makes its way back

to Carriage Road in a more leisurely manner. The parking area is 0.1 mile to the left.

SHORTENING YOUR HIKE
Many hikers ascend Belknap Mountain from a parking area at the upper end of Carriage Road. Any combination of the Red, Green, and Blue trails can be used to complete a loop in the 2-mile range. Be aware that the road can be rough and the gate is not always open.

66 Ossipee Mountains

RATING/ DIFFICULTY	LOOP	ELEV GAIN/ HIGH POINT	SEASON
***/4	14.5 miles	2800 feet/ 2990 feet	Year-round

Map: USGS Melvin Village; **Contact:** Lakes Region Conservation Trust; **Note:** Private conservation land; **GPS:** 43.731994, -71.324468

Surrounding the Castle in the Clouds historic mansion, a popular tourist destination, and offering 30 miles of trails open year-round to hikers, the 5381-acre Castle in the Clouds Conservation Area protects the core of New Hampshire's Ossipee Mountain Range. This spectacular property is owned and managed by the Lakes Region Conservation Trust, a membership organization with numerous preserves in the region. While the recommended loop is long, it traverses miles of easy trails to a series of breathtaking vistas.

GETTING THERE
From the junction of Routes 171 and 109 in Moultonborough, drive 0.5 mile east on Route 171 and then turn left onto Ossipee

Turtleback Mountain lies beneath Mount Shaw.

Park Road. Drive 1.3 miles and park on the right (before the gate).

ON THE TRAIL

Hike past the gate and follow the paved road east. Down a short hill, the road forks. Stay right and head toward Shannon Pond. Turn left and walk across the earthen dam to the trailhead. Numerous trails depart here. Pick up the Lower Bridle Path. As with most routes within the preserve, this path winds gradually up a wide corridor. In 0.6 mile, a spur trail departs left and climbs 0.1 mile to the top of a scenic knoll. The main trail swings right and wraps around the steep slope before ending in 0.4 mile.

Follow the Faraway Mountain Trail left and hike 0.2 mile to the start of the Upper Bridle Path on the right. This narrower path rises aggressively at first. Weave 0.7 mile up and over a wooded bump and then drop easily to a junction with the Oak Ridge Cutoff. Follow this path right for 0.5 mile. It ascends to an intersection with the High Ridge Trail.

The High Ridge Trail lives up to its name. Veer right and follow it 2.2 miles to Mount Shaw, the range's highest peak. Pay close attention to the route's many turns. The well-marked path leads gradually to the partially open summit, 0.4 mile beyond an intersection with the Black Snout Trail. In addition to being a fine picnic location, Mount Shaw offers exquisite views of Mount Washington and other White Mountain peaks to the north.

Return to the Black Snout Trail and stay left. Heading south, the path descends easily 0.3 mile to a side trail on the left. Hike 0.2 mile to the top of Black Snout to enjoy a vista

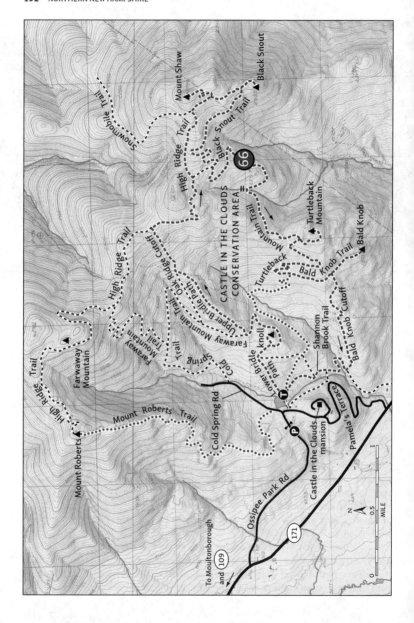

of New Hampshire's Lakes Region. Rejoin the Black Snout Trail and bear left. It rambles another 1.5 miles, with minor elevation change, before ending.

Turn left onto the Turtleback Mountain Trail. This wide path proceeds 1.1 miles to a brook crossing and small cascades. Continue another 0.9 mile across the rolling terrain. After swinging sharply right, reach a 0.5-mile spur on the left. Follow it to the rocky summit of Turtleback Mountain, which looks back at Mount Shaw and Black Snout.

Beyond the spur, the main route enters a series of switchbacks and in 0.8 mile arrives at an intersection with the Bald Knob Trail. Stay left and enjoy this mostly level path for 0.8 mile to the preserve's most dramatic bluff and spectacular views of Lake Winnipesaukee and the Belknap Range.

Retrace your steps 0.4 mile and then head left onto the Bald Knob Cutoff. This rugged 1-mile trail descends a rocky slope, passes the remains of the mountain's volcanic history, and then rises to a second open knoll with the day's final views.

Drop steadily into the dark forest toward the banks of Shannon Brook. At a junction, follow the Shannon Brook Trail right. This red-blazed path parallels its namesake and leads past numerous side trails. In 0.7 mile, return to the shores of Shannon Pond. Turn left to return to your car.

SHORTENING YOUR HIKE

While the terrain along the described hike is not difficult, 14.5 miles is a lengthy excursion. Limitless other loops are available. Consider a much shorter trek to Turtleback Mountain and Bald Knob. Another option, popular with visitors, is the 2.3-mile trail to the open summit of Mount Roberts that leaves from the same parking area.

67 Mount Cardigan

RATING/ DIFFICULTY	LOOP	ELEV GAIN/ HIGH POINT	SEASON
****/3	3.8 miles	1250 feet/ 3121 feet	May–Nov

Map: USGS Mount Cardigan; **Contact:** New Hampshire Division of Parks and Recreation; **GPS:** 43.644342, -71.935412

South Ridge Trail's rocky landscape

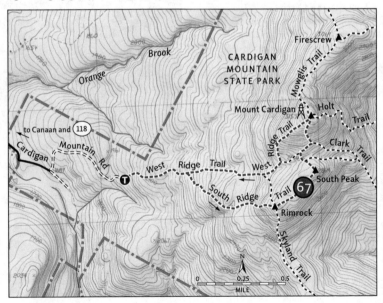 *Few mountains in New England provide more spectacular views for such a relatively modest effort. While this hike is understandably popular with visitors of all ages, do not underestimate the terrain or the exposure to the elements. Choose a great day and feast on the abundant scenery.*

GETTING THERE

From the junction of US Route 4 and Route 118 in Canaan, drive north on Route 118. In 0.6 mile, turn right onto Cardigan Mountain Road. Follow this road 3.4 miles into Cardigan Mountain State Park. Stay left and drive 0.6 mile to the large parking area.

ON THE TRAIL

The West Ridge Trail begins near a large sign. Swinging gently up the mountain, the well-used path leads up and over a small knoll. After descending briefly, rise to an intersection and the start of the day's loop, 0.5 mile from the start.

Turn right onto the 1.5-mile South Ridge Trail. This less-traveled portion of the hike climbs steadily through changing vegetation. In a rocky evergreen forest to start, the path's footing becomes less rugged as it enters a world of birch and beech. The evergreen forest soon returns and the trail rises more aggressively up a mossy, ledge-covered slope. Take your time and watch your footing. Before long, emerge atop a flatter landscape of smooth granite ledges.

Reach Rimrock, a partially open summit with the hike's first views, and an intersection with the Skyland Trail, which diverges left and right. Continue straight on the South Ridge Trail, formerly blazed in red but now

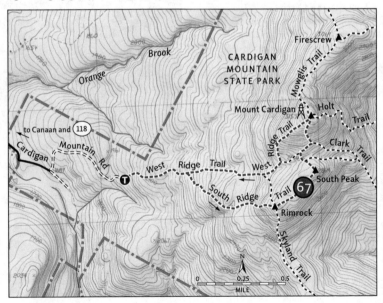

marked with white paint. As the route heads easily across the semi-open landscape, the summit tower comes into view. In 0.3 mile, arrive on Mount Cardigan's South Peak, which offers sweeping views of New Hampshire's Lakes Region.

After a brief drop into a small, forested saddle, return to exposed granite. Stay right and proceed to an intersection near a fire lookout cabin. Turn left onto the Clark Trail to begin the final 0.2-mile climb. This area, which is very steep, can be extremely tricky if wet or icy. Otherwise, it is a fun scramble up the increasingly open landscape.

From the 3121-foot high point, 360-degree views include the White Mountains to the north, the Green Mountains to the west, and Mount Monadnock to the south. In season, there is a fire tower open to visitors, but with no trees in sight it does little to augment the views. While the often-windy summit is a great place to enjoy a picnic lunch, stay alert. There is little cover should threatening storms arise.

The trek down follows the 1.5-mile West Ridge Trail exclusively. Be sure you are heading down the correct route; many trails that end atop Cardigan begin at distant parking lots. The West Ridge Trail is well marked and blazed in bright red. Remain in the open for about a half mile, and enjoy the many views during the initial descent.

Swinging left, the trail enters the forest. Watch your footing; in places the terrain can be slippery. Stay right at a large cairn near a junction with the Skyland Trail. The West Ridge Trail drops steadily, but it is easy to navigate. Take your time to identify the flowering plants and colorful mushrooms at your feet, as well as the melodious songbirds calling from the surrounding canopy.

68 Mount Osceola

RATING/ DIFFICULTY	ROUND-TRIP	ELEV GAIN/ HIGH POINT	SEASON
***/4	6.4 miles	2100 feet/ 4340 feet	May–Nov

Maps: USGS Waterville Valley and USGS Mount Osceola; **Contact:** White Mountain National Forest; **Note:** Access road closed in winter; **GPS:** 43.983183, -71.558831

Surrounded by Abenaki place names, this prominent peak in the southern White Mountains is named in honor of a nineteenth-century Seminole leader from Florida. The popular trail that leads to its high point, though rugged in places, is one of the easier routes up a New Hampshire 4000-foot mountain and features mesmerizing views from atop its summit ledges.

GETTING THERE
From Route 49 just south of the village of Waterville Valley, turn left onto Tripoli Road. In 1.2 miles, stay right (the road left leads to the Waterville Valley Ski Area) and continue 3.6 miles into Thornton Gap. The trailhead is located on the right just beyond the road's high point.

ON THE TRAIL
Pick up the Mount Osceola Trail and head across the flat, boulder-covered terrain. The path swings right and then up a rocky slope. While not steep, the terrain is uneven and requires extra care. Eventually, the route turns abruptly left, but then soon straightens. It continues to rise modestly up the valley as the footing slowly improves.

A little more than a mile from the start, the trail bends left and weaves to the top of Breadtray Ridge. With the incline moderating, take advantage and recharge before the next climb. The surrounding forest is home to mushrooms and other flora that thrive in this birch forest, which is slowly being overshadowed by a growing canopy of young spruce trees.

Hike in an easterly direction and make your way to a small stream, 0.9 mile from the summit. Beyond, the terrain becomes more challenging again. As the path winds up the mountain's southern slope, there are numerous ledges to navigate. Watch your step, especially if the surface is wet or icy. Fortunately, the difficult sections are interspersed with less demanding ones, and overall the grade is not rigorous.

One last right turn is soon followed by the relaxing final stretch to Mount Osceola's 4340-foot high point. Surrounded by trees, the top has no views. Follow the muddy trail a few hundred feet ahead to an open ledge. This former fire tower site is perched high above a precipitous cliff. Enjoy the inspiring views of the Tripyramids and other nearby peaks surrounding Waterville Valley, as well as more distant summits including Mount Carrigain and the Presidential Range looming to the north. This is a great place to hang out and enjoy lunch before returning 3.2 miles back to the trailhead.

EXTENDING YOUR HIKE
For a worthwhile 2-mile extension, venture farther along the Mount Osceola Trail to the 4156-foot summit of the mountain's East

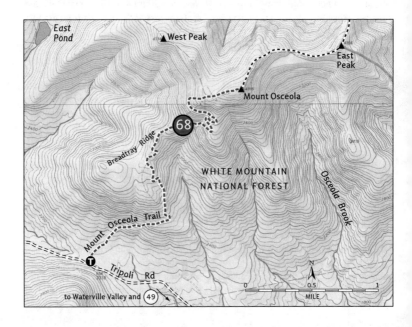

Views north to the Pemigewasset Wilderness

Peak. Although the terrain is challenging in places between the two, the scenery is well worth the trip. Turn around at the mostly wooded high point and check another 4000-foot mountain off your list.

69 Mount Moosilauke

RATING/ DIFFICULTY	LOOP	ELEV GAIN/ HIGH POINT	SEASON
****/4	7.9 miles	2600 feet/ 4802 feet	May–Nov

Maps: USGS Mount Moosilauke and USGS Mount Kineo; **Contact:** Dartmouth Outing Club; **GPS:** 43.993522, -71.815126

Standing prominently on the western edge of the White Mountains, Mount Moosilauke boasts numerous routes leading to its wide-open 4802-foot summit. Beginning at least as early as 1685, when Abenaki Chief Water-nomee is believed to have stood upon its summit, the mountain has lured many to its broad ridges and deep ravines in search of outdoor adventure and striking natural beauty.

GETTING THERE

From Route 25 in Warren, follow Route 118 (Sawyer Highway) north 5.8 miles. Turn left onto Ravine Road (dirt surface). Travel 1.6

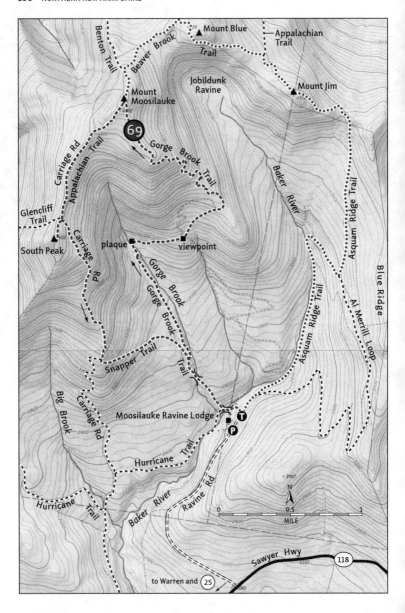

South Peak's quiet high point

miles to a turnaround area. After turning around, park along the right side of the road, facing out. Do not park in the turnaround area.

ON THE TRAIL

This challenging and popular hike, which leaves from Dartmouth's Moosilauke Ravine Lodge, travels through 4600 acres of land owned and managed by the college. The lodge is usually open to the public from mid-May to mid-October. People are welcome to make arrangements to stay overnight, or stop by for a snack and to fill water bottles. For more information, contact the Dartmouth Outing Club.

Hike to the road's turnaround area where a large kiosk marks the start of the Asquam Ridge Trail. Follow this path at first, but immediately turn left onto the Gorge Brook Trail. Drop 0.1 mile to the Baker River and cross a wooden bridge. Stay left, paralleling the rushing water,

and soon reach an intersection where the Hurricane Trail departs left. Bear right and rise gradually 0.3 mile over rocky terrain to the banks of the path's namesake natural feature. Use the bridge to safely cross the water and proceed 0.1 mile to a new junction with the Snapper Trail. This is the start of the day's loop.

Turn right, remaining on the Gorge Brook Trail. With modest elevation gain, continue 1 mile to a plaque marking the McKenney Memorial Forest and the last views of the brook. The summit is still 2.1 miles away and nearly 1500 feet above. While more challenging, the remaining ascent is straightforward throughout. Beyond an eastern viewpoint, switchbacks wind increasingly higher up the slope. Catch your breath at the many vistas along the way. Soon the Franconia Range can be seen towering to the north.

Level off atop a semi-open bump and catch the first glimpse of the day's destination. A brief descent is followed by a slightly longer climb to the mountain's treeless high point. On a clear day, peaks can be seen in all directions. Mount Moosilauke offers a great perspective of Vermont and exquisite views of the White Mountains, including the Presidential Range. While exploring, stay on marked trails to avoid trampling the summit's fragile alpine vegetation. If the wind is howling, take advantage of the rock-pile remains of summit structures that welcomed overnight guests more than a century ago.

The loop continues south along the Carriage Road, which coincides 0.9 mile with the Appalachian Trail (AT). Descending quickly into the boreal forest, the Carriage Road leads pleasantly along a flat, narrow ridge. At a four-way junction where the AT departs right down the Glencliff Trail, follow a short spur that rises straight 0.2 mile to the top of the mountain's South Peak. This picturesque spot offers a much quieter alternative to its higher northern neighbor.

Return to the four-way junction and veer right, rejoining the Carriage Road. The wide and scenic path squeezes through two boulders and then descends rapidly 1.2 miles to a forested junction where the Snapper Trail leaves left. Originally designed for downhill skiing, the Snapper Trail has been rerouted and now descends much more gradually. Follow it 1 mile to the Gorge Brook Trail to complete the circuit. Continue 0.5 mile to return to the trailhead.

EXTENDING YOUR HIKE

From the summit, descend using the Beaver Brook and Asquam Ridge trails as an alternative. This option adds nearly 2 miles to the loop but is easier on the legs and traverses less-traveled terrain.

70 Lincoln Woods

RATING/ DIFFICULTY	ROUND-TRIP	ELEV GAIN/ HIGH POINT	SEASON
**/2–3	8 miles	550 feet/ 1590 feet	Year-round

Map: USGS Mount Osceola; **Contact:** White Mountain National Forest; **Note:** Fee; **GPS:** 44.063843, -71.587928

This excursion to the edge of the Pemigewasset Wilderness is a great introduction for those new to the White Mountains. Choose this popular, mostly flat trail midweek for greater solitude as you explore roaring waterfalls, rushing rivers, placid ponds, and acres of maturing hardwood forests.

GETTING THERE

From Interstate 93, take exit 32 near Lincoln. Drive 5.4 miles east on Route 112, also called the Kancamagus Highway. Cross the East Branch Pemigewasset River and turn left into the large parking area.

ON THE TRAIL

At the US Forest Service's Lincoln Woods Visitor Center, turn left and immediately cross a large suspension bridge over the impressive East Branch Pemigewasset River. On the opposite side, follow the Lincoln Woods Trail as it bears sharply right onto a former rail bed. More than a century ago, this area was heavily logged. While the forest has grown significantly in subsequent years, there are still signs of this bygone era, including former logging camps and rail ties. The level of harvesting that once occurred here fostered the political support that led to

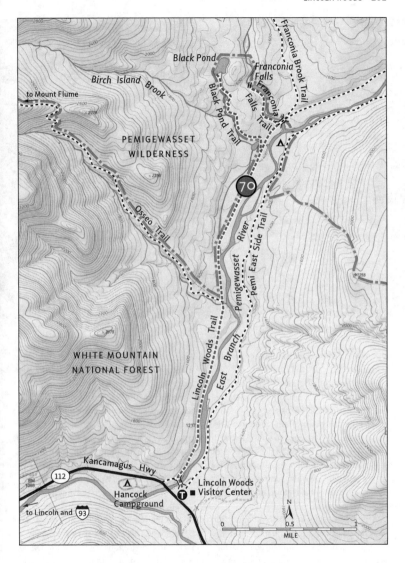

Black Pond

Franconia Falls

Franconia Brook Trail

Birch Island Brook

to Mount Flume

Black Pond Trail

Franconia Falls Trail

PEMIGEWASSET WILDERNESS

70

Osseo Trail

Pemigewasset River

Pemi East Side Trail

Lincoln Woods Trail

East Branch

WHITE MOUNTAIN NATIONAL FOREST

Kancamagus Hwy

112

to Lincoln and 93

Hancock Campground

Lincoln Woods Visitor Center

N

0   0.5   1
MILE

Franconia Brook above the falls

the creation of the White Mountain National Forest in 1911.

Hike north on the Lincoln Woods Trail. Paralleling the river, usually at a distance, the trail occasionally passes spots with more intimate views of the rushing water. In 1.4 miles, reach a junction on the left with the Osseo Trail. This 4.1-mile route rises easily at first and then more aggressively to the scenic 4328-foot summit of Mount Flume—a more challenging alternative to this described hike.

Continue straight and arrive at a junction with the Black Pond Trail, 2.6 miles from the start. Turn left onto this more traditional hiking path. After swinging around the shore of a diminutive wetland, veer right and follow a small stream 0.7 mile to the secluded pond.

Approach the shoreline quietly; perhaps a moose or another forest denizen awaits discovery.

Return to the Lincoln Woods Trail and turn left. Hike 0.2 mile to the edge of Franconia Brook. A bridge leads across to trails that enter the Pemigewasset Wilderness, a popular destination for backpackers. Rather than crossing the bridge, turn left onto the Franconia Falls Trail. Well-manicured at first, the path winds 0.4 mile to the dramatic falls. Watch your footing near the end as well as around the roaring cascades. The rocks can be slippery. This is a great spot to enjoy a picnic and the tranquil sounds of the falling water. When you are ready to head back, retrace your steps to the Lincoln Woods Trail. Turn right and proceed 2.8 miles to the start.

71 Mount Pemigewasset

RATING/ DIFFICULTY	ROUND-TRIP	ELEV GAIN/ HIGH POINT	SEASON
**/3	3.6 miles	1200 feet/ 2557 feet	Year-round

Map: USGS Lincoln; **Contact:** New Hampshire Division of Parks and Recreation; **GPS:** 44.097733, -71.681661

   This low but prominent peak in the heart of New Hampshire's Franconia Notch State Park is more famous for the Native American profile that is supposedly formed by the mountain's summit cliffs. While this geologic feature is fascinating to gaze upon from below, the stunning scenes from atop the precipitous cliffs are far more alluring.

GETTING THERE

From northbound Interstate 93, take exit 34A onto US Route 3. Drive 0.2 mile and turn right into the Franconia Notch State Park's Flume Visitor Center parking area. Proceed to the northern section of the parking lot (to

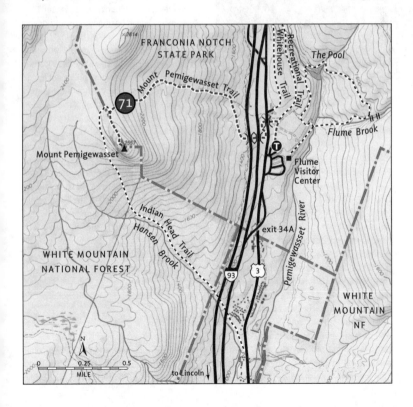

then veer left. With the sound of automobiles farther in the distance, listen for the more melodious sounds of resident songbirds or perhaps the hammering of a woodpecker.

A little more than two-thirds of the way to the top, pass a large, mossy boulder on the right. Soon after, encounter a growing number of spruce and birch trees, the first sign that the rocky summit is nearing. Heading south, the blue-blazed path reaches a junction with the Indian Head Trail. This path departs right and leads 1.9 miles to US Route 3, roughly 1 mile south of the Flume Visitor Center parking area.

Remain on the Mount Pemigewasset Trail. The final 0.1 mile has minor ups and downs as it leads across an increasingly rocky landscape. Before long, emerge atop the impressive ledge. The views west to Kinsman Mountain, south to Mount Moosilauke, and east toward Waterville Valley are breathtaking. While there are plenty of places to enjoy the view, be sure to watch your step near the edge. It is a long way down.

The trail continues left around the corner and rises to the mountain's high point. Here, find decent views of the Franconia Range; however, the growing trees are slowly blocking this vista. To complete the hike, return along the same route. Be sure to stay right at the intersection with the Indian Head Trail.

Kinsman Mountain rises up above Mount Pemigewasset.

the left after entering) and the start of the Franconia Notch Recreational Trail.

ON THE TRAIL

Head up the Recreational Trail, a paved route used by bicyclists and others. In a couple hundred feet, turn left onto the Mount Pemigewasset Trail. Follow this well-used trail 0.3 mile through a series of three tunnels that lead under US Route 3 and I-93. Beyond the highways, a rock staircase leads into the forest and soon reaches a small stream.

Cross the stream and swing right. The trail rises steadily under a canopy of beech trees. While not difficult, the tread is rocky and uneven in places. Climb more steeply near the banks of a seasonal streambed and

72 Franconia Notch

RATING/ DIFFICULTY	LOOP	ELEV GAIN/ HIGH POINT	SEASON
***/3	6.2 miles	1300 feet/ 2750 feet	Year-round

Maps: USGS Lincoln and USGS Franconia; **Contact:** New Hampshire Division of Parks and Recreation; **GPS:** 44.119426, -71.681380

❄ 🏔 🥾 *Finding solitude in Franconia Notch State Park can be difficult. Its beauty and accessibility have resulted in many well-trodden trails. Fortunately, there are still less-traveled locations in the notch to explore. This loop visits popular destinations, but it also passes through Franconia Notch's quieter places, where thick spruce forests cast shadows over cascading mountain streams and darting critters escape to dark cavities hidden in gnarled yellow birches.*

GETTING THERE

From Lincoln follow Interstate 93 north. Drive 2 miles past exit 34A. Take the Basin exit, which quickly turns into a parking area.

ON THE TRAIL

From the parking area, follow the signs leading under the highway to the Basin, a smooth circular rock that the river continues to shape on its journey to the sea. The loop begins just west of the Basin, at the intersection of the Pemi and Basin-Cascades trails. Continue straight on the Basin-Cascades Trail and enjoy a 1-mile journey beside a scenic mountain brook. Initially very popular, the trail quickly becomes less crowded as the incline increases and the footing roughens. Many natural features are along the way, including Kinsman Falls at 0.4 mile and Rocky Glen Falls at 0.9 mile. Near the halfway point, a brook crossing provides a small challenge, especially in the spring.

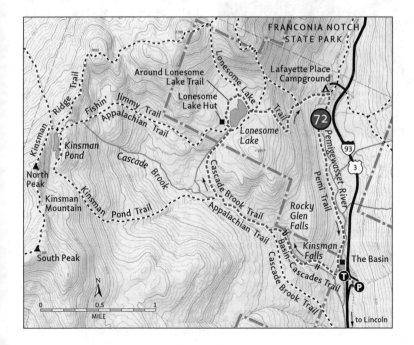

Franconia Ridge from Lonesome Lake

large rocks scattered about, including a lichen and moss-covered boulder on the left.

Returning to the brook's side once again, the trail climbs more aggressively until it reaches the shores of Lonesome Lake. Turn left and cross the small bridge. While the lake's name is rarely applicable, it quickly becomes evident why so many are drawn to its shore. With Cannon Mountain and the Franconia Ridge providing a surreal backdrop, few lakes this size and at this elevation boast a finer view.

To the left, the AT joins the Fishin' Jimmy Trail up a small incline to the Appalachian Mountain Club's Lonesome Lake Hut and beyond to Kinsman Mountain. Stay right, near the shoreline, and pick up the Around Lonesome Lake Trail. This flat trail skirts the edge of the lake, crosses boardwalks, and leads through marshy areas providing optimum wildlife viewing opportunities.

Upon reaching the Lonesome Lake Trail, turn right and travel nearly a quarter mile to another trail junction. Here a short path leads to the east shore of the lake and views of Kinsman Mountain. Stay on the Lonesome Lake Trail, which heads east away from the water. The frequently used trail descends south along moderate grades but eventually swings north toward Lafayette Place Campground.

Upon entering the campground, intersect the Pemi Trail. Turn right and follow this path past campsites back into the forest. The quiet 2-mile stroll along the banks of the Pemigewasset River is easy on the legs and ends at the Basin. Surrounded by tall, mature trees, a carpet of wildflowers, and the soothing sound of the rushing water, the Pemi Trail is a perfect way to cap off the day's journey. Before heading back

Upon reaching the Cascade Brook Trail/ Appalachian Trail (AT), turn right and immediately arrive at the final bridgeless water crossing of the day. Use caution hopping across the rocks; you will be rewarded with a pleasant path on the other side. After passing a junction with the Kinsman Pond Trail, briefly leave the noisy yet tranquil proximity of the running water. Take this opportunity to scan the dense forest for winter wrens, whose long flutelike call is more often heard than seen. In so doing, you will certainly see many of the to your car, check out the many displays, cascades, and natural features exhibited around the Basin.

73 Potash Mountain

RATING/ DIFFICULTY	ROUND-TRIP	ELEV GAIN/ HIGH POINT	SEASON
***/3	4.4 miles	1500 feet/ 2700 feet	Year-round

Maps: USGS Mount Tripyramid and USGS Mount Chocorua; **Contact:** White Mountain National Forest; **Note:** Fee; **GPS:** 43.994372, -71.369415

Lying in the shadows of much taller peaks in all directions, Potash Mountain's summit ledges offer inspiring views of New Hampshire's White Mountains. Relatively short but challenging in places, this hike serves as a nice tune-up for anyone planning to tackle the higher summits that surround it.

GETTING THERE

From the junction of Routes 112 and 16 in Conway, drive 14.1 miles west on Route 112 (Kancamagus Highway). Turn left (across from the US Forest Service Passaconaway Campground) and head 0.1 mile to the parking area. If coming from the west, drive 7.6 miles east of Kancamagus Pass to reach the entranceway on the right.

ON THE TRAIL

At a gate, head south on the Downes Brook Trail. Hike straight through a junction

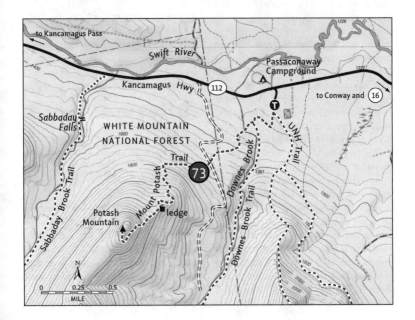

Mount Passaconaway's quite impressive northern slopes

where the UNH Trail diverges left and proceed 0.1 mile up a small incline to a trail sign. Turn sharply right and continue 0.2 mile over level ground. Bend left, then bear right onto the 1.9-mile Mount Potash Trail.

Head west 0.1 mile through an inviting hemlock forest to the banks of Downes Brook. Cross the rocky stream carefully, as it can be very difficult when the water is high. Swing left on the far side. The yellow-blazed trail quickly rises away from the water and moderates. Less than 0.5 mile from the brook, hike straight across a logging road and enter a young hardwood forest.

The trail is occasionally rough as it winds gradually up the slope. Still a mile from the summit, bear left and rise up a steep slope that is eroded in places. The path slowly becomes less demanding as it approaches the edge of the ridge. Swing right and

climb to an open ledge with intimate views of Mount Passaconaway and more distant shots of Mount Chocorua.

Leading though an inviting spruce forest, the trail offers a brief reprieve. Ascend a rocky slope to a small sign with an arrow directing hikers left. Rough footing continues as the trail wraps 0.1 mile along the slope to the mountain's southern side and additional exposed granite ledges. Here, the path bends abruptly right and makes the final 0.2-mile climb to the summit.

Difficult at first, the ascent to the rocky high point becomes less demanding and more scenic with every step. Continue over the summit to the trail's end for exceptional views of the Pemigewasset Wilderness and the Presidential Range. Follow the same route back to conclude the hike.

EXTENDING YOUR HIKE

A nice way to complement a day on Potash Mountain is to drive west along the Kancamagus Highway 1.5 miles to the Sabbaday Brook Trail. This very popular trail leads 0.3 mile to a picturesque waterfall.

74. Boulder Loop

RATING/ DIFFICULTY	LOOP	ELEV GAIN/ HIGH POINT	SEASON
***/3	3.2 miles	1100 feet/ 1750 feet	Year-round

Map: USGS North Conway West; **Contact:** White Mountain National Forest; **Note:** Fee; **GPS:** 44.005012, -71.239241

  This popular and aptly named loop visits numerous immense boulders as it follows a well-maintained path across ledge-covered

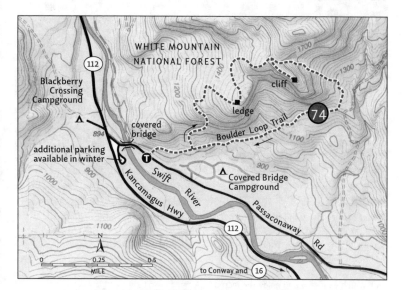

mountain slopes. While the area's geology is impressive, it is overshadowed by the awe-inspiring views from a cliff-top perch near the loop's halfway point.

GETTING THERE

From the junction of Routes 16 and 112 in Conway, drive west on Route 112 (the Kancamagus Highway). In 6.2 miles, turn right onto Passaconaway Road toward the US Forest Service Covered Bridge Campground. Cross the covered bridge in 0.1 mile and reach the large parking area, on the right, 0.1 mile farther. The covered bridge is closed to automobiles during winter, but parking is available just before the river.

ON THE TRAIL

The hike leads north on the Boulder Loop Trail from the parking area and crosses Passaconaway Road. Up a wooden staircase,

the trail swings right and immediately lives up to its name. Weave through impressive boulders under the cool shade of a maturing forest. In 0.2 mile, reach a junction and the start of the loop.

Stay left and join the 1.1-mile northern branch of the Boulder Loop Trail. Climbing steadily, the yellow-blazed path quickly arrives at the base of an impressive lichen-covered ledge. Veer right, stay below the steep rock face, and rise steadily up the slope. The incline remains challenging, but the well-used route is easy to tackle. Beyond a stand of eastern hemlock, enter a brighter forest. Ahead, a ledge with views of Mount Chocorua awaits.

The loop continues north along a more inviting stretch of trail and drops briefly. Curve right and ascend the rocky corridor, occasionally aided by steps. Here, a 0.2-mile spur leaves right to a spectacular vista. Initially, the side trail rises to an open knob with

Mount Passaconaway and the Tripyramids rise high above the Kancamagus Highway.

scenes of the southern White Mountains. Follow the route down through a narrow gap in the ledge. The spur ends at the edge of a cliff. Watch your step and enjoy the incredible panorama.

Return to the Boulder Loop Trail and turn right. The route descends east under a fern-draped ledge but soon leaves the rocky landscape behind. Drop steeply at first and then more moderately into a tranquil hardwood forest. After the trail swings west and crosses a small stream, the boulders return in earnest. In one spot a large rock forms a small tunnel near the trail. Continue to the end of the loop, 1.2 miles from the cliff spur trail. Stay straight to reach the parking area.

EXTENDING YOUR HIKE

A few miles west on the Kancamagus Highway, find the Rocky Gorge Scenic Area. Here the Swift River carves an interesting channel through the bedrock. Check out this popular natural feature and the 1-mile Lovequist Loop that circles Falls Pond beyond.

75 Middle Sister

RATING/ DIFFICULTY	LOOP	ELEV GAIN/ HIGH POINT	SEASON
****/4	8.6 miles	2800 feet/ 30 feet	Year-round

Map: USGS Mount Chocorua; **Contact:** White Mountain National Forest; **Note:** Fee; **GPS:** 43.953394, -71.213563

It is not uncommon for large crowds of hikers to pile atop nearby Mount Chocorua—and for good reason. Venture to Middle Sister to enjoy a similar destination with relative solitude. While challenging, this loop features outstanding views along Carter Ledge and from atop the mountain's rocky summit.

GETTING THERE

From the junction of Routes 112 and 16 in Conway, drive 5 miles southwest on Route 16 and then turn right into the US Forest Service White Ledge Campground. Park in the campground's picnic area. When the road is gated, park at the entrance.

ON THE TRAIL

The Carter Ledge Trail begins on the south side of the campground's southern loop road. Follow the yellow-blazed trail as it rises quickly away from the sounds of Route 16. Across the rocky landscape, the trail's first mile climbs gradually, a refreshing start to the day. Stay straight at an intersection with the Middle Sister Trail and begin the next 1-mile stretch. Up and over the spruce-covered landscape, reach a junction with the Nickerson Ledge Trail.

With the easiest and least scenic portion of the hike complete, remain on the Carter Ledge Trail and veer right. After descending briefly into a saddle, rise more steeply for 0.4 mile. Carefully make your way up the slope; it is tricky in spots. The thinning forest is one of the few places in the White Mountains where pitch

pine grows. Visiting one ledge after another, emerge onto the open ridge with exceptional views of Mount Chocorua to the southwest.

Catch your breath; the remaining 1.5-mile climb is the day's most challenging. Drop into the boreal forest. One last level stretch is soon followed by an increasingly aggressive ascent. In places, the exposed ledge demands extra care, especially when wet or icy. The ever-expanding scenery rewards your hard work. Swinging under a steep cliff, the trail soon bends left and scales one last rocky pitch. Continue to a junction straight ahead.

Turn left onto the Middle Sister Trail. A steep 0.1-mile climb leads to the top of the Third Sister and splendid views north to the Presidential Range. Minor ups and downs continue 0.2 mile to the top of 3340-foot Middle Sister. Bask in the panorama that extends in all directions. The Middle Sister Trail continues south 0.3 mile to the First Sister. Consider this extension if time permits.

Mount Chocorua from Carter Ledge

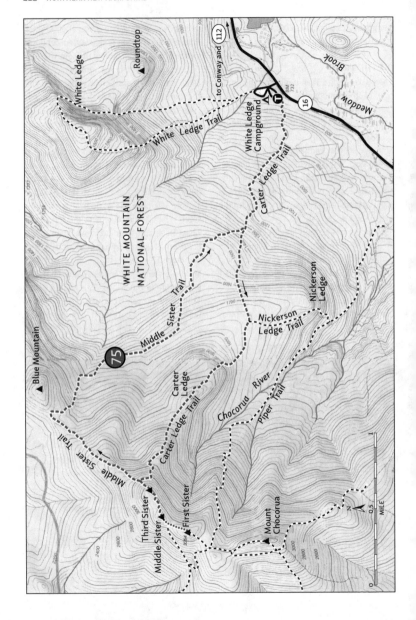

Otherwise retrace your steps back up and over Third Sister.

Continue straight past the Carter Ledge Trail and descend rapidly 0.5 mile down the Middle Sister Trail to open ledges and pleasant views. The route drops another 0.4 mile to a saddle on the ridge. Veer sharply right and head down the boulder-strewn hillside. Initially, the path loses elevation steadily, but it soon moderates. The final 2-mile stretch traverses gradual terrain, with minor ups and more frequent downs. Turn left at the Carter Ledge Trail to complete the hike in 1 mile.

76 North Moat Mountain

RATING/ DIFFICULTY	LOOP	ELEV GAIN/ HIGH POINT	SEASON
****/4	10.5 miles	2900 feet/ 3195 feet	Year-round

Map: USGS North Conway West; **Contact:** White Mountain National Forest; **Note:** Fee; **GPS:** 44.074573, -71.164065

🦴 🗑️ 📶 ⚙️ *Leveling out at just under 3200 feet, North Moat Mountain is often skipped by those seeking to scale the forty-eight New Hampshire mountains that rise higher than 4000 feet. While not high enough for some, North Moat offers scenery as beautiful and natural features as abundant as many of the peaks that rise above it.*

GETTING THERE
From the junction of Route 16/US Route 302 and River Road in North Conway, follow River Road west. In 1 mile stay right on West Side Road. Continue 1.4 miles and then turn left into a large parking area for Diana's Baths.

ON THE TRAIL
Beginning under the shade of tall white pines and lofty red oaks, follow the Moat Mountain Trail 0.6 mile over flat, well-manicured ground. The trail is maintained to serve the many people who visit Diana's Baths, an old mill site with numerous cascades and small swimming holes. Upon reaching the popular destination, turn right for a 0.5-mile walk along an old woods road that briefly swings away from the brook before returning to its banks. After crossing a small tributary, arrive at the 3.6-mile Red Ridge Trail, the start of the day's loop.

Red Ridge Trail viewpoint

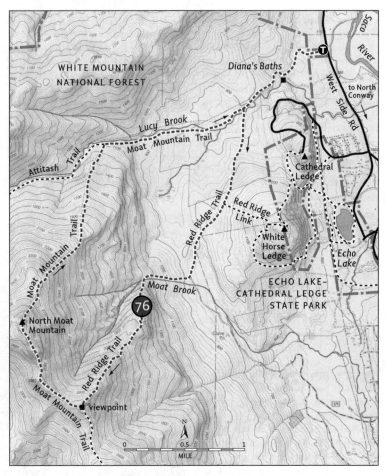

Take the trail left and cross Lucy Brook. You may get a little wet if the water is high, but there are rocks offering assistance and the current typically moves slowly. On the other side, begin a methodical 2-mile journey that ends at a crossing of Moat Brook. A 1.6-mile ascent up Red Ridge quickly ensues. At first the climb is fairly steep and slightly eroded; however, as the forest thins, the terrain moderates. Pass occasional views en route to the base of a 0.5-mile section of bare ledge. The stunted vegetation that has found a way to survive within the seams of the solid rock does little to obstruct the spectacular views that unfold across the Mount Washington Valley. Reenter the forest and reach a scenic pinnacle at a junction with the Moat Mountain Trail in 0.2 mile.

Turn right. Initially dropping into an evergreen forest, the 1.1-mile route to North Moat Mountain ascends over and skirts around a number of small ledges and rock outcroppings. The short scrambles are not too difficult, unless wet or icy. With each climb more expansive views appear, including glimpses toward the Swift River and the Kancamagus Highway. The final scramble leads to 360-degree views from the wide-open summit—the views of the Presidential Range are especially enticing.

Descend north from the summit, down a steep, rocky slope. The path quickly falls beneath the trees, levels off, and reaches the top of a long series of scenic ledges. Take your time, watch your step, and enjoy the backdrop; the shallow soil is a preferred location for many wildflowers such as bunchberry, Labrador tea, and lady slippers.

Drop rapidly into an evergreen forest. The footing remains tricky in places, and your knees will definitely feel the pressure. Arrive at an intersection 1.9 miles from the summit, where the Attitash Trail leaves to the left. Stay right for the final 2.4-mile stretch. The terrain, much easier now, allows for optimum viewing of the nearby cascading brook. Feel free to cool off in the refreshing waters of Diana's Baths, but be prepared to have company.

Young hikers atop Peaked Mountain

77 Green Hills Preserve

RATING/ DIFFICULTY	LOOP	ELEV GAIN/ HIGH POINT	SEASON
***/3	5.6 miles	1750 feet/ 1857 feet	Year-round

Map: USGS North Conway East; **Contact:** The Nature Conservancy, New Hampshire Chapter; **GPS:** 44.045026, -71.111584

Established in 1990 via a generous donation to the New Hampshire chapter of The Nature Conservancy, this nearly 5000-acre oasis contains several options for exploring. The loop to Peaked and Middle mountains is a great introduction to the area, as it provides pleasant forested paths along streams, panoramic views of the Mount Washington Valley, and ample exposure to many of the rare plants and natural communities that call this place home.

GETTING THERE

Starting in downtown North Conway near the train station, follow Route 16/US Route 302 south for 0.5 mile and turn left onto Artist Road. Travel 0.4 mile, pass under a rail bridge, and then turn right onto Thompson Road. Follow Thompson Road 0.3 mile to a small parking lot on the right. Look for signs indicating Conway Municipal Land and Pudding Pond.

ON THE TRAIL

From the parking area, follow the woods road south 0.2 mile to an information kiosk.

To the right lies a flat 1.6-mile loop to Pudding Pond. Turn left and follow the signs pointing to Middle and Peaked mountains. In 0.5 mile, at the top of a small incline, reach another trail junction. This is where The Nature Conservancy's Green Hills Preserve begins and Conway municipal property ends. It is also the start of the day's loop.

Stay left on the Peaked Mountain Trail as it ascends a short gully. Through a welcoming stand of northern hardwoods, the route remains relatively level over the next 0.5 mile. Here is a perfect opportunity to get your binoculars out and scan the forest undergrowth for colorful warblers, vireos, and other songbirds.

At a second informational kiosk and four-way intersection, turn right and head

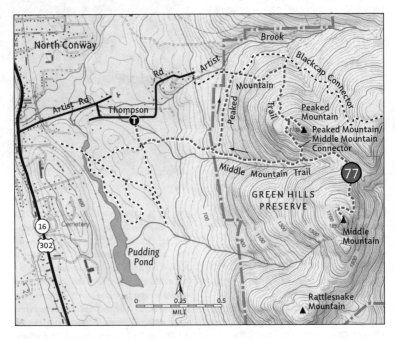

up Peaked Mountain's steep slopes. The trail that heads straight leads to Blackcap Mountain, the highest point in the preserve—a longer hike for another day. The climb up Peaked begins quickly but slowly levels off as the trail hugs the northern side of the mountain. After passing a junction where a trail leads left, the path veers sharply to the right. Suddenly, the soil becomes shallower and rockier, more amenable to the white, red, and pitch pines that thrive here.

With only 0.6 mile left to reach the 1739-foot summit, the remaining climb, although moderately steep, offers many ideal spots to catch your breath and enjoy the views of Mount Washington posing majestically to the north, the Moats stretching gracefully across the valley, and the walls of Crawford Notch looming impressively in the distance. Upon reaching the Peaked Mountain/Middle Mountain Connector, turn left onto the 0.2-mile spur trail that leads to Peaked Mountain's summit. With a few steep, rocky sections, the trail is lined with rare plants, including silverling, a small plant that grows in the cracks of the exposed granite. Be sure to stay on the trail to protect the fragile vegetation. Peaked Mountain is a great place to enjoy lunch and distant views before heading to the next destination.

Return to the junction with the connector trail and stay left. Follow the blazes down through a series of short switchbacks that conclude at the Middle Mountain Trail. Veering left, work your way gradually up to a small stream crossing. Rise past a modest viewpoint and follow the trail as it curls up the rocky slopes to the narrow 1857-foot summit of Middle Mountain. Drop down to an excellent view of Chocorua Mountain from the peak's south side.

The final 2.1-mile leg of the journey begins by returning to the connector trail junction. Continue straight on the Middle Mountain Trail and head through a charming narrow ravine where a small stream runs parallel to the footpath. You will soon reach the junction with the Peaked Mountain Trail and the loop's conclusion. Retrace your steps back to the start.

78 Arethusa Falls and Frankenstein Cliff

RATING/ DIFFICULTY	LOOP	ELEV GAIN/ HIGH POINT	SEASON
***/3–4	5 miles	1700 feet/ 2530 feet	Year-round

Maps: USGS Crawford Notch and USGS Stairs Mountain; **Contact:** New Hampshire Division of Parks and Recreation; **GPS:** 44.148645, -71.366842

 This enjoyable half-day adventure leads to a cool, refreshing mist at the base of New Hampshire's highest falls and to the precarious edge of a 600-foot-high cliff with breathtaking views of the Saco River valley. Generally along easy to moderate terrain, the hike has one steep section that becomes a faded memory as wildflowers, balsam-scented forests, and choruses of songbirds quickly instill more lasting memories.

GETTING THERE
From the center of Bartlett, head west on US Route 302 toward Crawford Notch. Travel 8.2 miles and turn left into the well-signed parking lot. There are two parking areas: a large one at the base of the hill and a second, smaller spot 0.1 mile up the road.

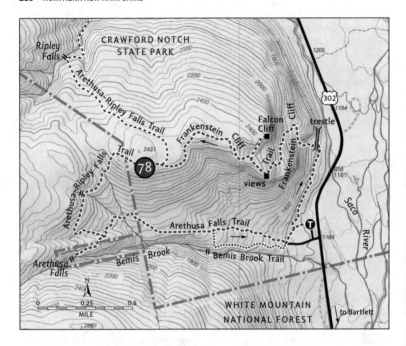

ON THE TRAIL

Leaving the lower parking area, the trail climbs 0.1 mile to the start of the loop. Turn right onto the Frankenstein Cliff Trail. Hike 0.5 mile along rolling terrain paralleling the railroad track to Frankenstein Trestle. This impressive bridge spans a small stream along the historic railroad line that leads through Crawford Notch.

Swing under the tracks and begin a steep climb up the loose, rocky soil. Gaining more than 800 feet in less than three-quarters of a mile, the challenging trail passes under sheer rock faces and ascends a small ledge before suddenly emerging atop the impressive and precarious cliff. Named for a German-born artist, not the famous monster creator, the cliff is

an excellent spot to gaze upon Arethusa Falls plummeting in the distance. More mesmerizing are the views of the Saco River and surrounding peaks.

Return to the forest and slowly hike away from the cliff's edge. In 0.3 mile, the route passes a lightly used spur that leads 0.3 mile right to Falcon Cliff, with a less dramatic vista than its neighbor's. The main route continues to climb steadily, eventually reaching the hike's high point near a ledge that once offered a splendid view of Mount Washington. Past the overgrown viewpoint, the path becomes much easier.

At a junction, stay left, joining the Arethusa–Ripley Falls Trail. Begin a 1-mile trek down the ridge, somewhat steep in places. Pass a small cascade and enter a dark evergreen forest where lady slippers flower in late spring. Upon reaching the Arethusa Falls Trail, turn right and drop 0.2 mile to Bemis Brook and the base of the massive falls. The water crashes over a short ledge before taking a final plunge to the deep pool below.

Begin the 1.5-mile conclusion by retracing your steps to the previous intersection. Stay right on the Arethusa Falls Trail. It winds across fairly level terrain before beginning a moderate descent. One mile from the falls, arrive at a junction with the Bemis Brook Trail. This slightly more difficult route drops

Bemis Brook Trail cascades

rapidly down to, then parallels, the cascading water. To the left, the Arethusa Falls Trail descends steadily and continues in the woods high above the brook. Both options meet up near the trail's end.

Upon reaching the trailhead, carefully cross the still-active railroad tracks. Walk through the upper parking area and pick up the trail that points toward Frankenstein Cliff. Once in the woods, you will quickly arrive at the junction where the loop began. Turn right to return to the parking area.

79 Tom, Field, and Avalon

RATING/ DIFFICULTY	LOOP	ELEV GAIN/ HIGH POINT	SEASON
***/4	7.2 miles	2850 feet/ 4340 feet	Year-round

Map: USGS Crawford Notch; **Contact:** White Mountain National Forest; **GPS:** 44.218119, -71.411419

This scenic loop visits a cascading brook before rising high above New Hampshire's Crawford Notch to numerous panoramic vistas. While the journey is challenging at times, much of it traverses moderate terrain. Choose this circuit if you are just beginning to tackle New England's 4000-footers. All or parts of this loop are also good options for snowshoeing in the heart of winter.

GETTING THERE
From the junction of US Routes 3 and 302 in Twin Mountain, drive 8.6 miles east on US Route 302. Turn right into the parking area near the train depot. Overflow parking is available along US Route 302. Parking at the AMC Highland Center is for guests only.

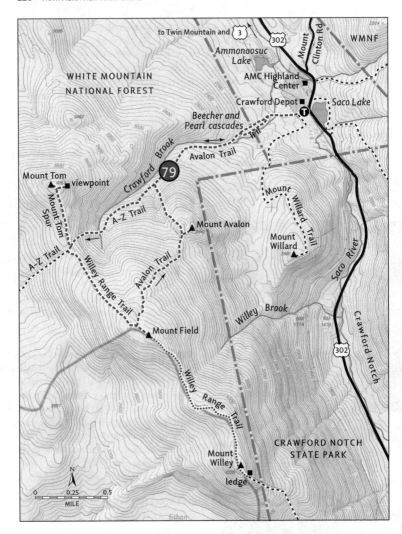

ON THE TRAIL

At the train depot, carefully cross the active railroad tracks and pick up the Avalon Trail. Hike 0.1 mile to a large kiosk, where the popular Mount Willard Trail departs left. Stay right as the trail meanders easily to Crawford Brook, where large stones ease the crossing. On the far side, turn left on a 0.2-

mile side path that parallels the main trail while visiting Beecher and Pearl cascades. Turn left upon reintersecting the Avalon Trail. The moderate ascent continues to a second Crawford Brook crossing. Beyond, rise steadily to an intersection, 1.3 miles from the start.

Veer right onto the A–Z Trail, a route that connects the Avalon and Zealand trails. Follow this straightforward path 1 mile. Occasionally descending to and crossing small streams, for the most part the trail rises steadily up the thick-forested slopes. A final push leads to a long, flat saddle. Turn right onto the 0.6-mile Mount Tom Spur and climb easily to the 4051-foot summit. It was once a viewless peak, but thanks to many trees succumbing to disease and wind, it offers many vistas today. From the high point, enjoy scenes south into the Pemigewasset Wilderness. In addition, just before the trail's end, diverge right on a path that ends at a bench and impressive views of Mount Washington.

Return to the A–Z Trail and turn right. In a few dozen feet, turn left onto the Willey Range Trail. This route rises modestly through a picturesque boreal forest, perfect habitat for Canada jays and spruce grouse. Hike 0.9 mile to the top of Mount Field. The final stretch, steep but short, occurs just beyond a junction with the Avalon Trail. Named in honor of Darby Field, the first European settler to set foot atop Mount Washington, this 4340-foot peak used to have more extensive views. Despite the growing forest, one can still catch a glimpse of summits to the north and west.

Drop back to the Avalon Trail junction and turn right. The 1-mile descent that follows is steady but not too difficult; watch your footing in places. Swinging left, reach

Snow blankets Mount Avalon.

a spur on the right that climbs steeply 0.1 mile to the top of Mount Avalon. While this is the lowest peak of the day, Avalon's rocky pinnacle offers the most spectacular scenery. Views of the Presidential Range and Crawford Notch are especially breathtaking.

Return to the Avalon Trail and bear right. Before long, head down the day's steepest slope. Drop 0.5 mile back to the A–Z Trail junction and then turn right to complete the journey.

EXTENDING THE HIKE

A great addition is to continue southeast along the Willey Range Trail from Mount Field to the summit of Mount Willey. Just beyond its high point, find a spur left that leads to an open ledge that offers a spectacular vantage point across Crawford Notch. The toughest part of this 2.8-mile round-trip journey is climbing back over Mount Field, but it is well worth the effort.

80 Middle and North Sugarloaf

RATING/ DIFFICULTY	ROUND-TRIP	ELEV GAIN/ HIGH POINT	SEASON
****/3	3.4 miles	1050 feet/ 2539 feet	Year-round

Map: USGS Twin Mountain; **Contact:** White Mountain National Forest; **Note:** Fee; **GPS:** 44.254841, -71.504013

Accessible by hikers of all ages, these two rocky summits provide exceptional 360-degree views of countless peaks that tower high above them. While the trail is especially glorious during peak fall foliage, venture here year-round to enjoy the White Mountains' ever-changing scenery.

GETTING THERE

From the junction of US Routes 302 and 3 in Twin Mountain, drive 2.2 miles east on US Route 302. Turn right onto Zealand Road and proceed 1 mile to the parking area on the right. Zealand Road is closed during winter, but a large parking area exists on US Route 302 east of its entrance. The unplowed road is easy to follow to the trailhead.

ON THE TRAIL

Follow the road south a hundred feet. After crossing over the Zealand River, arrive at the trailhead on the right. The Trestle and Sugarloaf trails coincide for 0.2 mile while remaining close to the babbling river. At an intersection stay left on the Sugarloaf Trail and climb gently away from the water. After crossing a dirt road, the route continues straight to a boardwalk leading through a forested wetland.

Rise onto drier ground to a series of immense lichen-covered boulders. The trail weaves in and around these impressive obstacles. Under the shade of a dense hardwood forest, the yellow-blazed route's moderate ascent eventually becomes more demanding. Fortunately, the challenge does not last long. Reach a saddle and intersection 0.9 mile from the start.

The Sugarloaf Trail diverges in two directions. First, follow the 0.3-mile right branch. The path soon swings left and descends a rocky slope—a necessary diversion to avoid North Sugarloaf's steepest ledges. Wrap around the peak's western side and then rise to the first views of the day. The trail turns south and ends atop a more open promontory with excellent views toward Crawford Notch.

Return to the previous junction, then make your way straight to Middle Sugarloaf. The 0.5-mile trek to the higher of the two peaks is slightly longer and a bit more demanding. The climb begins pleasantly, but soon short switchbacks lead up the increasingly steep, rocky terrain. The final pitch is conquered with help from a long wooden staircase. This section could be difficult with snow or ice.

From the mostly open summit of Middle Sugarloaf, the panorama of the many higher surrounding peaks is exceptional. There are countless places to hang out and take in scenery that includes Mount Washington to the north and even the Green Mountains on the western horizon. Follow the Sugarloaf Trail back to the start when you have had your fill.

EXTENDING YOUR HIKE

There are two nearby options to extend this hike. The first is to venture along the Trestle Trail. This path follows the Zealand River en route to and then through the Sugarloaf Campground. The bridge that once spanned the river has washed out, making this 0.8-mile option more difficult. A second choice, only 0.4 mile round-trip, is to hike up the forest road that heads east across from the trailhead's parking area. Stay straight and then right (this route is not well-marked). Reach a wooden walkway that leads to a small pond with a view of Middle Sugarloaf. It is also a great place to spot wildlife.

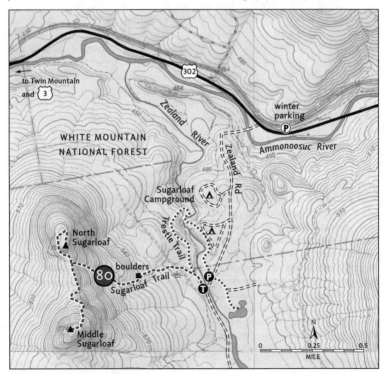

Middle Sugarloaf's barren summit

81 Mount Jefferson

RATING/ DIFFICULTY	LOOP	ELEV GAIN/ HIGH POINT	SEASON
*****/5	10.2 miles	4300 feet/ 5716 feet	June–Oct

Map: USGS Mount Washington; **Contact:** White Mountain National Forest; **Note:** Trail begins on private property; **GPS:** 44.357582, -71.344488

When Thomas Jefferson *drafted the Declaration of Independence, he spoke of three inalienable rights. Standing atop his namesake peak in New Hampshire's Presidential Range, with the wind in your face and the sun's warm rays above, where could you feel more alive? Scaling the steep face of Castle Ravine, heart pumping and muscles flexing, where could you feel more liberated? Descending a barren ridge with views in all directions and recalling the day's accomplishment, how could you feel any happier?*

GETTING THERE

From the junction of US Route 2 and Route 16 in Gorham, follow US Route 2 west 7.5 miles and then turn left onto a dirt driveway. The parking area is immediately on the right. Beginning at the junction of US Route 2 and Route 115 in Jefferson, drive 4.6 miles east on US Route 2. Turn right and find the parking area immediately on the right.

ON THE TRAIL

With Mount Jefferson's peak looming nearly 4500 feet above, pick up the Castle Trail along an old rail bed. At a gate, turn left. Soon after, pass under a power line and enter the White Mountain National Forest. The trail veers left and follows the Israel River a few hundred feet before reaching a crossing that can be difficult, especially during high water. Jumping from stone to stone, carefully make your way to the other side and continue the gradual ascent, paralleling the river once again. At 1.3 miles, reach a junction and the start of the loop.

Follow the Israel Ridge Path left 0.4 mile and then turn right onto the Castle Ravine

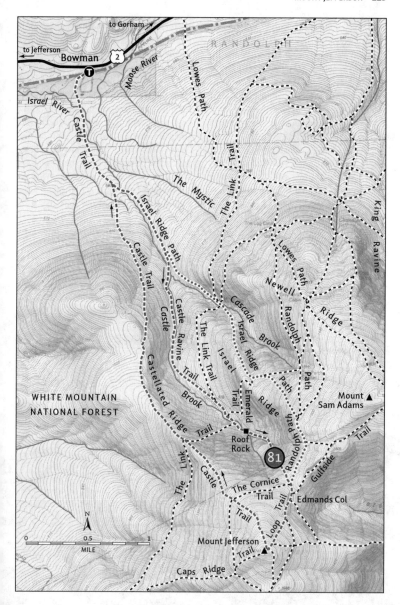

Trail. For 2.1 miles this route leads steadily up a narrowing valley. While the footing is occasionally rough and numerous stream crossings require extra attention, the incline is mostly moderate. Hike through a thick, moss-covered spruce-fir forest and pass three intersections before reaching Roof Rock, an imposing boulder that forms a natural tunnel on the trail.

Now the hike's most difficult stretch begins, as the Castle Ravine Trail climbs 1300 feet in less than a mile. This is the best place to turn around if the weather is uncooperative. Rise quickly above tree line. Take your time ascending the boulder-covered slope. Few trails in the Presidential Range are harder or less crowded, and few offer more spectacular scenery. Finally reaching the headwall, pass a small wetland before arriving at a four-way intersection with the Cornice trail and the Randolph Path.

Continue straight on the Randolph Path to Edmands Col, where a small plaque honors J. Rayner Edmands, a pioneer trail-maker who left his mark on this region in the late 1800s.

The final 0.7-mile climb to the summit begins to the right on the Gulfside Trail. In 0.2 mile turn right again, this time on the Loop Trail. The ascent is demanding but straightforward. Arrive at a junction just below the summit. Follow the Caps Ridge Trail a few dozen feet to the high point and incredible views in all directions. Enjoy the well-earned rewards, but remember: while it is all downhill from here, your work is far from over.

The descent follows the 5-mile-long Castle Trail throughout. The first third heads down an open ridge, whose views distract you from the pounding of foot to rock that transpires. Before dropping below tree line, pass over and around a number

Scaling the Castle Ravine Trail

of small knobs that look like castle turrets. Each provides stunning views, especially into the ravine. The final views of the day are followed by a short, steep drop that culminates at a junction with the Link Trail. Continue straight through the intersection as the trail moderates significantly along a pleasant forested ridge. Eventually, the route veers right and begins to drop more aggressively to the valley below. Small switchbacks ease the descent a bit, and as the Israel River becomes louder, the trail becomes more gradual. After reaching the loop's end, complete the final 1.3 miles to the trailhead.

OTHER OPTIONS

A good alternative ascent is to bypass Castle Ravine and continue on the Israel Ridge Path. This trail, in combination with the Randolph Path, adds 0.3 mile to the loop. While still challenging, this loop is less demanding than the route described above. In the winter, consider using the Castle Trail for both the climb and the descent—an arduous but exhilarating out-and-back hike if the weather is cooperative.

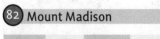

82 Mount Madison

RATING/ DIFFICULTY	LOOP	ELEV GAIN/ HIGH POINT	SEASON
*****/5	9.3 miles	4300 feet/ 5367 feet	Year-round

Map: USGS Mount Washington; **Contact:** White Mountain National Forest; **Note:** Route passes AMC Madison Spring Hut; **GPS:** 44.371714, -71.288853

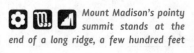

Mount Madison's pointy summit stands at the end of a long ridge, a few hundred feet lower than its neighbors. Consequently, like the fourth United States president, for whom the peak is named, Mount Madison's prominence tends to be overlooked. Yet a hike to the summit of Mount Madison is as awe-inspiring and rewarding as scaling any of the nearby mountains that rise above it.

GETTING THERE

Beginning at the intersection of Route 16 and US Route 2 in Gorham, travel west 5.3 miles on US Route 2. Look for the large parking area on the left.

ON THE TRAIL

Head up the Valley Way, but quickly turn left onto the much quieter Maple Walk. Rising moderately, this 0.2-mile trail leads to a junction above Gordon Fall, the first of many impressive cascades along the loop. Turn left onto the Sylvan Way and carefully cross Snyder Brook, especially difficult with high water. Follow Sylvan Way as it ascends moderately 1 mile before ending at an intersection with the Howker Ridge Trail. To the left, find Coosauk Fall, a small cascade along Bumpus Brook.

Turn right onto the Howker Ridge Trail. Past a junction with the Kelton Trail, the path leads left 0.2 mile into a steep valley and scenic Hitchcock Fall. Cross the brook and climb a few hundred feet to a spur leading right to the Bear Pit, a narrow gap in the rock. The climb becomes increasingly steep. After passing a limited northern outlook, traverse a narrow ridge that culminates atop the First Howk ("howk" is the name given to the series of small peaks on the ridge). Enjoy restricted views of Madison's rock-covered summit. Descend briefly before climbing to the Second Howk's more open ledge. Down

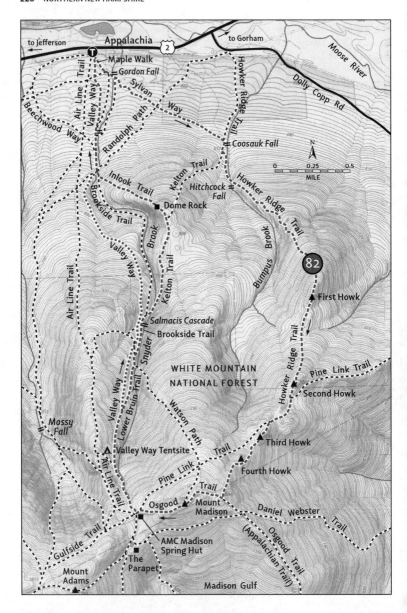

to Jefferson

Appalachia

to Gorham

Moose River

Dolly Copp Rd

Maple Walk

Gordon Fall

Beechwood Way

Air Line Trail

Valley Way

Randolph Path

Sylvan Way

Howker Ridge Trail

Coosauk Fall

N

0   0.25   0.5
MILE

Inlook Trail

Kelton Trail

Hitchcock Fall

Brookside Trail

Dome Rock

Howker Ridge Trail

Brook

Valley Way

Kelton Trail

Bumpus Brook

Air Line Trail

82

First Howk

Salmacis Cascade

Brookside Trail

Snyder Brook Trail

WHITE MOUNTAIN
NATIONAL FOREST

Lower Brun Trail

Valley Way

Watson Path

Howker Ridge Trail

Pine Link Trail

Second Howk

Mossy Fall

Valley Way Tentsite

Pine Link Trail

Third Howk

Fourth Howk

Air Line Trail

Osgood Trail

Mount Madison

Daniel Webster Trail

Gulfside Trail

AMC Madison Spring Hut

Osgood Trail (Appalachian Trail)

The Parapet

Mount Adams

Madison Gulf

the slope, the path converges with the Pine Link Trail, 2.1 miles from Hitchcock Fall.

Follow the two trails as they coincide for 0.4 mile, then stay left, remaining on Howker Ridge. While extremely challenging, the final 0.7-mile climb is the trail's most scenic section. Scramble to a wide-open peak, Third Howk, featuring expansive views north and east. A short drop and another steep climb later ends at the fourth and final Howk. Rise out of the stunted forest and across the rocky terrain to reach the Osgood Trail (Appalachian Trail). Turn right and ascend 0.3 mile to attain the summit. Enjoy the glorious views of Mount Washington, Mount Adams, and countless other mountains in all directions. Looking into the chasm of the Great Gulf is especially mesmerizing.

For the descent, head west along the Osgood Trail and drop 0.5 mile across numerous boulders to the grassy, protected saddle where the Appalachian Mountain Club's Madison Spring Hut is located. This popular overnight facility, available by reservation only, is surrounded by numerous places to explore, including the Parapet, a prominent rock above Madison Gulf with scenic views.

From the hut, the most straightforward route down exclusively follows the 3.8-mile Valley Way. While somewhat steep at first, it gradually moderates and is the safest trail to use, especially during bad weather or in the winter.

To opt for a more adventurous and scenic alternative, follow the Valley Way 1 mile, then turn right onto the Lower Bruin Trail. Drop steeply 0.2 mile before joining the Brookside Trail. Follow this path 0.5 mile past a series of cascades and larger waterfalls. After Salmacis Cascade, turn right onto

the Kelton Trail and carefully cross Snyder Brook (this could be difficult with high water). The next 0.8 mile is relatively level. Veer left onto the 0.7-mile Inlook Trail. You will likely have the place to yourself while descending, sometimes steeply, over a series of scenic ledges. The trail ends at the banks of Snyder Brook.

Use caution crossing the brook one last time and turn right, rejoining the Valley

Mount Madison's pointy peak

Way for the final 1-mile stretch back to the parking area. The trail parallels the rushing water. There are also a handful of paths diverging right, allowing exploration of small cascades and deep pools.

SHORTENING YOUR HIKE

If you are looking for a half-day excursion, combine the Maple Walk, Sylvan Way, Howker Ridge, Kelton, and Inlook trails with the Valley Way to complete a 4-mile loop with great views, picturesque cascades, and little company.

Scrambling up the Lion Head Trail

83 Mount Washington

RATING/ DIFFICULTY	LOOP	ELEV GAIN/ HIGH POINT	SEASON
*****/5	9.3 miles	4350 feet/ 6288 feet	May–Oct

Map: USGS Mount Washington; **Contact:** White Mountain National Forest; **GPS:** 44.257076, -71.252974

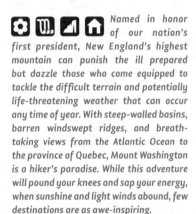

Named in honor of our nation's first president, New England's highest mountain can punish the ill prepared but dazzle those who come equipped to tackle the difficult terrain and potentially life-threatening weather that can occur any time of year. With steep-walled basins, barren windswept ridges, and breathtaking views from the Atlantic Ocean to the province of Quebec, Mount Washington is a hiker's paradise. While this adventure will pound your knees and sap your energy, when sunshine and light winds abound, few destinations are as awe-inspiring.

GETTING THERE

From the junction of Route 16 and US Route 302 in Glen, drive 11.8 miles north. Turn left into the Appalachian Mountain Club's Pinkham Notch Visitor Center parking area.

ON THE TRAIL

Behind the visitor center, follow the Tuckerman Ravine Trail. This very popular, wide, and easy-to-follow route climbs 0.2 mile to the roaring waters of Crystal Cascade. Remain on the Tuckerman Ravine Trail for 2 additional miles. It rises aggressively up a rocky corridor and passes numerous trail junctions along the way. As you near the base of the ravine,

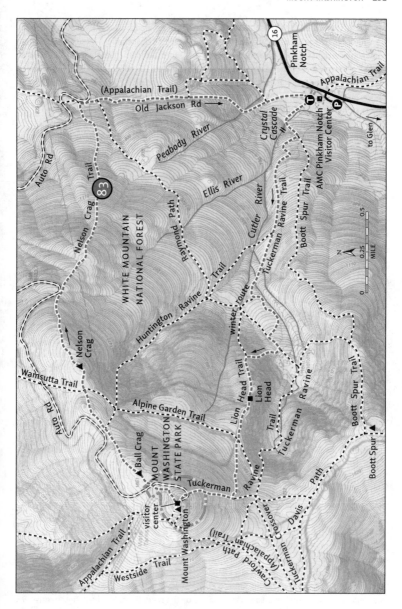

reach the start of the Lion Head Trail and turn right (note: the Lion Head Trail winter route departs right 0.5 mile earlier).

Rising steeply out of the ravine, the Lion Head Trail ascends 0.4 mile to the edge of the alpine zone. Here the winter route enters from the right. This location is a good place to turn around if the weather is not cooperating. Otherwise, continue left up the increasingly rocky ridge. Watch your footing up the steep incline. A 0.4-mile stretch leads to the summit of Lion Head and spectacular views of Tuckerman Ravine below.

Proceed 0.3 mile across the flat landscape to an intersection with the Alpine Garden Trail. This area is noted for its flowers in early summer. Stay straight and hike 0.5 mile up the boulder-covered route to another junction with the Tuckerman Ravine Trail. Turn right and head up the increasingly steep incline. With persistence, rise 0.5 mile to the top of New England. While covered by buildings as well as tourists arriving by car and train, the 6288-foot summit is still an exhilarating spot from which to view the surrounding peaks and valleys. In season, the summit includes a visitor center with services available, including restrooms.

When you are ready to leave the crowds behind, join the Nelson Crag Trail. It crosses the cog railway track near the summit and descends 0.1 mile to the auto road. Head cautiously across both transportation corridors and then up to the small pinnacle of Ball Crag. Still over 6000 feet in elevation, this quiet location offers remarkable views of the northern Presidential Range.

Remain on the Nelson Crag Trail as it drops a little more than 1 mile across the open landscape. The path is rugged in places and occasionally steep, but the vistas are endless. After approaching the auto road a second time, stay right and soon descend

back into the forest. Take your time; in many respects descending Mount Washington is more difficult than climbing it. The trail continues 1.5 miles, still dropping steadily, before ending at a junction with the Old Jackson Road (Appalachian Trail).

Turn right; the final 1.7-mile stretch of the loop is the easiest. Remain on the Old Jackson Road throughout. The wide path leads past many intersections as it meanders over the gently rolling landscape, a perfect way to end a glorious day atop New England.

84 Imp Face

RATING/ DIFFICULTY	LOOP	ELEV GAIN/ HIGH POINT	SEASON
****/3–4	6.5 miles	2150 feet/ 3350 feet	Year-round

Map: USGS Carter Dome; **Contact:** White Mountain National Forest; **Note:** Fee; **GPS:** 44.323469, -71.216848

There are few places in New England with more jaw-dropping views than Imp Face, an impressive rocky knoll on the western slope of the Carter Range. While many head to the Presidential Range peaks that cast shadows upon it, this adventure is a great alternative for a less demanding trek or when cold winds are creating less-than-hospitable conditions on the higher summits.

GETTING THERE
The two trailheads for this hike are 0.2 mile apart. From the junction of Route 16 and US Route 2 in Gorham, follow Route 16 south 5.2 miles to park at the northernmost trailhead. Parking is available on the left (east) side of the road. From Pinkham Notch, drive 5.3

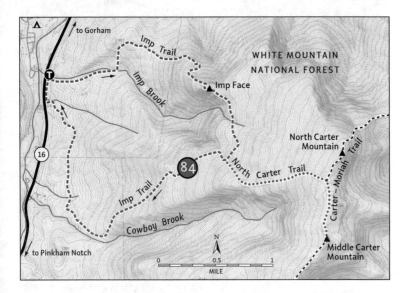

miles north on Route 16 to reach the same trailhead on the right side of the road.

ON THE TRAIL

The Imp Trail begins under a dark canopy of tall hemlock trees high above a bubbling mountain stream. The gradual grade remains until the trail crosses two small sections of Imp Brook in 0.8 mile. Since the valley is quite narrow, the second crossing can be a bit tricky with heavy rainfall or abundant snowmelt. The forest quickly brightens as the trail ascends to a hardwood-covered plateau. Up the slight incline, the trail veers left and then the climb becomes more intense.

Make your way up the side of the slope. Turning sharply to the right, the route uses a series of short switchbacks to reach the rocky, wide-open Imp Face, 2.2 miles from the start. From this vantage point—roughly half the elevation of Mount Washington—the ravines, gulfs, and rock summits of the Presidential Range stand impressively before

you. This spot is also a great place to scan the sky, above and below, for hawks, falcons, and ravens circling in the cool mountain air.

The hike continues east, near the side of the ledge, and soon reenters the forest for good. Cross numerous small brooks around the rim of a deep valley. There is not much overall elevation change, but the terrain is uneven in places and some of the stream crossings can be slippery. A brief descent leads to a junction with the North Carter Trail. This spot is slightly less than the half-way point of the loop.

Stay right on the Imp Trail for the 3.4-mile descent. At first the route parallels a small stream, and occasionally the footing can be quite wet. Heading in a southerly direction, the trail gradually winds down the ridge, soon skirting a fairly steep slope. Approach Cowboy Brook and then swing north along the increasingly level terrain. For a little more than a mile, the trail concludes along relaxing grades. Reach Route

Imp Face's mesmerizing views

16 and then follow the paved road right 0.2 mile to your car.

EXTENDING YOUR HIKE

If you are looking for a little longer workout or are interested in conquering a 4000-foot mountain, extend this loop by ascending the North Carter Trail. This path leads 1.2 miles steadily up the mountain through classic high-elevation forests. Once on the ridge, turn right and head 0.5 mile to the rocky summit of Middle Carter Mountain, where there are excellent views in most directions.

85 Percy Peaks

RATING/ DIFFICULTY	LOOP	ELEV GAIN/ HIGH POINT	SEASON
*****/4	6.7 miles	2600 feet/ 3420 feet	May–Oct

Map: USGS Percy Peaks; **Contact:** New Hampshire Division of Forest and Lands; **Note:** Access road is used by logging trucks; **GPS:** 44.665384, -71.457835

As the hiking centerpieces of the nearly 40,000-acre Nash Stream State Forest, the rounded summits of North and South Percy peaks offer tantalizing shots of New Hampshire's remote North Country. While significant portions of the hike are easy to moderate, at times the route is extremely rugged and very demanding—making the views that much more rewarding.

GETTING THERE

From the intersection of Nash Stream Road and Northside Road in Stark, drive 2.6 miles north on Nash Stream Road to the small parking area on the right. Nash Stream Road, a well-maintained dirt road, is closed during the winter.

ON THE TRAIL

From the parking area, walk north on Nash Stream Road for a few hundred feet. After crossing Slide Brook, turn right onto the 2.2-mile Percy Peaks Trail. Steep at first, the orange-blazed trail levels off and offers an occasional glimpse of North Percy Peak's precipitous western slope through a dense canopy of birch, beech, and maple.

Return to Slide Brook and parallel its banks, climbing more steadily. The path winds up a narrow ridge to a large rock just before this trail's halfway point. This is a good location to prepare for the extremely challenging ascent that follows. Swing left and then switchback up the steep slope. As the forest transitions to evergreens, rise near an exposed granite ledge that offers limited western views. Watch your step; the trail is very steep as well as wet and slick in spots.

Make your way to the top of the ledge and veer right. While the trail rises more slowly, the footing is rough, with many rocks and exposed roots. Still demanding, the terrain slowly becomes easier to navigate. Over a forested ledge, bear left and before long reach a junction with the Cohos Trail, a 162-mile path that traverses New Hampshire's largest county from Crawford Notch to the Quebec border. Today's loop will complete 2.5 miles of its route.

Turn right onto the Old Summer Club Trail/Cohos Trail and drop 0.1 mile into a thick meadow of ferns. Veer right onto the lightly used and slightly overgrown spur that climbs 0.3 mile to the top of South Percy Peak. Exposed ledges on and around the high point provide excellent views of North Percy Peak and the White Mountains.

Return to the Old Summer Club Trail/ Cohos Trail, stay straight, and return to the

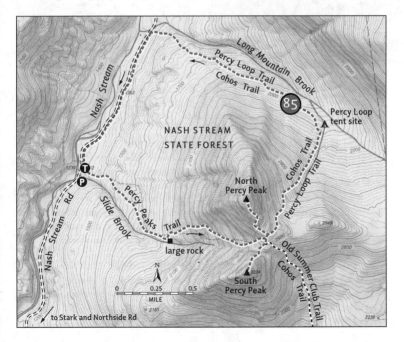

Ascending North Percy Peak (Photo by Maria Fuentes)

Percy Peaks Trail. Turn right onto the Percy Peaks Trail/Cohos Trail and hike 0.1 mile north to a junction with the Percy Loop Trail/Cohos Trail. Stay left and follow the Percy Peaks Trail as it ascends 0.5 mile to the summit of North Percy Peak. Straightforward at first, the route soon rises very steeply up exposed rock. Very difficult if wet or icy, the incline moderates significantly at the end. Throughout, there are amazing views in all directions and few signs of civilization.

Carefully retrace your steps back to the Percy Loop Trail/Cohos Trail junction. Join this yellow-blazed 2.3-mile path to the left as it winds pleasantly through a high-elevation boreal forest. After a short climb, begin a steady descent. The footing is loose in spots. Soon the path reaches a small brook, where a spur right leads to the Percy Loop tent site. Beyond, the route drops to an old woods road and turns sharply left. The final 1.5 miles to Nash Stream Road take advantage of this wide and easy-to-follow corridor. After a few minor ups and downs, the trail descends rapidly through an impressive hardwood forest.

Conclude the day's circuit by turning left following Nash Stream Road 1.1 miles to the trailhead. The dirt road includes a few small hills and offers intimate views of its namesake waterway. Keep your eyes open for moose and other resident fauna.

86 Dixville Notch

RATING/ DIFFICULTY	LOOP	ELEV GAIN/ HIGH POINT	SEASON
****/3–4	5.2 miles	2000 feet/ 2600 feet	Year-round

Map: USGS Dixville Notch; **Contact:** New Hampshire Division of Parks and Recreation; **Note:** Portions of loop are on private land; **GPS:** 44.865355, -71.313177

This challenging loop in northern New Hampshire features precarious cliff-top vistas, cascading brooks, and rugged natural beauty. In addition to being the first place to cast ballots in US presidential elections, Dixville Notch has a remoteness that makes this hike that much more alluring.

GETTING THERE
From the junction of US Route 3 and Route 26 in Colebrook, drive 10 miles east on Route 26 to the trailhead on the right. Park on the right (south) side of the road.

ON THE TRAIL

The western half of the day's loop traverses land owned by the Balsams Grand Resort. This classic turn-of-the-last-century hotel has been in transition in recent years. Fortunately, the trails remain open to the public. Join the Table Rock Trail as it climbs steadily through the hardwood forest. Switchbacks and rock steps ease the way. In 0.7 mile, reach an intersection with the Cohos Trail, a long-distance route through New Hampshire's northernmost county. To the right, the Cohos Trail follows the Mount Gloriette Trail to the top of a nearby ski area.

Turn left, remaining on the Table Rock Trail, now joined by the Cohos Trail along its journey north. Drop quickly to an intersection where the Three Brothers Trail leaves right. Stay straight and head down a steep pitch into a narrow saddle and a

junction. (Here, the Table Rock Trail turns sharply right and leads 0.3 mile to Route 26 near the Sanguinary Ridge Trailhead. Some visitors scale this extremely steep route, but it is not recommended.) Follow the spur path straight ahead and immediately climb atop Table Rock, which juts out from the mountain like a peninsula. Proceed with caution as it narrows near the tip. Both sides fall off precipitously, but the eagle-eye views will leave you speechless.

Return to the Three Brothers Trail (Cohos Trail) and turn left. Swing past the Ice Cave, a narrow gap in the ledge, and climb over a wooded peak. The trail then descends moderately. Reach a spur that leads left to Middle Brother Outlook, 0.5 mile from Table Rock. This lightly used 0.1-mile path descends rapidly before climbing to a scenic perch above the notch.

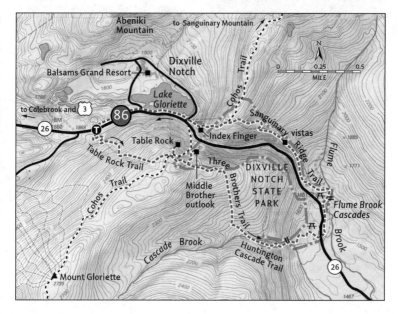

Capturing dramatic views atop Table Rock

swings left and crosses a bridge. Continue straight to a picnic area and parking lot.

Stay right and follow the entranceway to a small cemetery that serves as the final resting place for some of this area's earliest settlers. Bear left on the Cohos Trail and hike a few hundred feet to Route 26. Safely cross the highway and rejoin the trail as it heads north. The yellow blazes wind 0.4 mile to the Flume Brook Cascades and picnic area. The path remains on the same side of Flume Brook throughout. At the picnic area, remain on the Cohos Trail as it joins the Sanguinary Ridge Trail.

Rise 0.1 mile past the scenic flume and then turn sharply left. For the next 0.6 mile, parallel a property boundary that, like the trail, is marked in yellow. While it can be confusing at times, the higher you rise, the more obvious the trail becomes. In 0.4 mile, reach the first of three scenic vistas that offer views of Dixville Notch and distant peaks. Beyond the final promontory, the trail bends right and climbs aggressively up the slope. Level off and hike to a junction, 1.2 miles from the flume. The Cohos Trail departs right and leads 3 miles to the top of Sanguinary Mountain.

Continue left on the Sanguinary Ridge Trail. The path drops steadily 0.3 mile through a dense evergreen forest. Emerge atop a ledge with picturesque views of Lake Gloriette and the Balsams Grand Resort. The final 0.3 mile meanders down an open landscape of loose rock and ledge. Watch your footing around the Index Finger, an aptly named rocky protrusion. A final stretch through the forest leads rapidly to the road. Follow Route 26 west. Take advantage of the wide shoulder and complete the loop in 0.6 mile.

The Three Brothers Trail continues another 0.4 mile. Shortly after entering Dixville Notch State Park, it ends at a stream crossing. Cross the water and pick up the 0.4-mile Huntington Cascade Trail (no sign). This increasingly steep path parallels the rushing water as it cuts through a narrow ravine. There are numerous cascades along the way; the most scenic are toward the bottom. Leveling off significantly, the trail

Pigeon Hill Bay's alluring shoreline, Petit Manan (Hike 99)

maine coast

The Maine coast is often described as a picturesque rocky shoreline, and it is a shoreline like no other in the eastern United States. Highlighted by 30,000-acre Acadia National Park, the 5000-mile coast also includes a number of state and privately owned conservation areas as well. Woven throughout the fabric of conserved lands are working fishing villages, scenic lighthouses, 4000 islands, and some of the finest seafood restaurants in the country.

Maine coastal hikes provide cool summer venues but are often more intriguing during the off-season when the crowds have subsided. Regardless of the time of year, a hiking adventure on the Maine coast will deliver incredible views, abundant wildlife, vibrant colors, and sufficient challenge.

87 Mount Agamenticus

RATING/ DIFFICULTY	LOOP	ELEV GAIN/ HIGH POINT	SEASON
***/3	6.7 miles	1150 feet/ 691 feet	Year-round

Map: USGS York Harbor; **Contact:** Mount Agamenticus Conservation Program; **Notes:** Many of these are multiuse trails. Some are open to motorized vehicles; **GPS:** 43.216820, -70.692060

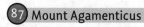 *For decades, the Mount Agamenticus to the Sea Conservation Initiative, local communities, and government agencies have been busy piecing together a 13,000-acre conservation area in this ecologically rich corner of Maine. View firsthand the results of their tireless efforts by venturing along this enticing loop to vernal pools, rocky hillsides, shady forests, and scenic summits.*

GETTING THERE
From the junction of US Route 1 and Mountain Road in York, follow Mountain Road 4.2 miles northwest to the parking area on the right (just before the right turn for the summit road).

ON THE TRAIL
The white-blazed Ring Trail rises 0.1 mile to a junction. Here the path forms a 2-mile loop

Ledges lead up Vultures View Trail.

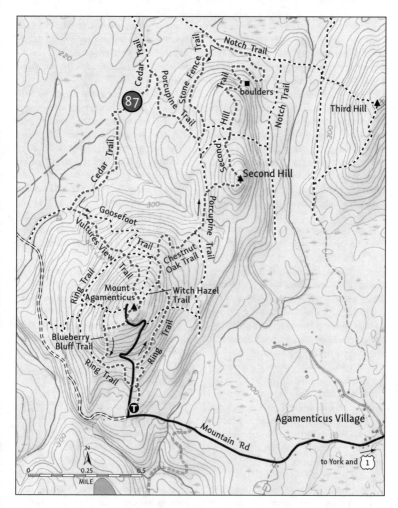

around the mountain. Stay right and follow the circuit's eastern branch 0.8 mile. Along the way, two trails diverging left lead 0.1 mile to the Mount Agamenticus summit. Save this destination for later. The Ring Trail ascends modestly through changing forests and then winds down a steep slope to a four-way intersection.

At the four-way intersection, turn right. Hike 0.3 mile along the Chestnut Oak Trail and then veer left onto the Porcupine Trail. Continue 0.2 mile to the start of the Second

Hill Trail. Bear right onto this 1.2-mile route. It meanders up the ledge-covered hillside and in 0.2 mile arrives atop the flat summit. Find limited views through the thin pine forest and keep your eyes open for resident snakes sunning themselves on the exposed rocks.

Continuing north, the Second Hill Trail descends rapidly 0.3 mile into a narrow gap before ascending gently once again. Head straight atop the ridge, ignoring the two paths departing left and one to the right. Once over a low summit, the trail drops off the ridge and wraps around to the base of its boulder-filled slopes before coming to an end.

Turn left onto the green-blazed Notch Trail. Follow this wide, multiuse route 0.3 mile to a junction with the Stone Fence Trail. Bear left onto this much narrower white-blazed path and climb steadily 0.6 mile along Second Hill's western slopes. After paralleling a rock wall and leveling off, stay right at an unmarked intersection. The trail soon drops rapidly to a second intersection. Turn right to rejoin the Porcupine Trail.

The hike proceeds gradually down the slope and, in 0.5 mile, arrives at a junction with the Cedar Trail. Bear left onto this woods road and begin a relaxing 0.8-mile jaunt to the base of the mountain's former ski area. Time to tackle the day's final climb: a 0.8-mile scramble to the 691-foot summit of Mount Agamenticus.

Begin left on the Goosefoot Trail, but in 0.1 mile bear right onto the Vultures View Trail. Climbing modestly at first, the trail eventually ascends a series of rock steps and granite ledges. Each step leads higher with increasing views, but watch your footing up the steep incline. Head straight across the Ring Trail. One final pitch leads to the summit's broad, and recently expanded, open meadows. Enjoy views of Mount Washington in one direction and the Atlantic Ocean in the other. While the scenery is delightful, be prepared for a lot of company. Many use the mountain's auto road to enjoy the panoramic views.

To descend, head to the top of the summit road. Follow the pavement a few dozen feet, then turn right onto the Blueberry Bluff Trail. After swinging to a bench with scenes to the west, which include New Hampshire's Pawtuckaway State Park, the trail turns left and descends swiftly into the forest. Make your way carefully down the rocky slope. In 0.3 mile, turn left onto the Ring Trail and follow this well-used path 0.3 mile. After crossing the pavement, reach one last junction. Turn right and hike 0.1 mile back to the parking area.

OTHER OPTIONS

There are many opportunities to either shorten or extend this hike. Consider the Ring Trail with a side excursion to the summit via the Witch Hazel Trail to complete a 2.5-mile trek.

88 Wells Reserve

RATING/ DIFFICULTY	LOOP	ELEV GAIN/ HIGH POINT	SEASON
***/1	4.5 miles	100 feet/ 60 feet	Year-round

Map: USGS Wells; **Contact:** Wells National Estuarine Research Reserve; **Note:** No dogs allowed, fee; **GPS:** 43.338374, -70.551010

With 7 miles of trails, numerous potential loops, and 1600 acres of diverse habitats, the Wells Estuarine Reserve is an oasis of open space on Maine's southern coastline. This loop leads through

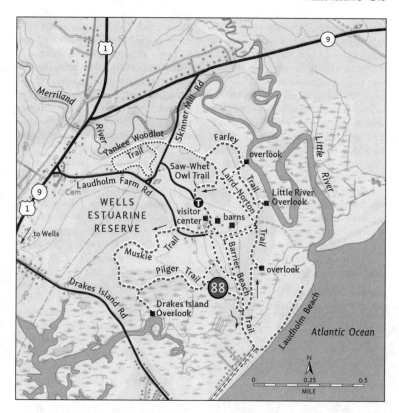

a representative cross-section of the reserve. Especially impressive in the spring during bird migration, the reserve's natural beauty is alluring twelve months a year.

GETTING THERE

From the northern junction of US Route 1 and Route 9 in Wells, drive 0.2 mile south as both roads coincide. Turn left onto Laudholm Farm Road. Continue 0.5 mile and then turn left onto Skinner Mill Road. The reserve's entrance is 0.1 mile on the right. Follow the driveway 0.3 mile to the parking area.

ON THE TRAIL

Designated in 1984, the Wells National Estuarine Reserve is a public-private partnership that relies, in part, on funding from the nonprofit Laudholm Trust. The reserve is jointly owned by federal, state, and local governments and was established to conduct research, convey findings to decision makers, provide natural-resource education, protect the land for wildlife and people, and conserve southern Maine's coastal resources.

Follow the walkway that leads between the barns and a nineteenth-century farmhouse that houses the reserve's visitor center. On the visitor center's southern side, a sign marks the start of the 0.8-mile Muskie Trail. Follow this route 0.1 mile through a meadow and then across Laudholm Farm Road. The path meanders around the edge of a field before entering a shady stand of large pines and oaks. It ends at a three-way junction with the Pilger Trail. Take the spur right and hike 0.1 mile to the Drakes Island Overlook, an observation deck on the edge of a pond frequented by waterfowl.

Retrace your steps and turn right onto the 0.6-mile Pilger Trail. Wind easily to expansive meadow views before ascending a grassy slope. After tunneling through the forest, the path ends at a four-way intersection with the Barrier Beach and Laird-Norton trails. Turn right onto the

Laird-Norton Trail boardwalk

Barrier Beach Trail. This narrow dirt corridor proceeds 0.2 mile to Laudholm Beach. Hike over a causeway, across a dirt road, and past a gate to reach the sandy shore. To the left the beach stretches nearly 0.5 mile to the mouth of the Little River. Laudholm Beach is home to the federally protected piping plover. Please watch your step and avoid disturbing these well-camouflaged, tiny shorebirds.

Return to the Laird-Norton Trail and swing right. For much of the next 0.5 mile, the hike remains atop an extensive network of boardwalks. Near the halfway point, a short spur departs right to the Laird-Norton Overlook, a good location to spot wading birds. As the main route emerges into a field, veer right onto the Farley Trail.

Return quickly to the forest, and in 0.2 mile reach the Little River Overlook. Beyond, the trail meanders 0.2 mile through field and forest before arriving at an intersection under an evergreen canopy. Remain on the Farley Trail as it bends right. Head down to the water's edge and one last scenic overlook. The trail swings inland. In 0.2 mile, head across an open field to a junction with the Laird-Norton Trail. To the right, the path leads through meadows and across Skinner Mill Road to a quiet forested loop. Consider adding this nearly 2-mile extension if you have the time.

Conclude the day's hike by bearing left. In 0.1 mile, turn right onto the Saw-Whet Owl Trail. This pleasant path weaves 0.2 mile to the entrance road. The parking area is a few hundred feet to the left. Before leaving, enjoy a picnic under one of the many large shade trees that surround the visitor center. The building houses a small museum with information about the area's human and natural history.

The Boundary Trail is lined with stone walls.

89 Bradbury Mountain

RATING/ DIFFICULTY	LOOP	ELEV GAIN/ HIGH POINT	SEASON
**/2	3.2 miles	360 feet/ 485 feet	Year-round

Map: USGS North Pownal; **Contact:** Maine Bureau of Parks and Lands; **Note:** Fee; **GPS:** 43.900394, -70.179201

Bradbury Mountain State Park is nearly 600 acres of open space within a half hour of Portland. With a campground, picnic tables, a small playground, and easy to moderate terrain, Bradbury Mountain is an ideal place to bring the whole family for a relaxing outing of nature exploration any time of year.

GETTING THERE

From the junction of Route 9 and Elmwood Road in Pownal Center, drive 0.3 mile north on Route 9. Turn left to enter the state park. There are two parking areas; the hike leaves from the northernmost one. To reach this parking area, turn right after passing through the entrance.

ON THE TRAIL

The park offers many different loop options from as little as 1 mile to as long as 3.5 miles. All the trails are well blazed and easy to follow, and many end atop the 485-foot summit of Bradbury Mountain. The quickest, steepest ascent is the Summit Trail. However, for greater variety, choose this more circuitous adventure that begins on the Northern Loop Trail.

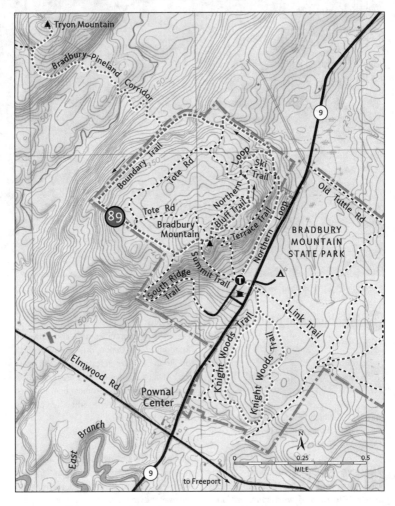

For a half mile, hike along the wide footpath across mostly level terrain while passing many historical features, including a cattle pound, stone walls, and a mine where feldspar was once gathered for china. After passing a junction with the Terrace and Ski trails on the left, continue straight to the start of the Boundary Trail, which departs right.

Traveling through a wide diversity of habitats, this orange-blazed trail lives up to its name by hugging the park's property line for most of its 1.5 miles. Tall red oaks and small wetlands line the trail's beginning.

After passing over small mounds, descend and cross over a tiny streambed. Soon after, arrive at a junction with the newly created Bradbury–Pineland Corridor Trail. Leaving north, this well-signed but lightly blazed route meanders 0.9 mile to a 0.1-mile spur that leads right to an abandoned feldspar quarry atop Tryon Mountain. Consider adding this pleasant 2-mile round-trip diversion to your day's itinerary.

Beyond the Bradbury-Pineland Corridor intersection, a short climb up a steep hemlock-covered slope follows. The path continues to rise, but more gradually. At the boundary's westernmost corner, turn sharply left. Proceed another 0.4 mile along the boundary and, after crossing over a rock wall, reach an intersection with the South Ridge Trail.

Turn left and ascend easily 0.2 mile to the 485-foot summit of Bradbury Mountain. From an expansive open ledge, views stretch south toward the ocean and Maine's largest city. Above, the skies are often frequented by hawks, falcons, and other raptors. This is a popular location for bird-watchers, especially during fall migration.

Depart the summit to the north and briefly follow the blue-blazed Northern Loop Trail. In 0.1 mile, turn right onto the Bluff Trail. Another 0.1 mile farther, remain left on the Bluff Trail. Descend gradually to the path's namesake feature and attractive views of the surrounding countryside. From the bluff, descend a few hundred feet and turn right, rejoining the Northern Loop Trail. Remain on this route as it makes its way down the mountain. As the path levels and passes the start of the Boundary Trail, stay right for the final 0.5-mile hike back to the parking area.

EXTENDING YOUR HIKE

If you are not ready to return to civilization, consider a short adventure on the 1.5-mile Knight Woods Trail. Located on the other side of Route 9, this loop provides an opportunity to enjoy more of Bradbury Mountain State Park's maturing forests, prolific wildflowers, and melodious birds.

90 Dodge Point

RATING/ DIFFICULTY	LOOP	ELEV GAIN/ HIGH POINT	SEASON
**/2	4.2 miles	350 feet/ 220 feet	Year-round

Map: USGS Bristol; **Contact:** Maine Bureau of Parks and Lands; **GPS:** 43.995241, -69.567511

With more than 500 acres adjacent to the Damariscotta River's tidal waters, the Dodge Point Preserve is a perfect location for a leisurely family hike. In addition to natural beauty, Dodge Point showcases human history including an old mill site and brickyard, cellar holes and rock walls, and stands of large trees grown under the watchful eyes of an owner whose trustees sold the small woodlot to the state in 1989.

GETTING THERE

From downtown Wiscasset, travel 6.2 miles east on US Route 1 into Newcastle. Turn right (the sign points to River Road) and in 0.2 mile turn right again onto River Road. Drive 2.5 miles to a sign and parking area on the left.

ON THE TRAIL

Begin on the Old Farm Road, a wide path that loops 2.2 miles around the preserve. Head up a small incline. In 0.1 mile, turn right onto the narrower Timber Trail.

Winding over boardwalks and through small wetlands, the trail proceeds easily. Stay left at a junction with the River-Link Trail. The River-Link Trail is the product of an initiative by multiple conservation organizations to connect the Sheepscot and Damariscotta rivers. With help from the Land for Maine's Future Program, this ambitious project has acquired several parcels and easements along a 4.5-mile trail and wildlife corridor. Consider exploring this path on a future excursion.

Continue along the Timber Trail and ascend a low hill. After passing over a small stone wall, the path ends. Turn right and rejoin the Old Farm Road.

Gradually make your way down the side of a steep hill. After the route levels, arrive at a junction where a sign points right to the shore. Turn right off of Old Farm Road onto this equally wide path and follow it 0.2 mile to a small dock on the river. During colder months, this is a great location to spot loons as well as long-tailed and bufflehead ducks. Both spend considerable time feeding beneath the water's surface.

Bear left and for the next 1.3 miles enjoy the Shore Trail's scenic journey as it winds along the riverbank. Level for the most part, the trail has minor ups and downs. Take your time and explore a trio of picturesque beaches along the way. All three are at the end of short spur trails. The final stop is Brickyard Beach, which is adjacent to a mudflat popular for shellfish harvesting. Aptly named, the beach is also strewn with the remains of bricks produced here as early as the 1600s. At one time there were nearly thirty brickyards in the region, employing 200 people. The trail eventually swings inland and returns once again to Old Farm Road.

Making memories along Shore Trail

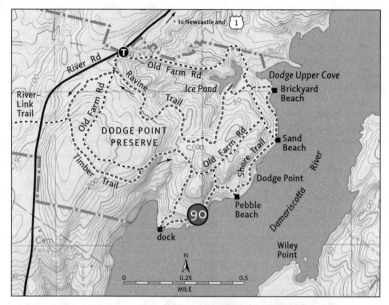

Follow the road right a few hundred yards to the start of the Ravine Trail on the left. Before taking this path, check out Ice Pond a few dozen feet ahead. This manmade water body is a good location to spot turtles sunning on fallen trees.

The 1.1-mile Ravine Trail wraps around the pond's shore and then slowly ascends along the edge of a diminutive ravine. After leveling off, the route swings right and cuts through a dark evergreen forest, emerging onto an old road lined with large sugar maples. Veer left off the road. Hike over a few small inclines and arrive one last time at the Old Farm Road. Turn right to complete the circuit. Before leaving, stop at the small kiosk for information about the Damariscotta River Association, a local land trust that helps the state manage the property.

91 Camden Hills

RATING/ DIFFICULTY	LOOP	ELEV GAIN/ HIGH POINT	SEASON
****/3	6.5 miles	1700 feet/ 1385 feet	Year-round

Maps: USGS Camden and USGS Lincolnville;
Contact: Maine Bureau of Parks and Lands;
GPS: 44.247201, -69.087663

This journey, which leads to a pair of popular Camden Hills destinations, completes a figure eight–shaped adventure while visiting some of the state park's quieter locations. Two loops in one, the hike can be completed as described or as shorter, separate treks. Whichever option you choose, you will not go home disappointed.

GETTING THERE

From US Route 1 in downtown Camden, follow Route 52 north. In 2.2 miles, just before approaching Megunticook Lake, turn right into a driveway that leads 0.1 mile to the parking area.

ON THE TRAIL

Beginning on town-owned land, the 0.8-mile Maiden Cliff Trail climbs steadily at first. Swing right and carve through a narrow rock-covered ravine. Under the shadows of tall conifers, ascend to a large boulder and trail junction 0.4 mile from the start. Stay left on the Maiden Cliff Trail and ascend the short switchbacks that culminate atop a flat oak-covered ridge.

Continue straight to a three-way intersection and follow the short spur left that ends atop a dramatic cliff. From this vantage point the views of Megunticook Lake are stunning. While not scary, it is potentially dangerous if you choose to wander down the steep slope. Heed the warning from the metal cross

erected in the memory of a young girl who plunged to her death here in 1864.

Return to the woods and veer left on the 0.4-mile Scenic Trail. This route leads up a short, steep slope to a series of wide-open ledges that offer extensive views and prime picnic locations. At the bottom of the final ledge lies a junction with the Ridge Trail. To the right, the path leads 0.6 mile down to the parking area, completing a 1.8-mile loop.

To tackle the longer hike, continue straight on the Ridge Trail. After a short descent, the route rises gradually 0.6 mile to an intersection with the Jack Williams Trail and the start of the second loop. Remain left on the Ridge Trail and proceed 1.2 miles to the wooded summit of 1385-foot Megunticook Mountain, the park's highest point. The route there rises aggressively at first, passes an intersection with the Zekes Trail, visits a small ledge featuring distant ocean scenes, and then levels off. Hike through a maze of ferns and rocks before tackling the final ascent.

Descending Ocean Lookout

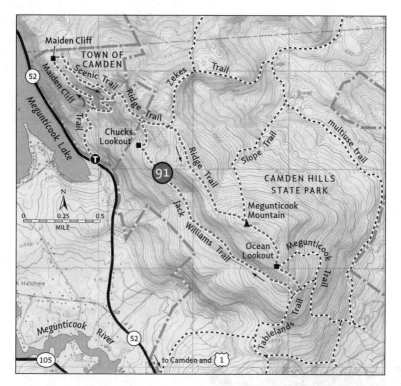

Rather than stopping at the viewless summit, press on 0.4 mile down the Ridge Trail to the spectacular Ocean Lookout. Perched atop a cliff face, this much-visited vantage point provides ample locations to spread out and enjoy the incredible scenery. Especially impressive are the countless islands and inlets of Penobscot Bay.

Resume the hike southeast, joining the Tablelands Trail for 0.3 mile. It descends through a forest of stunted oaks. Watch your step in spots and enjoy the abundant views. Bending right, the path heads down a rocky slope to an intersection. Turn right onto the 1.6-mile Jack Williams Trail. This path quickly

swings beneath the base of the impressive Ocean Lookout Cliff and then continues with minor elevation change before easily climbing back to the Ridge Trail. As you approach the end of the Jack Williams Trail, a short path leads left to Chucks Lookout, a viewpoint similar in appearance to, but not as popular as, Maiden Cliff.

Once back on the Ridge Trail, turn left. At the intersection with the Scenic Trail, turn left again. Down open ledges and past impressive vistas, descend steeply 0.2 mile to a small streambed. After swinging right, reach the Maiden Cliff Trail. Stay left and hike 0.4 mile back to the trailhead.

92 Holbrook Island Sanctuary

RATING/ DIFFICULTY	LOOP	ELEV GAIN/ HIGH POINT	SEASON
***/2–3	7.6 miles	650 feet/ 300 feet	Year-round

Map: USGS Cape Rosier; **Contact:** Maine Bureau of Parks and Lands; **Notes:** Open daily 9:00 AM to sunset year-round; **GPS:** 44.360056, -68.792822

In 1971, Anita Harris donated the 1230-acre Holbrook Island Sanctuary to the state "to preserve for the future a piece of the unspoiled Maine" that she used to know. Today, lovers of nature are invited to explore the family-friendly trails of this coastal gem and marvel at diverse habitats that are home to a wide variety of plants and animals.

Cobble beach on Penobscot Bay

GETTING THERE
From the junction of Cape Rosier Road and Route 176 in Brooksville, drive 1.6 miles west on Cape Rosier Road and then turn right onto Back Road. Follow this dirt road 0.8 mile before turning right onto Indian Bar Road. Continue 0.1 mile to the parking area on the left.

ON THE TRAIL
This recommended itinerary features three separate hikes. Each can be done individually, and each has its own trailhead parking. Improvise as appropriate; the trailheads are well marked.

Hike 0.1 mile south along Indian Bar Road and then turn left onto Back Road. In a few hundred feet reach the start of the Ice Works Trail on the right. This relatively flat route proceeds 1 mile, weaving between small rocky hillsides. Beginning in a damp forest of cedar and spruce, the trail eventually rises gently to the shore of Fresh Pond.

Fresh Pond is a haven for wildlife. Scan the sky for bald eagles on the hunt and the water for ducks raising young. Turn right to begin the 1.3-mile circuit of the large pond. The easy-to-follow trail hugs the shoreline most of the way, with minor ups and downs. Nearly three-quarters of the way around, arrive at an intersection where a branch of the Fresh Pond Trail swings right to an alternative parking area. Turn sharply left to complete the loop. Enjoy the last few scenes of the pond before retracing your steps along the Ice Works Trail.

Upon returning to Back Road, turn right. Hike less than 0.1 mile, then bear right onto

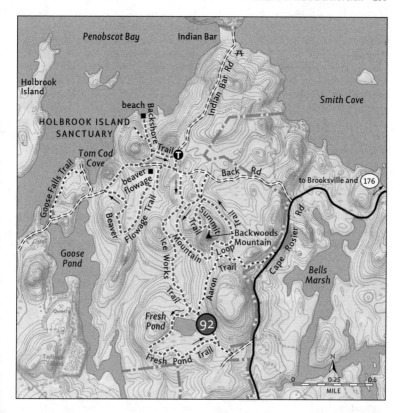

the Mountain Loop Trail. This path rises 0.1 mile to an intersection and the start of the day's second loop. Follow the trail right. For the next 1.2 miles, enjoy a pleasant woods walk. While gradually ascending a forested slope, stay alert for the pounding of woodpeckers and the soothing calls of hermit thrushes. The circuit concludes with a gentle descent to an intersection with the Summit Trail.

Turn left and hike 0.3 mile to the top of the just-circled Backwoods Mountain. Easy at first, the trail becomes quite steep at the end. Carefully rise up the ledge-covered

slopes and scan the surroundings for signs of porcupine. Near the top, enjoy modest views of Castine Harbor through the tree branches. Retrace your steps down the Summit Trail and continue 0.1 mile to Back Road.

Turn left and head to the third component of the day's hike. Remain on Back Road beyond its junction with Indian Bar Road. Drop 0.1 mile to the start of the Beaver Flowage Trail on the left. This 0.9-mile corridor circles a broad, marshy wetland. Be alert for great blue herons and the colorful flashes of red-winged blackbirds. Hugging the water to start and occasionally crossing wooden bridges, the loop concludes after rising through a pine forest. Bear right to join Back Road one last time.

Walk 0.3 mile along the dirt road before turning left onto the Backshore Trail. This path leads into the fields of a former estate. In 0.2 mile, the portion of the trail that leads back to the parking area veers right. For now, continue straight and wind past a small cemetery to another intersection. Follow the main route straight ahead; it leads 0.1 mile directly to a beach on the shores of Penobscot Bay. This is a peaceful spot to grab a snack and scope the waters for harbor seals and eider ducks. Retrace your steps 0.2 mile before turning left. Head across the open meadow and then up a small rise to reach the trailhead.

93 Champlain Mountain

RATING/ DIFFICULTY	ROUND-TRIP	ELEV GAIN/ HIGH POINT	SEASON
***/3	5.5 miles	1400 feet/ 1058 feet	June–Oct

Map: USGS Seal Harbor; **Contact:** Acadia National Park; **Note:** Fee; **GPS:** 44.362457, -68.207687

Automobiles have traditionally been the preferred mode of transportation in Acadia National Park, a park too often plagued by air pollution, traffic, and overflowing parking areas. Leave these worries behind and hop aboard an Island Explorer shuttle to tackle this scenic excursion. The described hike rises atop a barren mountain ridge with exquisite views of Mount Desert Island before stopping at the park's most visited sites.

GETTING THERE

The primary Island Explorer routes begin at the Bar Harbor Village Green on Route 3. While there is limited public parking available, the green is within walking distance of many overnight establishments and can be reached using the Island Explorer shuttle service from a number of other locations including the national park visitor center in Hull's Cove. Take an Island Explorer shuttle to Sieur de Monts Spring to reach the trailhead.

ON THE TRAIL

The Sieur de Monts Spring offers short trails that weave through a collection of plant species illustrative of those found on the island. Just beyond a small natural history museum, turn left and follow the Jesup Path as it leads 0.3 mile to the Tarn. At the north shore of the large pond, bear left again. Rise quickly to the side of Route 3 and carefully cross the busy highway to reach the start of the Beachcroft Trail.

The 1.4-mile Beachcroft Trail gradually switchbacks up a steep slope and features stunning views from numerous rocky vantage points. The footing for much of the trail amazingly consists of a series of flat stones laid out perfectly. Circling around Huguenot Head, a small peak on the ridge, the path descends to a saddle before climbing steeply up rock ledges to the summit of Champlain Mountain. The mountain, named for the French explorer who discovered and named Mount Desert Island in 1576, stands at 1058 feet high above Frenchman Bay.

A relaxing stroll down Champlain's attractive South Ridge Trail ensues. Duck in and out among the stunted pine trees that have established roots within the inhospitable rocky surface, and follow the trail as

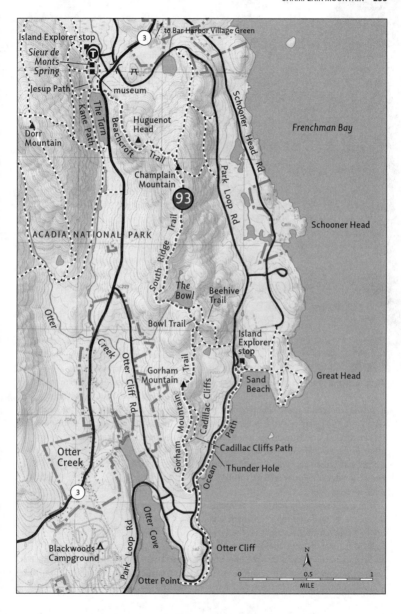

Island Explorer stop
Sieur de Monts Spring
Jesup Path
to Bar Harbor Village Green
3
T
museum
Kane Path
The Tarn
Beachcroft Trail
Huguenot Head
Dorr Mountain
Champlain Mountain
93
Schooner Head Rd
Park Loop Rd
Frenchman Bay
Schooner Head
ACADIA NATIONAL PARK
South Ridge Trail
229
The Bowl
Beehive Trail
Bowl Trail
Island Explorer stop
Otter Creek
Otter Cliff Rd
Gorham Mountain
Gorham Mountain Trail
Cadillac Cliffs
Ocean Path
Cadillac Cliffs Path
Thunder Hole
Sand Beach
Great Head
Otter Creek
3
Blackwoods Campground
Park Loop Rd
Otter Cove
Otter Point
Otter Cliff

N

0   0.5   1
MILE

The Beachcroft Trail is a work of art.

mile veers right, joining another branch of the trail. Climb more steadily to the summit of Gorham Mountain. Although topping out at only 525 feet above sea level, the peak's proximity to the ocean provides excellent views and cool, refreshing breezes. Heading south down the ridge, quickly reach the Cadillac Cliffs Path on the left, a route that weaves around a series of rock faces once submerged beneath the sea. Take the slightly more difficult Cadillac Cliffs Path or continue straight on the Gorham Mountain Trail; the two routes rejoin in 0.3 mile.

Upon reaching the Gorham Mountain Trail's conclusion, pick up the Ocean Path on the opposite side of the Park Loop Road. The Ocean Path is a flat and well-manicured trail that passes many popular natural attractions. Otter Cliff, a scenic ledge rising above the ocean, lies along the Ocean Path 0.2 mile to the right.

To complete the hike, turn left. Hike past Thunder Hole, where the ocean crashes loudly between the rocks, especially as the tide rises. Continue to beautiful Sand Beach where Island Explorer shuttles arrive every half hour, offering a return trip to the Village Green. If you have the time and energy, Sand Beach and the 1.5-mile loop to Great Head that begins on the beach's eastern end are both enjoyable destinations.

it steadily descends past countless ocean vistas. In 1.2 miles arrive at the Bowl, a large, secluded pond that is home to beaver and other resident wildlife. With the assistance of a boardwalk, make your way along the shore and at a three-way intersection, turn right onto the Bowl Trail.

The trail rises easily and then descends through a birch forest of white bark and bright green leaves. Stay right on the Bowl Trail at a junction with the Beehive Trail and then, shortly after, turn right onto the Gorham Mountain Trail. This path ascends gradually up the rocky landscape and in 0.1

94 Dorr Mountain

RATING/ DIFFICULTY	LOOP	ELEV GAIN/ HIGH POINT	SEASON
****/3	6.5 miles	1400 feet/ 1265 feet	April–Nov

Maps: USGS Seal Harbor and USGS Bar Harbor; **Contact:** Acadia National Park; **Note:** Fee; **GPS:** 44.362457, -68.207687

Named for George Dorr, one of Acadia National Park's most influential founders, this rugged mountain features exceptional views and stunning natural beauty that are fitting tributes to his legacy. This loop connects sprawling forested wetlands with broad granite ridges. While generally across easy to moderate terrain, the trail has a few sections that can be challenging, especially if the weather is inclement.

GETTING THERE

From the Village Green in downtown Bar Harbor, drive 2.1 miles south on Route 3. Turn right to reach the Sieur de Monts Spring parking area in 0.2 mile. Alternatively, take advantage of the Island Explorer shuttle when it is available.

ON THE TRAIL

Sieur de Monts Spring features Wild Gardens of Acadia, a collection of native plants. Hike straight past the displays to reach the Jesup Path. Turn right and follow this well-manicured path that soon arrives at an intersection with a dirt road. Veer left and follow the dirt road 0.3 mile.

Turn left onto the Hemlock Trail, but immediately veer right onto the Stratheden Path. This lightly used route leads 0.7 mile below Kebo Mountain's rocky ridge. Pass through a section of large boulders and make your way across the Park Loop Road. Proceed quickly to the Kebo Brook Trail and turn left. In 0.1 mile, turn left again, this time onto the Kebo Mountain Trail.

Cross over the Park Loop Road one last time and rise quickly 0.3 mile to the top of 407-foot Kebo Mountain. Covered in pine trees, the diminutive peak offers modest views of Frenchman Bay from a spot just

before the summit. Continue south 0.6 mile. The trail winds over a rolling landscape of ledges and loose rocks before dropping into a narrow saddle.

Stay straight on Dorr Mountain's North Ridge Trail. Rising aggressively at first, it gains a lot of elevation over the first half of its 1-mile course. Near the halfway point, the forest canopy begins to open, offering increasing views north and east. At the same time, the granite ledges begin to rise less steeply. Pass straight through a four-way junction and reach the 1265-foot summit in 0.1 mile. From the giant cairn atop Dorr Mountain there are wonderful views in all

Views abound on the Kane Path.

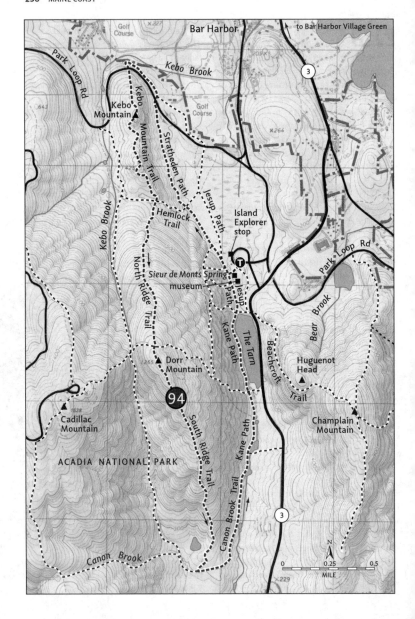

Dorr Mountain's massive cairn

directions. The shots of Cadillac Mountain to the west are especially noteworthy.

Begin the descent along the mountain's sweeping south ridge. Follow its namesake trail and descend toward the open ocean. In the beginning, the 1.5-mile route weaves easily in and out of the stunted evergreens, revealing one extraordinary vista after another. Toward the end, it becomes more difficult. Watch your step while heading down the rocky surface as the path sinks beneath the forest canopy.

Turn left onto the Canon Brook Trail. This last leg of the loop is much more relaxing. After dropping 0.1 mile east, the path swings north toward an extensive series of wetlands. Hike 0.6 mile to a beaver pond with intimate views of Champlain Mountain. Stay straight, joining the Kane Path. It leads easily 0.3 mile to the southern end of the Tarn. Over this next 0.5 mile, the route remains close to the scenic pond's western shore. Although level, the trail traverses a boulder field that requires added attention. At the Tarn's outlet, follow the Jesup Path 0.3 mile straight to reach the Sieur de Monts parking area.

95 Norumbega Mountain

RATING/ DIFFICULTY	LOOP	ELEV GAIN/ HIGH POINT	SEASON
**/3	3.8 miles	800 feet/ 850 feet	Year-round

Map: USGS Southwest Harbor; **Contact:** Acadia National Park; **Note:** Fee; **GPS:** 44.325796, -68.291353

This scenic circuit above the eastern shore of Somes Sound is a good tune-up hike to prepare for more rigorous adventures in Acadia National Park. Although the journey is challenging at first, much of it enjoys easy to moderate terrain. There are countless viewpoints throughout, as well as ample opportunity to observe wildlife within many diverse habitats.

GETTING THERE

From the junction of Routes 102 and 3/198 in Somesville drive 4.1 miles southeast on Route 3/198 to the parking area on the right.

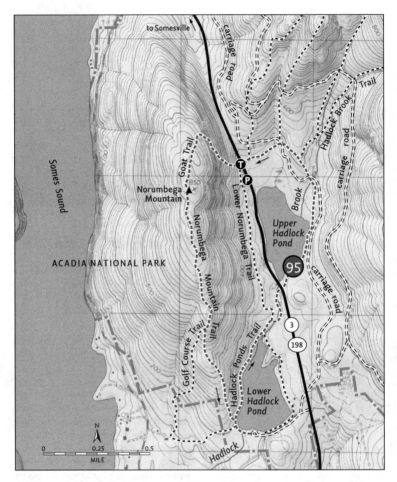

ON THE TRAIL

Just north of the parking area, the Goat Trail enters the forest left and immediately reaches a junction. Stay straight and proceed up the steep slope. The path employs numerous rock steps and short switchbacks to ease the way, but the route is difficult nonetheless. In 0.4 mile, rise out of the forest onto semi-open ledges. Swing south and ascend more gradually. During the final 0.2-mile stretch to Norumbega Mountain's 850-foot summit, there are many views east to Sargent Mountain.

Named for a fabled city of riches that famed Acadia explorer Samuel de Champlain searched for in the early sixteenth century,

Norumbega Mountain offers limited views from its high point. However, if you continue south along the Norumbega Mountain Trail, western panoramas quickly emerge. Enjoy the surroundings as you make your way in and out of the forest over the next 0.8 mile. Stay straight at a junction where the Golf Course Trail departs right. Descend more rapidly into the thicker evergreen forest. In 0.6 mile, the route ends at an intersection with the Hadlock Ponds Trail.

Continue the loop left, but first walk a few dozen feet ahead to a small dam on the shores of Lower Hadlock Pond. This reservoir is used for public drinking water. While swimming is prohibited, photographing the reflective waters and nearby peaks is allowed.

Return to the Hadlock Ponds Trail and turn right. With little elevation change, hug the pond's western shoreline for 0.5 mile.

The route continues north an additional 0.3 mile while following the small stream that descends from Upper Hadlock Pond. Pass a junction with the Lower Norumbega Trail. This path departs left and offers a shorter, alternative route back. Stay on the Hadlock Ponds Trail. It leads quickly to the side of Route 3/198.

Safely cross the busy highway and rejoin the trail as it leads to Upper Hadlock Pond's eastern shore. Over the next 0.3 mile, enjoy intimate views of the pond and Bald Peak rising high above it. Boardwalks keep your feet high and dry. Leave the picturesque pond behind and hike 0.2 mile to a carriage road. Hike across this wide corridor that is popular with bicyclists and cross-country skiers. The Hadlock Ponds Trail rises gently 0.2 mile before ending. Turn left onto the Hadlock Brook Trail to tackle the final 0.3-mile hike back to the parking area.

Upper Hadlock Pond's idyllic shoreline

96 Acadia Mountain

RATING/ DIFFICULTY	LOOP	ELEV GAIN/ HIGH POINT	SEASON
****/3	4.5 miles	1300 feet/ 681 feet	April–Nov

Map: USGS Southwest Harbor; **Contact:** Acadia National Park; **Note:** Fee; **GPS:** 44.321710, -68.332854

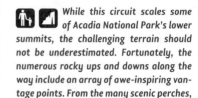 *While this circuit scales some of Acadia National Park's lower summits, the challenging terrain should not be underestimated. Fortunately, the numerous rocky ups and downs along the way include an array of awe-inspiring vantage points. From the many scenic perches, gaze out over Somes Sound and marvel at the loftier peaks in the distance.*

GETTING THERE
From the junction of Routes 102 and 3/198 in Somesville, drive 3.4 miles south on Route 102 to the parking area on the right. Alternatively, take advantage of the Island Explorer shuttle when it is available.

ON THE TRAIL
Carefully cross the busy road. The trail climbs easily 0.1 mile to a junction and the start of the day's loop. Turn left onto the St. Sauveur Trail and drop 0.2 mile to the Man O' War Road (a dirt road not open to vehicles). Cross the road to the start of the Acadia Mountain Trail and begin a steady 0.6-mile ascent up the well-used corridor. After heading over roots and scaling small ledges, the path eventually levels off. A final climb leads to the top of Acadia Mountain's 681-foot rocky summit and views in most directions.

The circuit resumes east at first, but it soon swings south. Weave through the thin evergreen forest. Initially easy to navigate, the trail's exposed granite surface becomes more challenging as the 0.7-mile descent unfolds. Take your time and soak in the spectacular scenes of Mount Desert Island's rugged slopes meeting the salty waters of the surrounding ocean. Nearing sea level, the path crosses Man O' War Brook. Here, a spur departs left 0.1 mile to a picturesque

Gazing across Somes Sound

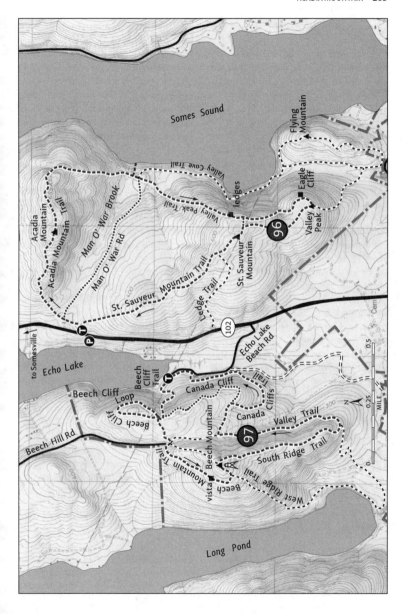

spot on the shoreline. Ahead, find a four-way intersection.

To the right, the Man O' War Road leads 1 mile back to the parking area. This is a good alternative to complete a shorter 2.7-mile hike. For those looking for more adventure, stay straight along the Valley Peak Trail. Wasting little time, this challenging route climbs aggressively 0.8 mile up the slopes of St. Sauveur Mountain. Near the halfway point, ascend a series of open ledges showcasing dramatic views of the park's eastern summits. Remaining in the open, the trail eases and reaches a junction.

While a shortcut leaves right, stay left on the Valley Peak Trail and descend 0.3 mile to the top of Eagle Cliff. From a perch high above Flying Mountain, this is the day's last stunning vista. Beyond Eagle Cliff, proceed a few hundred feet to an intersection with the St. Sauveur Trail.

Turn right and climb easily 0.4 mile to the wooded summit of the trail's namesake peak. Hike across the rolling terrain 0.3 mile farther to a junction with the Ledge Trail. Stay straight on the St. Sauveur Trail for the final 1-mile stretch. Slithering across the rolling, rocky landscape, the route crosses one ledge with limited northern views before dropping steadily. Turn left at the end of the loop and hike 0.1 mile to return to the trailhead.

97 Beech Cliff and Mountain

RATING/ DIFFICULTY	LOOP	ELEV GAIN/ HIGH POINT	SEASON
***/3–4	4 miles	1100 feet/ 831 feet	April–Nov

Map: USGS Southwest Harbor; **Contact:** Acadia National Park; **Note:** Fee; **GPS:** 44.314827, -68.336743

Not for those afraid of heights, this loop ascends steep metal ladders to start. However, much of the remaining trek traverses far less strenuous terrain. There are numerous spectacular vistas along the way, including countless views of neighboring summits, nearby lakes, and surrounding ocean scenery.

GETTING THERE
From the junction of Routes 102 and 3/198 in Somesville, drive 4.2 miles south on Route 102. Turn right onto Echo Lake Beach Road. In 0.3 mile, stay right and drive 0.2 mile to the parking area. Alternatively, take advantage of the Island Explorer shuttle when it is available.

ON THE TRAIL
The 0.5-mile Beech Cliff Trail starts in a cul-de-sac at the parking area's northern end. As the path reaches the base of the mountain, swing left and climb a series of rock steps. In 0.2 mile a spur right rises to a ledge with an aerial view of Echo Lake. Beyond, the real fun begins. The trail rises 0.3 mile up a seemingly impenetrable slope. Weave under precipitous ledges and carefully ascend long metal ladders. The final pitch leads to an open granite ledge and incredible views.

Turn right onto the 0.4-mile Beech Cliff Loop. The route remains close to the cliff's edge for 0.2 mile, passing alluring vantage points of Echo Lake and east to Acadia's highest peaks. Swing left into the forest and then head south to complete the small circuit.

Turn right and hike 0.2 mile down a well-manicured path that ends at the southern tip of Beech Hill Road and a small parking area. The Valley Trail leaves the parking area

Long Pond from Beech Mountain Trail

to the left. Find the Beech Mountain Trail, which departs right, offering two options to the summit. Follow the longer, more scenic 0.7-mile western branch by staying right. The trail is forested at first but emerges into the open near the halfway point. Enjoy the exceptional western panorama of Long Pond, Mansell Mountain, and Blue Hill Bay. Stay left at a junction with the West Ridge Trail and proceed 0.1 mile to the 831-foot summit.

Beech Mountain offers splendid views from its rocky high point and fire tower (the cabin is not always open). In the autumn, many venture here to scan the skies for migrating raptors.

Resume the hike along the 0.8-mile South Ridge Trail. In and out of the thin forest, the path's mostly gradual descent occasionally traverses ledges that require extra attention. With the last of the vistas behind, descend a rock staircase that leads to an intersection with the Valley Trail.

Turn left and follow this route 0.6 mile. Straightforward to start, the Valley Trail soon snakes through an inviting collection of moss- and fern-draped boulders. At a junction with the Canada Cliffs Trail, veer right and hike 0.2 mile to a three-way junction (all three routes are branches of the Canada Cliffs Trail). Follow the path right. It parallels a small stream to start and then descends easily, well below the steep mountain slope. In 0.6 mile, arrive at the Echo Lake parking area and the end of the loop.

OTHER OPTIONS

If the ladders and ledges of the Beech Cliff Trail are too intimidating, begin and end the hike using the Canada Cliffs Trail. On the ascent, turn right at the first intersection and rise past numerous scenic outcrops en route to the top of the Beech Cliff Trail. This option adds 0.5 mile to the described route.

98 Tunk Mountain

RATING/ DIFFICULTY	ROUND-TRIP	ELEV GAIN/ HIGH POINT	SEASON
★★★★/3–4	4.5 miles	1100 feet/ 1400 feet	Year-round

Map: USGS Tunk Mountain; **Contact:** Maine Bureau of Parks and Lands; **Note:** Toilet at trailhead; **GPS:** 44.624733, -68.088940

Tunk Mountain's steep slopes are challenging to ascend, but from the wide-open granite ledges that flank its highest point, the scenes of surrounding peaks, ponds, and forests are breathtaking. This half-day adventure also showcases fascinating geology and provides ample opportunity to spot resident wildlife as the trail weaves through ever-changing habitat.

GETTING THERE

From the junction of Routes 182 and 200 in Franklin, follow Route 182 east 8.5 miles to the large parking area on the left.

ON THE TRAIL

The Tunk Mountain Trail starts pleasantly over rolling terrain. Across small wetlands, swing right and wind over a low ridge carpeted in ferns and dotted with lichen-draped

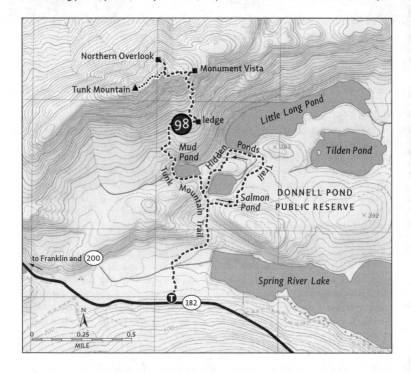

A rock staircase climbs above Mud Pond.

boulders. In 0.5 mile, reach an unsigned junction and the start of the 1-mile Hidden Ponds Trail.

Turn right and ascend a small incline. Follow the path as it winds around Salmon Pond. It descends toward, but does not approach, the shore. Continue over mostly level but rocky terrain to a second and larger body of water, Little Long Pond. Two short spurs lead right to the water's edge. The first arrives atop a steep cliff. A second leads to a safer viewing location. Both vistas showcase the pond's picturesque shoreline and dramatic surroundings. Paralleling a small bubbling brook, the trail rises 0.1 mile back to Salmon Pond. Check out the short path that departs left to the water's edge. The loop quickly ends 0.1 mile north of its start at a junction with the Tunk Mountain Trail.

Swing right and climb 0.1 mile to Mud Pond, a narrow body of water that lies nestled beneath Tunk Mountain's steep slopes. The trail leads west and remains along the shore. At the pond's northwestern corner, the principal climb commences. Head up a rock staircase and through an evergreen forest of spruce and cedar. The trail steadily meanders 0.5 mile up the slope to an open ledge with impressive views of the ponds below.

The next 0.5-mile stretch becomes more demanding and difficult with each step, especially if conditions are wet or icy. In one location, three metal rungs aid the ascent. Through the thinning forest, the trail switchbacks and rises to one spectacular viewpoint after another. Hike through a narrow gap in the ledge to a junction. Here a short spur leads right to Monument Vista. It ends at a memorial for the generous landowner who donated the property to the state years ago.

The main trail continues to climb for 0.2 mile, but now at a more moderate pace. Crossing open granite ledges, enjoy the day's most expansive panorama, including the peaks of Acadia National Park on the southwestern horizon. As the trail levels off, keep your eyes open on the left for an unofficial red-blazed route. It leads 0.2 mile to Tunk Mountain's summit and a small communications building. Consider adding this optional extension. Either way, be sure to follow the blue-blazed trail 0.1 mile straight ahead. It ends at the Northern Overlook, an immense ledge providing expansive views across the blueberry barrens, isolated mountains, and wind turbines of interior Hancock County. Conclude the hike by following the Tunk Mountain Trail 1.8 miles back to the parking area.

99 Petit Manan

RATING/ DIFFICULTY	ROUND-TRIP	ELEV GAIN/ HIGH POINT	SEASON
***/2	5.5 miles	300 feet/ 115 feet	Year-round

Map: USGS Petit Manan Point; **Contact:** Maine Coastal Islands National Wildlife Refuge; **GPS:** 44.439249, -67.893564

The Maine Coastal Islands National Wildlife Refuge includes more than 8000 acres of conservation land. Many of the preserve's properties are offshore islands that are nesting sites for puffins, terns, and razorbill auks, among other seabirds. This excursion consists of two mainland hikes where sandpipers, nuthatches, and eider ducks are the avian species more likely to be encountered.

GETTING THERE
From downtown Milbridge, drive 2.4 miles west on US Route 1 and turn left onto Pigeon Hill Road. Drive 5.7 miles to the wildlife refuge entrance. Continue 0.2 mile straight to the parking area on the right.

ON THE TRAIL
The refuge's 2195-acre Petit Manan Point division offers two easy-to-follow hiking trails that begin at neighboring parking areas. Begin the adventure on the 4-mile-round-trip Birch Point Discovery Trail. Heading north, the wide path transects a large meadow and passes the first of many signs describing the area's natural features. Briefly swing through a birch forest before emerging into a second open field. Return to

Relaxing near Carrying Place Cove (Photo by Maria Fuentes)

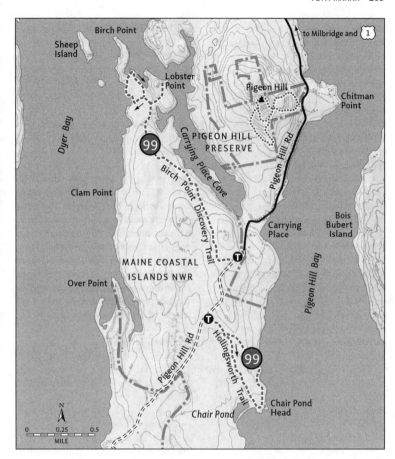

the forest for good and in 0.7 mile, reach a spur that leads a few hundred feet right to a bench and views of a secluded cove.

Beyond the spur, the main trail swings left and rises over a low ridge. Boardwalk and bog bridging lead across a wet landscape shaded in birch and fir. Hike north 0.8 mile to a well-marked junction. Take the trail right. It leads 0.2 mile to scenic Lobster Point. This rocky peninsula provides views of Carrying

Place Cove's placid waters and peaks rising in the distance.

Retrace your steps back to the previous junction and join the path leaving right that leads to Birch Point. In 0.1 mile, the route divides and forms a 0.5-mile loop. Head left to complete the circuit in a clockwise direction. The trail offers scenic views of Dyer Bay, explores a rocky beach, and visits a ledge-lined cove. Listen and look for signs of resident bald eagles. Turn left to return to the main trail, then right. Hike 1.5 miles back to the start.

To reach the second trail, drive 0.4 mile south on the dirt road to a parking area on the right. Pick up the 1.5-mile Hollingsworth Trail on the opposite side of the road. This trail is named in honor of a couple who dedicated much of their lives to support the nation's national wildlife refuges through photography, writing, and advocacy. The path, a fitting tribute to Karen and John Hollingsworth, leads through a field and up a rocky ridge to start. In 0.2 mile, arrive at an intersection where a 1.1-mile loop begins.

Stay right and hike 0.5 mile to the shores of Pigeon Hill Bay. En route, traverse ledges lined with blueberries and cross boardwalks through small cedar swamps. The footing is rough in places but the trail is easy to follow. The views from the shore are spectacular, first enjoyed from the edge of a large crescent-shaped beach. Swinging left, the trail parallels the edge of the water north.

Along the way, stop at rocky beaches and granite promontories where there are ample places to spot wildlife and enjoy cool ocean breezes. The route eventually leads inland to complete the circuit. Stay straight and hike 0.2 mile back to your car.

EXTENDING YOUR HIKE

Visit the nearby Pigeon Hill Preserve. Located a little more than 1 mile to the north of the Birch Point trailhead on Pigeon Hill Road, this 170-acre Downeast Coastal Conservancy preserve features a well-marked network of trails. A less than 1-mile round-trip trek leads to the summit of Pigeon Hill and amazing views of Acadia National Park and countless islands and inlets.

100 Bog Brook Cove

RATING/ DIFFICULTY	ROUND-TRIP	ELEV GAIN/ HIGH POINT	SEASON
***/2–3	4.7 miles	600 feet/ 170 feet	Year-round

Map: USGS Moose River; **Contact:** Maine Coast Heritage Trust; **GPS:** 44.716887, -67.136774

 *This 1770-acre Maine Coast Heritage Trust preserve showcases moderate trails to a diverse collection of natural features including a sandy beach, a boggy pond, rocky knolls, and a bold headland. This described hike includes stops at the preserve's two principal trailheads. Either can be done separately, but together the two form complementary treks for a wonderful day on the Maine coast.*

GETTING THERE

The main parking area is on Route 191 in Trescott Township. From the junction of US Route 1 and Route 191 in East Machias, drive 18.5 miles east on Route 191 to the parking area on the right. To reach the second parking area, continue 1.5 miles northeast on Route 191 and turn right onto Moose River Road, a paved road that turns to gravel. Drive 0.6 mile and continue straight through the intersection. The parking area is in 0.6 mile, at the end of the road.

ON THE TRAIL

Leaving the Route 191 parking lot, the Norse Pond Trail winds over bog bridging and through the young forest. Up and over low ridges, the blue-blazed path leads past small wetlands to a trail junction in 0.6 mile. Stay right and hike 0.2 mile to a scenic bluff that offers expansive views of Norse Pond. Seemingly hidden from civilization, this boggy pond provides ideal habitat for numerous songbirds, including the sleek-flying cedar waxwing.

Continue east along the main trail. It eventually leaves the pond behind and approaches the ocean, which is visible through the trees. Swing north and parallel the coast 0.3 mile to an intersection. Follow the 0.1-mile path that departs right and drops rapidly to the shore. Watch your step; the incline is steep. Once on the shore, cross the mouth of Bog Brook to reach the secluded sand beach. Especially impressive

are the smooth rock formations beneath the steep bluff. High above the beach lies a private residence. Please respect the owner's privacy.

Return to the main trail and turn right. Pass a junction where a path diverges right. Continue left on the Norse Pond Trail. It rises over rocky knolls before completing its loop in 0.5 mile. Stay right to return to the parking area.

Drive to the next trailhead, at the end of Moose River Road. Here, a handicapped-accessible trail leads easily 0.1 mile toward the salt water. Just beyond the start of the Ridge Trail, reach a scenic bluff. On a clear day, enjoy views across the rolling ocean waves to the dramatic cliffs of Grand Manan

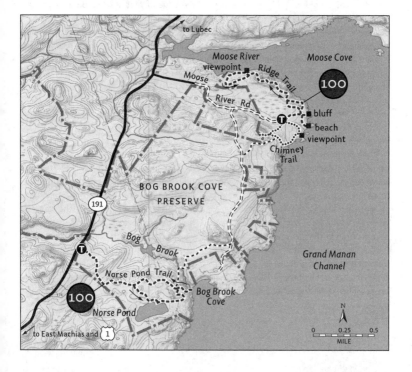

Calm day on the Bold Coast

Island. To the right, a path leads a few hundred feet to the rocky shore. Watch your step while exploring this rugged coastline of cobble beaches and gnarly promontories.

Back at the bluff, pick up the Ridge Trail, a 1.8-mile round-trip journey. The path departs the bluff to the northwest and quickly forms a small loop. Stay right on the more challenging half of the circuit and rise quickly to the top of a small peak that provides stunning views of incredible Bold Coast scenery. This part of Maine is noteworthy for its steep, photogenic shoreline. The path drops down a wooden staircase and the small loop ends. Stay right on the Ridge Trail.

Meander across the rolling landscape. Over rock and around ledges, the path swings through the pleasant coastal forest. It leads 0.5 mile to the start of a second small loop. Stay right and gradually descend. The route soon arrives at a short spur right that leads to the shoreline and intimate views on the edge of Moose Cove. Be alert for bald eagles soaring high above in search of prey as well as shorebirds feeding during low tide.

The loop meanders to the west and follows a small brook before ending. Follow the main route back toward the beginning. Upon reaching the initial loop, stay right and wind more easily around the base of the rocky knoll. Bear right to return to the bluff and the parking area.

EXTENDING YOUR HIKE

If time permits, explore the 0.7-mile Chimney Trail. It begins at the Moose River Road parking area and forms a small loop providing exquisite views of the coast at first before swinging inland to modest viewpoints. For more information on treks in eastern Washington County, contact Cobscook Trails, a partnership that manages dozens of incredible hiking trails throughout the region.

Big Moose Mountain towers above Big Moose Pond (Hike 109).

northern maine

A land of endless forests, bountiful lakes, rushing rivers, and rolling mountains, northern Maine is wilder than any other place in New England. Its hiking crown jewels, 200,000-acre Baxter State Park and the Appalachian Trail corridor, are surrounded by a patchwork of conservation lands that continues to grow each year.

A region that has always been more famous for its booming timber industry, northern Maine offers a great variety of hiking opportunities to those who are patient enough to uncover them. Visit here during the summer and fall, when trails are more accessible, moose are more visible, the weather is more comfortable, and amenities are more available. Be prepared for fewer comforts and conveniences than other places offer, but revel in greater expanses and remoteness.

101 Androscoggin Riverlands State Park

RATING/ DIFFICULTY	LOOP	ELEV GAIN/ HIGH POINT	SEASON
**/2	5.2 miles	350 feet/ 400 feet	Year-round

Map: USGS Lake Auburn East and USGS Turner Center; **Contact:** Maine Bureau of Parks and Lands; **Note:** Part of this route follows multiuse trails open to ATVs and snowmobiles; **GPS:** 44.261163, -70.188055

🚶 🦴 🎿 🏔 🏠 *Maine's newest state park, this 2675-acre densely forested expanse along the shores of the Androscoggin River has been the focus of conservation efforts for the past four decades. Much of the land was farmed years ago, but in 1925 the installation of the Gulf Island Dam forced settlers to abandon their land in search of drier ground. Today, miles of trails afford hikers of all ages wildlife viewing opportunities throughout the year.*

GETTING THERE
From Route 117 in Turner, follow Center Bridge Road east 1.8 miles and then turn right onto the state park's dirt driveway (Center Bridge Road continues 0.3 mile east to a boat launch on the Androscoggin River). Drive 0.1 mile into the large parking area.

ON THE TRAIL
Pick up the Old River Road as it departs south from the parking area. Up a small hill, the wide multiuse route reaches an intersection with the Homestead Trail in 0.1 mile. Turn left onto this much narrower corridor. The 2.3-mile Homestead Trail is open only to hikers. Never straying too far from the banks of the Androscoggin River, the route leads gently across mostly level terrain.

In maturing forest, pass an impressive granite foundation in 0.5 mile. The trees also shade a number of large moss-covered boulders, stone walls, and other remnants left by previous residents. Follow the trail to a secluded cove and the first intimate views of the river. Beyond a junction with the Harrington Path (no sign), emerge into an open meadow and picnic area, 1.3 miles from the start. Follow a spur left to the tip of the peninsula to enjoy expansive views of the wide, slow-moving river.

Remain on the Homestead Trail and continue the trek south 1 additional mile. As you leave the picnic area, a few unofficial trails can be confusing, but the maintained route eventually becomes obvious as it swings around a narrow cove. Head away

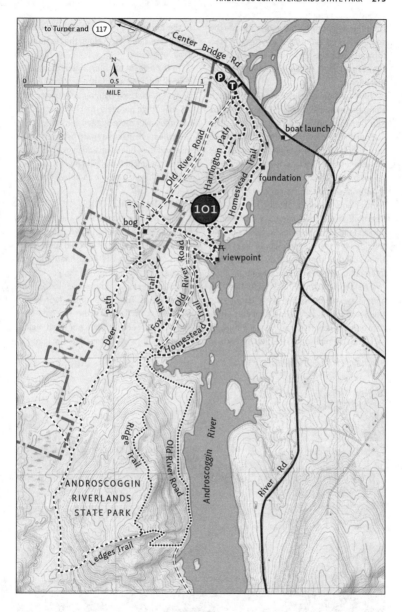

from the water briefly, but soon return to the shore at an excellent spot to scan the area for waterfowl, osprey, and bald eagles. The Homestead Trail ends at a junction with Old River Road.

Turn right and hike less than 0.1 mile north along the multiuse corridor. Pick up the Fox Run Trail (no sign) as it departs left and stays just north of a marshy wetland. This 1.1-mile trail is a bit more challenging to follow than the Homestead Trail as it meanders with fewer blazes through a young forest into an interior section of the park. After staying right at an unmarked intersection with the Deer Path in 0.7 mile, rise up a sandy slope into a stand of white pines. Parallel a bog to the right and then veer right onto a dirt road. Upon reaching the trail's end, swing right to intersect Old River Road once again.

The shortest route back is to turn left and hike a little more than 1 mile back to the trailhead. However, opt for a quieter alternative and follow the road right 0.2 mile. At an intersection of roads, stay left and return to the picnic area on the banks of the river. From here, head north along the Homestead Trail.

In 0.1 mile, at an intersection marked by a small boulder, stay left and join the Harrington Path. Used by mountain bikers, this 1.2-mile route parallels the Homestead Trail but goes over more rugged terrain. Wide at first, the route makes a sharp right turn in 0.3 mile and then heads up and over a low rocky ridge. At a junction with Old River Road, turn right and hike 0.1 mile to complete the trek.

EXTENDING YOUR HIKE

A quiet 2.5-mile extension to the described route begins at the southern intersection of the Homestead Trail and Old River Road. Head south along Old River Road and turn immediately right onto the Ridge Trail. It rises 1 mile to an impressive ledge with limited views. Turn left at the high point and descend 0.3 mile down the steep Ledges Trail. Upon reaching Old River Road, near a viewpoint, turn left to complete the loop.

Androscoggin River from the Homestead Trail

Hikers enjoy views of Maine's Belgrade Lakes region.

102 Kennebec Highlands

RATING/ DIFFICULTY	LOOP	ELEV GAIN/ HIGH POINT	SEASON
**/3	4.5 miles	900 feet/ 1100 feet	Year-round

Map: USGS Belgrade Lakes; **Contact:** Maine Bureau of Parks and Lands; **GPS:** 44.529911, -69.922194

The Kennebec Highlands encompass more than 6000 acres of young forestland assembled thanks to the leadership of the Belgrade Regional Conservation Alliance and the state's Land for Maine's Future Program. This loop is a great introduction to an area that is home to the county's highest peaks, as well as numerous small ponds and wetlands.

GETTING THERE

From the junction of Routes 27 and 225 in Rome, drive 1.1 miles north on Route 27. Turn left onto Watson Pond Road and continue 3.8 miles south. Turn right, near a junction with Prescott Road, into the parking area.

ON THE TRAIL

The Round Top Trail heads west from the parking area and quickly rises up a rocky hillside. Level off atop the low ridge and enjoy a more leisurely stroll. The surrounding mixed forest is prime habitat for scarlet tanagers, rose-breasted grosbeaks, and other colorful avian residents. Watch your footing while descending across a semi-open ledge. The blue-blazed path descends gradually to a five-way intersection and the start of a 2.1-mile loop, nearly 1 mile from the trailhead.

Turn right onto the Round Top Trail's eastern branch as it coincides for 0.8 mile with the multiuse Kennebec Highlands Trail. Following an old woods road, the route is wide and rises gently. Be sure to pay close attention to signs and other markings to avoid turning onto unmaintained side trails.

At an obvious intersection where the Kennebec Highlands Trail continues straight, turn sharply left and remain on the Round

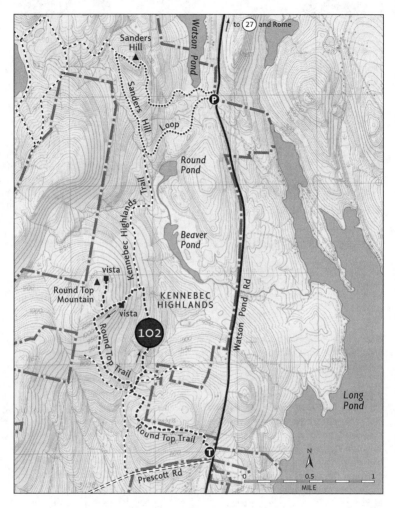

Top Trail. Swinging west, for the next 0.5 mile the route becomes more challenging but also more inviting. Slither around immense lichen-covered boulders, ascend rugged surroundings, and pass through a landscape of lady slippers and other showy wildflowers.

The forest slowly thins as the path leads to an open ledge and small bench. Enjoy the soothing views of the Belgrade Lakes with forested hills and ridges beyond.

The trail rises to a height of land where a spur leads right 0.3 mile. With little elevation change, this short diversion meanders to a pair of northeasterly vistas just below Round Top Mountain's 1133-foot summit. Beyond the spur trail, the main route descends 0.8 mile. Gradual at first, the route drops past a collection of large rocks, then falls more steadily. Hike straight through the intersection with the Kennebec Highlands Trail as the loop ends. Follow the Round Top Trail 0.9 mile back to the start.

EXTENDING YOUR HIKE

The Kennebec Highlands features another family-friendly hiking opportunity 2.5 miles farther north on Watson Pond Road. Here, the 2.9-mile Sanders Hill Loop heads west from the road. It visits wetlands, climbs a wooded but rocky ridge, and provides access to multiuse trails that lead deeper into the highlands.

103 Speckled Mountain

RATING/ DIFFICULTY	LOOP	ELEV GAIN/ HIGH POINT	SEASON
****/3–4	8.6 miles	2500 feet/ 2906 feet	Year-round

Maps: USGS Wild River and USGS Speckled Mountain; **Contact:** White Mountain National Forest; **Note:** Fee; **GPS:** 44.267171, -71.003815

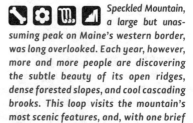 *Speckled Mountain, a large but unassuming peak on Maine's western border, was long overlooked. Each year, however, more and more people are discovering the subtle beauty of its open ridges, dense forested slopes, and cool cascading brooks. This loop visits the mountain's most scenic features, and, with one brief*

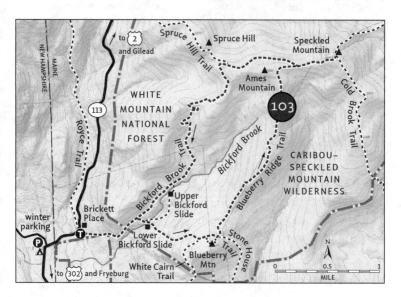

Impressive views from Blueberry Mountain

exception, traverses moderate terrain to make for a great hike any time of year.

GETTING THERE

From the junction of Route 113 and US Route 302 in Fryeburg, drive 18.8 miles north on Route 113 and turn right into the parking area. Alternatively, from the junction of Route 113 and US Route 2 in Gilead, follow Route 113 south 10.5 miles and turn left into the parking area (this route closes in the winter). Winter parking is available on Route 113 near the Cold River Campground entrance, 0.3 mile southwest of the trailhead.

ON THE TRAIL

The Bickford Brook Trail climbs steadily for 0.3 mile and then turns right onto the route fire wardens once used to access the former summit tower. Shrouded by a canopy of large oaks, maples, and yellow birch, the path soon enters the Caribou–Speckled Mountain Wilderness and, 0.7 mile from the start, reaches a trail intersection.

Turn right onto the Blueberry Ridge Trail and descend 0.1 mile to the top of the cascading Lower Bickford Slide. Before the trail crosses the brook, a lightly used path leads left and parallels the water 0.3 mile upstream

to the picturesque Upper Bickford Slide. Continuing on the Blueberry Ridge Trail, walk across the slippery surface of Bickford Brook and immediately begin a demanding 0.7-mile climb. Rock stairs eventually lead to open ledges and the first mountain views of the day. Just beyond a junction with the White Cairn Trail, a 0.3-mile loop leaves right to the top of Blueberry Mountain and an impressive southerly view above an imposing rock face. This optional diversion returns to the main route 0.3 mile ahead, near a junction with the Stone House Trail.

The remaining 2.2-mile hike along the Blueberry Ridge Trail begins as a short descent but quickly becomes a steady, gradual climb that traverses a series of open and semi-open ledges. There are limitless places to hang out, partake of the blueberries in late summer, and marvel at the exceptional views. Most impressive are the scenes of Evans Notch, Kezar Lake, and the Presidential Range towering in the distance. After entering a spruce-fir forest, the trail climbs aggressively before ending at an intersection with the Bickford Brook Trail.

Turn right for the final 0.5-mile climb to the Speckled Mountain summit. Level at first, the path briefly enters an open meadow but soon returns to the thick forest. Wind quickly to the high point and panoramic views in most directions, including north to the Mahoosucs and Maine's western mountains.

The hike down the Bickford Brook Trail is very gradual, offers good footing, and is refreshingly easy on the legs. Once past the upper intersection with the Blueberry Ridge Trail, the path hugs the northern slopes of Ames Mountain. Continue to a junction with the Spruce Hill Trail, 1.3 miles from the summit.

Remain left on the Bickford Brook Trail. The evergreen forest slowly transitions to hardwoods down a series of short switchbacks. Head over a streambed. Here, the path widens and remains so all the way back. Upon returning to the parking area, check out the Brickett Place, a former homestead that is now the site of a wilderness information center.

104 Caribou Mountain

RATING/ DIFFICULTY	LOOP	ELEV GAIN/ HIGH POINT	SEASON
*****/3–4	6.9 miles	2000 feet/ 2850 feet	May–Oct

Map: USGS Speckled Mountain; **Contact:** White Mountain National Forest; **Note:** Fee; **GPS:** 44.335986, -70.975422

From its open summit, Caribou Mountain offers tremendous views in all directions, and throughout the forests that blanket its slopes, cascading brooks and wildlife abound. This loop, though challenging at times, is a great introduction to the White Mountains for hikers of all ages.

GETTING THERE

From the junction of Route 113 and US Route 2 in Gilead, drive 4.7 miles south on Route 113. Turn left and drive 0.1 mile to the parking area. Access to the trailhead is not maintained during the winter.

ON THE TRAIL

The 3.4-mile ascent to the summit heads up the Mud Brook Trail. Enter the forest to the right, near an information kiosk, and enjoy a gradual beginning that affords ample opportunity to loosen up. Approaching the banks of Mud Brook, bear left and parallel its course through a small, secluded valley. The trail briefly rises away from the water and

Hardwood trees shade Mud Brook Trail.

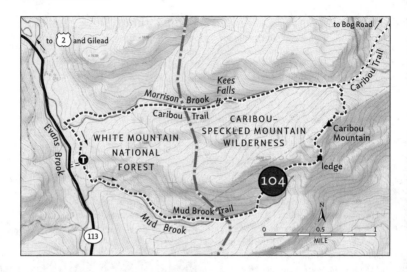

then crosses the brook without much difficulty. Enter the Caribou–Speckled Mountain Wilderness 1.4 miles from the start. Established in 1990, this area includes more than 12,000 acres and nearly 25 percent of the White Mountain National Forest in Maine. Continue 0.5 mile beyond the wilderness boundary and bounce over the rocks of Mud Brook one last time.

The trail rises steadily out of the valley, steeply at first. With every step, the soil becomes rockier. Continue through the increasingly shady forest, now dominated by spruce and fir. Arrive onto an open ledge, 0.5 mile from the summit. Enjoy dramatic views south and east toward Speckled Mountain, Kezar Lake, and the Oxford Hills. The final climb demands added attention as the trail ascends the ledge-covered mountain. Caribou's summit consists of two open peaks; the second one is slightly higher, but both provide splendid 360-degree views. Even on days when hikers are plentiful, there are

more than enough places to find solitude and cherish the surrounding beauty.

The 3.6-mile descent remains on the Mud Brook Trail to start. Follow the yellow blazes down the mountain's wooded northern ridge. Gradual at first, the incline quickly steepens. Past craggy rock formations and gnarly birch trees, a final pitch leads to a junction with the Caribou Trail. To the right, the route rambles 2.5 miles to Bog Road. Today's adventure leads left and soon descends rock steps along the banks of Morrison Brook. The footing becomes a bit rougher as the trail drops more rapidly near the first of many brook and stream crossings. Two crossings of note include one that passes the base of a fairly large cascade on the left and another that occurs near the top of Kees Falls, where Morrison Brook tumbles a few dozen feet to a deep pool below.

Beyond Kees Falls the trail continues for 2 miles. After exiting the wilderness, the path levels off considerably. The relaxing grade and the tranquility of the hemlock-shaded brook make for a soothing end to the day's journey. Before reaching Route 113, turn abruptly left and make one final crossing of Morrison Brook. A short climb and 0.5 mile later, the circuit is complete.

OTHER OPTIONS

With the Route 113 access closed, a great option in the winter is to hike the eastern side of the Caribou Trail. From US Route 2 in West Bethel, Maine, drive 2 miles south on Bog Road. The road is plowed to within a mile of the trailhead. This mostly gradual climb to the summit is 8 miles round-trip in the winter.

Young hikers traverse open summit ledges.

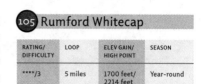

105 Rumford Whitecap

RATING/ DIFFICULTY	LOOP	ELEV GAIN/ HIGH POINT	SEASON
****/3	5 miles	1700 feet/ 2214 feet	Year-round

Map: USGS East Andover; **Contact:** Mahoosuc Land Trust; **Note:** The preserve is surrounded by private land, so please remain on the marked trails; **GPS:** 44.550020, -70.683868

 *This bald summit rises above the Androscoggin and Ellis rivers and*

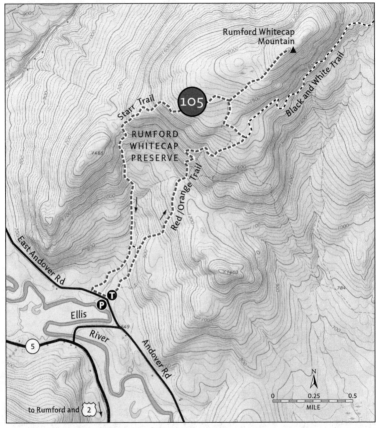

showcases exceptional views of the area's much larger mountains. A great choice for hikers of all ages, Rumford Whitecap is the centerpiece of an expanding 751-acre Mahoosuc Land Trust preserve with forests frequented by colorful warblers and filled with equally vibrant wildflowers.

GETTING THERE

From the junction of Route 5 and US Route 2 in Rumford, follow Route 5 north 3.1 miles and then turn right onto Andover Road. Drive 0.3 mile before turning left onto East Andover Road. A large parking area is located 0.2 mile on the left.

ON THE TRAIL

Follow the Red/Orange Trail as it enters the forest on the other side of the road and initially traverses private land. The well-marked route enters a log yard in 0.1 mile. Hike left through the open area. The wide path reenters the forest and climbs quickly into the Mahoosuc Land Trust's Rumford Whitecap Preserve. Pass a connector trail that departs left. Stay straight and ascend at a moderate grade. As the path narrows, the hike becomes a bit more challenging, but switchbacks and rock steps offer assistance.

The forest slowly transitions from hardwoods to evergreens. At 1.4 miles, rise to an open ledge with two boulders that provide a place to sit and catch your breath. As you continue, still surrounded by trees, views are scarce, but not for long. Through a thinning canopy, reach a junction where the Black and White Trail leaves right and heads a couple miles to the summit of nearby Black Mountain. Stay left, drop into a small depression, and then ascend the increasingly open landscape to another junction, 2 miles from the start.

The yellow-blazed Starr Trail heads left. Use this route for the descent, but first continue straight to the summit of Rumford Whitecap. Across exposed granite throughout, the final 0.5-mile climb to Rumford Whitecap can be tricky if weather conditions are bad; however, the incline is not demanding. Pay close attention to the cairns that mark the way through the abundant blueberry bushes and other low-lying plants. With each step, the scenery becomes more expansive until the path ends atop the mountain's barren high point. Enjoy a picnic lunch and 360 degrees of views that include the Mahoosucs, Tumbledown Mountain, and the Presidential Range.

Retrace your steps back to the 2.1-mile Starr Trail and turn right. The upper half of this route is easy to follow as it traverses additional open areas bordered by a stunted pine forest. There are numerous western viewpoints that entertain, especially one

impressive vista 0.5 mile from the junction. Dropping rapidly down the ledge-covered slope, watch your footing as you reenter the deciduous forest. This 0.4-mile stretch is the loop's most difficult section, especially if the footing is wet or icy.

Leveling off, the trail turns sharply left. After briefly paralleling an overgrown woods road, the path heads straight across it and then rises gently before swinging left. Descend steadily past rocks and through small openings in the young forest. The trail winds down and eventually returns to the now-more-inviting woods road. Follow it right 0.7 mile to the trail's end. Remain on the wide route throughout; it occasionally intersects unmarked logging roads that depart right.

Past the connector to the Red/Orange Trail, emerge into an open field. Continue straight to reach East Andover Road. Turn left and follow the pavement 0.1 mile to the parking area.

106 Little Jackson

RATING/ DIFFICULTY	LOOP	ELEV GAIN/ HIGH POINT	SEASON
*****/4	9.1 miles	3200 feet/ 3470 feet	May–Oct

Map: USGS Roxbury; **Contact:** Maine Bureau of Parks and Lands; **GPS:** 44.729160, -70.532329

Little Jackson Mountain is lower than Big Jackson Mountain, its wooded neighbor to the east, and less popular than Tumbledown Mountain, its diminutive, ledge-covered neighbor to the south. Yet those who make the journey to its summit will revel in spectacular scenic ledges, mesmerizing 360-degree views, and rugged natural beauty.

GETTING THERE

From Weld, follow Route 142 north 2.3 miles and turn left. Drive 0.5 mile, then veer right onto a dirt road (Byron Notch Road). In 2.3 miles, stay right at the intersection. Continue 1.6 miles to the parking area on the left (just beyond the trailhead on the right).

ON THE TRAIL

Find the start of the Brook Trail and Little Jackson Connector on the north side of the road. Join the Little Jackson Connector as it

Departing Little Jackson's high point

diverges right at the trailhead. It leads 1.1 miles over gently rolling terrain to a junction with the Parker Ridge Trail. Turn right and quickly reach a stream. Your feet may get wet, but the crossing is usually straightforward. Follow the path straight and reach the Little Jackson Trail a few hundred feet ahead.

Turn sharply left. A steady climb commences immediately. Rising through the hardwood forest, the trail follows an old woods road 1.5 miles. Two sections have been recently rerouted. These improvements help to lessen the incline. First the path departs left, but after rejoining the old road, it veers sharply right. Wind up the rocky landscape. After rejoining the woods road a third time, continue to a junction.

The Pond Link Trail proceeds straight; turn right for now, remaining on the Little Jackson Trail. Narrowing significantly, the path crosses numerous small streams and then heads up a steep slope through a spruce-fir forest. In 0.8 mile from the junction, emerge atop the day's first open ledge. Enjoy views of Webb Lake and rolling hills to the south.

The final 1-mile stretch weaves across exposed granite ledges surrounded by fewer and fewer trees. Take your time and be sure to follow the cairns and blazes carefully, as they are not always obvious. After passing a 0.7-mile spur that leads right to Big Jackson Mountain, the blue-blazed path swings left. Past a narrow notch, the climb resumes up a knoll. Drop steadily to a small stream and climb steeply up the other side. The hike becomes easier as you approach the barren 3470-foot summit. It is surrounded by peaks, lakes, and forests in all directions. The scenes are breathtaking, and the sense of remoteness will leave you speechless.

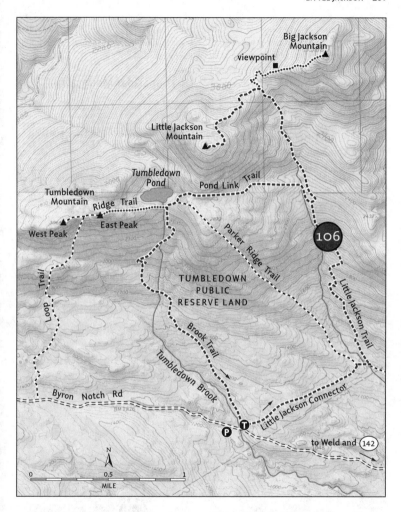

Return to the Pond Link Trail and turn right. This 0.9-mile route rises moderately through a birch forest carpeted in ferns. Beyond the path's halfway point, head across a saddle and then drop quickly to a junction with the Parker Ridge Trail. Turn right and hike 0.1 mile to the shore of scenic Tumbledown Pond. This popular destination is one of Maine's most photogenic.

The circuit's final 1.8-mile segment uses the Brook Trail. Staying left of and parallel-ing Tumbledown Brook, the trail descends ruggedly down rock and ledge. In 0.5 mile swing right, cross the running water, and, soon after, enter a series of switchbacks. The trail eventually coincides with an old woods road. Rocky at first, the tread becomes easier and less steep with each step. Enjoy the relaxing conclusion to a spectacular day within this more than 26,000-acre natural paradise conserved with help from the Tumbledown Conservation Alliance, the state's Land for Maine's Future Program, and the US Forest Service Forest Legacy Program.

EXTENDING YOUR HIKE
There are two opportunities to extend the hike by 1.4 miles. The first is to follow the quiet spur trail to Big Jackson Mountain. The mostly wooded trail passes a scenic ledge near the halfway point. For a more picturesque extension, follow the Ridge Trail west from Tumbledown Pond. This popular option leads to Tumbledown Mountain's wide-open East Peak.

107 Sugarloaf Mountain

RATING/ DIFFICULTY	ROUND-TRIP	ELEV GAIN/ HIGH POINT	SEASON
***/4	6.6 miles	3100 feet/ 4250 feet	May–Oct

Map: USGS Sugarloaf Mountain; **Contact:** Maine Bureau of Parks and Lands; **GPS:** 45.043767, -70.346552

Maine's highest peak outside of Baxter State Park, Sugarloaf Mountain is well known for its world-class ski slopes. Located a mere half mile from the Appalachian Trail, its alpine summit also

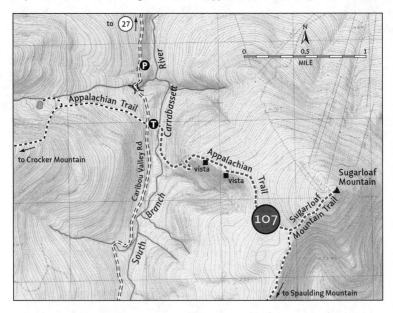

Crocker Mountain views from the Appalachian Trail

features comprehensive 360-degree views from Mount Katahdin to the White Mountains. *This challenging excursion rises beside a dramatic cirque before tunneling through a dense boreal forest alive with Bicknell's thrush and spruce grouse.*

GETTING THERE

From the main entrance to the Sugarloaf ski area, follow Route 27 west. In 1 mile, atop a hill, turn left onto Caribou Valley Road (no sign). Follow this dirt logging road 3.9 miles and park on the left, just before a metal bridge. The road is lightly maintained and, while it is usually accessible for most cars, you will have better chances with a higher-clearance vehicle.

ON THE TRAIL

Continue the journey up the Caribou Valley Road on foot. Across the metal bridge, the wide route rises gently and then levels off. In 0.5 mile, reach an intersection with the Appalachian Trail. The white-blazed long-distance path departs right to Crocker Mountain. Turn left to reach Sugarloaf.

The Appalachian Trail drops 0.1 mile to the banks of the South Branch Carrabassett River. This crossing poses the first significant obstacle along the journey. During high water, it can be dangerous. At the very least, it requires extra care and attention. After rock hopping, walk across a long plank to complete the traverse.

Once safely on the other side, begin a moderate 0.5-mile climb. Paralleling the river upstream at first, the route quickly leads away from the water. Eventually, swing left and climb more aggressively up the increasingly rocky slope. Use caution over the next 0.4 mile as the trail weaves steeply up ledges and over boulders. After passing a few views of Crocker Mountain through the trees, enter a wide-open expanse on the edge of a large cirque. The scenes of the scarred mountain walls nearby as well as distant shots toward Saddleback Mountain are stunning.

The path swings back into the woods and ascends more modestly through a picturesque forest of birch and spruce. Lined with bunchberry and blue-bead lily, this 0.3-mile stretch soon leads to a second perch higher above the rugged cirque. These are the last significant views until the summit.

Enter the evergreen forest and proceed 1 mile to a junction with the Sugarloaf Mountain Trail. While this section of the hike includes minimal elevation gain, it is far from straightforward. Uneven footing and numerous small stream crossings await. Take your time and scan the lush vegetation for snowshoe hare and the latest crop of colorful mushrooms.

At a well-signed intersection where the Appalachian Trail bears sharply right and leads 2.2 miles to the summit of Spaulding Mountain, veer left onto the Sugarloaf Mountain Trail. Climbing steadily, the 0.5-mile path slowly plods its way to the high point. Scenes of faraway mountains appear through the thinning canopy, and soon after, the tops of summit communications towers are in view. The final 0.1 mile heads across an alpine landscape of rock and fragile plants. Beyond the surrounding ski-area infrastructure, there are incredible views in all directions. When you have had your fill, retrace your steps to complete the adventure.

EXTENDING YOUR HIKE

Follow the Appalachian Trail to Spaulding Mountain. This extension adds 4.4 miles to the hike, leads to one of New England's 4000-foot mountains, and provides fine

views from a quiet peak. Another option to consider from this trailhead is to scale the two summits of Crocker Mountain. This peaceful and rigorous out-and-back hike is 7.2 miles round-trip.

108 Bigelow Mountain: Avery Peak

RATING/ DIFFICULTY	ROUND-TRIP	ELEV GAIN/ HIGH POINT	SEASON
*****/4–5	9 miles	3100 feet/ 4088 feet	June–Oct

Maps: USGS The Horns and USGS Little Bigelow Mountain; **Contact:** Maine Bureau of Parks and Lands; **GPS:** 45.165156, -70.236522

Bigelow Mountain's Avery Peak honors the visionary conservationist Myron Avery, who was instrumental in establishing the Appalachian Trail, which extends from Georgia to Maine. This challenging and rugged hike leads to the 4088-foot summit through one of the quieter sections of the 36,000-acre Bigelow Mountain Preserve.

GETTING THERE

From the junction of Long Falls Dam Road and Route 16 in North New Portland, drive 17.3 miles northwest on Long Falls Dam Road and then turn left onto East Flagstaff Road. Follow this dirt road 4.9 miles to the Safford Brook Trail parking area on the right.

ON THE TRAIL

The 2.4-mile Safford Brook Trail enters the forest and swings by the edge of a marshy wetland with views of Bigelow Mountain's imposing ridge. The recently rerouted path

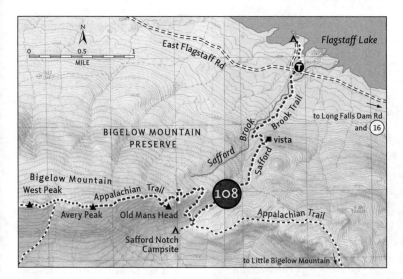

continues to Safford Brook and crosses it over a bridge. Swing right and parallel the bubbling brook up the gradual slope. At a register box, turn sharply left and rise more steadily. Near the blue-blazed path's halfway point, reach an imposing boulder where a spur leads left a few hundred feet to a vista with limited views.

The Safford Brook Trail maintains a modest ascent, occasionally leveling off, before rising into a secluded notch. Across an increasingly rocky landscape, meander up and over small inclines while passing a number of boggy wetlands to the left. As the route narrows, reach an intersection with the Appalachian Trail (AT). Catch your breath and fuel up; the remaining 2-mile climb is far more demanding.

Turn right onto the AT and enter a world of large rocks and hidden caves. Finding the course of least resistance, the path swings up the steep slope, often up rock steps and

sometimes through narrow passageways. Check out the short side trails that lead to vistas, as each offers tremendous views of distant peaks and nearby cliffs. The trail ascends methodically to a sharp right turn. Here a spur departs 0.1 mile left to the top of Old Mans Head, the day's most scenic ledge. For optimum lighting, save this diversion for the hike down and enjoy its breathtaking views north to Baxter State Park.

The final 1-mile climb to the summit of Avery Peak is less steep and more straightforward, but do not take it lightly. Ascend the shrinking ridgeline. As the thick canopy of spruce and fir trees thins and becomes more stunted, the white-blazed trail emerges into the alpine zone. Dominated by gnarly rocks and fragile vegetation, the last stretch offers incredible scenery in all directions. Especially mesmerizing is the view north over Flagstaff Lake. As hard as it is to reach this spot, on a gorgeous day it is often more

In the alpine zone near Avery Peak

109 Big and Little Moose Ponds

RATING/ DIFFICULTY	LOOP	ELEV GAIN/ HIGH POINT	SEASON
***/2–3	4 miles	700 feet/ 1825 feet	May–Oct

Map: USGS Big Squaw Pond; **Contact:** Maine Bureau of Parks and Lands; **GPS:** 45.462303, -69.686302

   *With its abundance of wildlife, northern Maine lures us to explore its vast forests, numerous lakes, and remoteness. Yet for many, especially those new to the area, the region may appear daunting. Adventuring for a half day in the Little Moose Public Reserve will provide even the most unfamiliar with a firsthand introduction and a wonderful snapshot of the flora, fauna, and beauty the region has to offer.*

difficult to leave. When necessary, retrace your steps back to East Flagstaff Road.

EXTENDING YOUR HIKE

There are two worthwhile extensions. The first is to hike 0.7 mile along the AT from Avery Peak to the slightly higher West Peak. While there is not a huge drop between the summits, the route is rocky. On a clear day, West Peak offers views from Mount Washington to Mount Katahdin. A more relaxing option is to follow the Safford Brook Trail 0.3 mile north from the parking area. This path swings gently to a camping area on Flagstaff Lake. A small beach offers a perfect backdrop to recall the day's adventure.

GETTING THERE

From Greenville, drive north on Routes 6 and 15. Cross under the railroad bridge in Greenville Junction and drive 3.6 miles to North Road, a dirt road on the left. Look for a sign indicating Little Moose Public Reserve Land. Follow this road 1.6 miles before turning left onto a narrower unnamed road. The trailhead is 1.1 miles on the left, with parking along the roadside.

ON THE TRAIL

The trail commences under the tall limbs of sugar maple trees. A long slate staircase soon leads into a valley where the trail passes a small wetland. At a junction, a path leaves straight to a campsite. Stay left and 0.4 mile from the start arrive on the rocky shore of Big Moose Pond. Above the water's

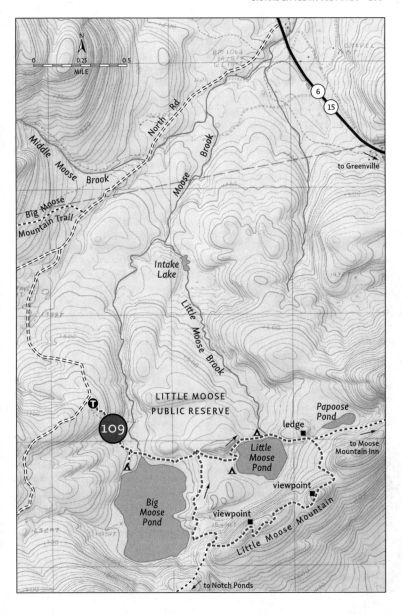

distant shore stand a ridge and many rock ledges, including a scenic destination that lies ahead on the day's journey. Cross over a cement dam at the pond's outlet and enter the woods where a 0.3-mile stroll leads to a trail junction and the start of a loop.

Follow the left branch 0.2 mile to Little Moose Pond. As you approach the shore, the route veers left and hugs the water's edge for 0.3 mile, passing a number of primitive campsites. While uneven, the going is not difficult. After crossing Little Moose Brook, climb out of the basin to the base of a large

Little Moose Pond

ledge. Quickly arrive at an intersection. The route left heads to tiny Papoose Pond and continues 2.4 miles over a wooded summit to Greenville's Moose Mountain Inn.

Continue the loop by turning right. For roughly a mile, the trail traverses a scenic ridge of Little Moose Mountain. Gradual at first, the slope becomes steeper and the terrain rockier. After passing up and over a small knoll, head downhill. At a sharp left turn, follow a spur straight to an open ledge perched high above Little Moose Pond. The ledge offers views toward Mount Kineo, Moosehead Lake, and Big Moose Mountain.

Remaining on the ridge, the trail ascends additional knolls, each with limited views, until it reaches a second spur trail on the right. This path leads a few hundred feet to the hike's finest viewpoint. From its open ledge, countless lakes and mountains are visible in most directions. Especially impressive is the perspective of the amphitheater-shaped valley below. With a little luck, the haunting calls of resident loons will welcome your presence.

Return to the main trail and turn right. Hike 0.1 mile west to a trail junction where a path leads left about 2 miles to the Notch Ponds. Stay right and wind down the main trail, which soon reaches a level surface. Arrive at the southern end of Big Moose Pond in 0.2 mile. The loop concludes in 0.3 mile over gently rolling terrain aided by a series of bog bridges. Bear left to return to your car.

Note: The ponds, streams, and mountains in this area originally used the term "squaw," a derogatory label to describe Native American women. In the early 2000s, the Maine Legislature renamed all squaw place names in the state. Today, these natural features use the term "moose."

View of Barren Mountain from West Peak

110 Borestone Mountain

RATING/ DIFFICULTY	ROUND-TRIP	ELEV GAIN/ HIGH POINT	SEASON
*****/3–4	5.2 miles	1500 feet/ 1981 feet	Year-round

Map: USGS Barren Mountain West; **Contact:** Maine Audubon; **Notes:** Fee for nonmembers, dogs prohibited; **GPS:** 45.377919, -69.430339

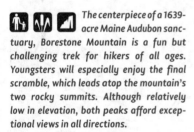 *The centerpiece of a 1639-acre Maine Audubon sanctuary, Borestone Mountain is a fun but challenging trek for hikers of all ages. Youngsters will especially enjoy the final scramble, which leads atop the mountain's two rocky summits. Although relatively low in elevation, both peaks afford exceptional views in all directions.*

GETTING THERE

Follow Route 15 north through Monson. A half mile from the center of town, turn right onto Elliotsville Road. Drive 7.7 miles and then turn left onto Mountain Road immediately after crossing Big Wilson Stream.

Continue 0.7 mile to the parking area on the left.

ON THE TRAIL

Enter Maine Audubon's Borestone Mountain Sanctuary on the opposite side of the road near a large gate. Immediately turn left onto the 0.9-mile Base Trail. Blazed with green triangles, this route wastes little time ascending the steep slope. Aided by numerous rock steps, it slowly winds through a dense evergreen forest that suggests a higher elevation. After the trail levels off, a spur leads right to the Greenwood Overlook. Visit this scenic spot on the descent. For now, proceed straight 0.4 mile to the Access Road. Stay left upon reaching this wider corridor and pass an outhouse on the right. Ahead, reach the visitor center on the picturesque shores of Sunrise Pond. Pay your entrance fee (Maine Audubon members enter for free) and check out the handful of displays.

Before heading to the summits, explore the 0.4-mile Peregrine Trail. This lightly used path lacks signage initially and is occasionally closed to accommodate guests staying at the sanctuary's lodges. It enters

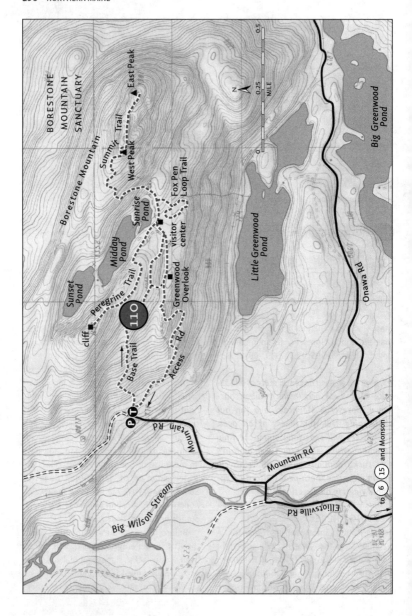

the forest across from the visitor center and stays close to Sunrise Pond's western shore. At a sign, the red-blazed route swings left and moderately rises to the top of a steep cliff. Watch your step near the edge; the views east over Midday Pond toward Borestone Mountain are amazing.

Back at the visitor center, join the 1-mile Summit Trail as it swings south of Sunrise Pond. A small bridge quickly leads over the pond's outlet. The path then climbs slowly over very rocky terrain. Soon, the incline steepens and numerous rock steps lead up the ledge-covered, root-filled trail. Take your time and watch your footing. The final pitch to West Peak's open summit is tricky in spots, but iron rungs have been installed to assist. Once atop the pointy pinnacle, marvel at the incredible panorama north across Onawa Lake to the rugged slopes of Barren Mountain.

To reach East Peak, the highest point on the ridge, follow the green-blazed Summit Trail 0.3 mile farther. A short drop is followed by a gradual climb. Less pointy, East Peak is more open and provides a larger area to hang out. The views are equally stunning from both summits.

Retrace your steps down the Summit Trail and use caution descending West Peak, especially if it is wet or icy. Before reaching the visitor center, take a slight detour onto the 0.4-mile Fox Pen Loop Trail. This short diversion crosses a small wetland before looping past a modest viewpoint and imposing ledge.

From the visitor center, rejoin the Access Road. Take advantage of this wide and easy-to-follow route for the descent. It leads 1.2 miles back to the parking area. Just before the halfway point, turn left onto the spur leading to the Greenwood Overlook for one last dose of scenery.

111 Chairback Mountain

RATING/ DIFFICULTY	LOOP	ELEV GAIN/ HIGH POINT	SEASON
***/4	11.2 miles	2800 feet/ 2320 feet	May–Nov

Map: USGS Barren Mountain East; **Contact:** Appalachian Mountain Club; **Note:** Fee charged to access road managed by North Maine Woods, Inc., www.northmainewoods .org; **GPS:** 45.467892, -69.310238

This all-day loop in the southern half of the Appalachian Mountain Club's 37,000-acre Katahdin Iron Works property combines newly developed trails with 7 miles of prime Appalachian Trail scenery in the

Monument Cliff

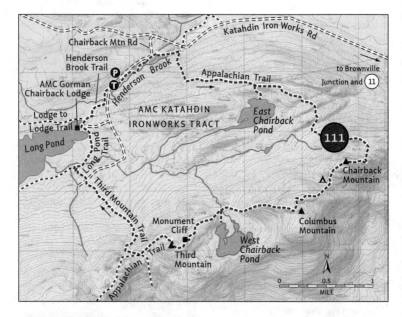

heart of Maine's 100-Mile Wilderness. Add this to your syllabus of upcoming hikes to experience a classic northern Maine adventure featuring cascading brooks, hidden ponds, and precipitous ledges.

GETTING THERE

From Brownville Junction, follow Route 11 north. After crossing the Pleasant River, drive 4.7 miles and turn left onto Katahdin Iron Works Road (KI Road). Continue 6.4 miles to the gatehouse and pay your entrance fee. Rejoin KI Road and head north toward Little Lyford Pond. Drive 7.2 miles and turn left onto Chairback Mountain Road. Proceed 0.8 mile to a parking area on the left.

ON THE TRAIL

Walk to the Henderson Brook trailhead a few hundred feet farther up Chairback Mountain

Road. Turn left and follow this newly developed trail 1 mile. It quickly descends into a narrow, deep valley and crosses the cascading Henderson Brook three times before ending at a junction with the Appalachian Trail (AT). This is the lowest point of the hike. Catch your breath: the toughest climb soon follows.

Bear right onto the white-blazed path. The AT rises aggressively under a canopy of hardwood trees. In 0.5 mile, the route bends left and begins to moderate significantly. Wind through the evergreen forest 0.7 mile to a wooded peak, where a 0.2-mile spur leads right. The spur descends steeply to the banks of East Chairback Pond. While it would be preferable to not lose so much elevation, the beautiful pond is well worth exploring.

The AT continues 1.7 miles southeast along a narrow ridge. There are numerous ups and downs before the route emerges atop an open landscape with scenic views of Whitecap Mountain to the north. Meander in and out of the thinning forest. The summit of Chairback Mountain, only 0.5 mile away, is accessed via a steep boulder-filled slope. Turn sharply right and follow the trail as it hugs the edge of an impressive ledge en route to the high point. The scenery is rugged, remote, and spectacular.

The next 2.2 miles south along the AT are short on dramatic natural features but long on solitude. Descend 0.6 mile into a saddle and shortly thereafter rise past a lean-to. Continue 0.7 mile toward the wooded summit of Columbus Mountain. Turn sharply right just west of the high point and begin a modest 0.9-mile descent. After crossing over a stream, find a side trail leading 0.2 mile left to West Chairback Pond. A much more level path than the one leading to its eastern counterpart arrives at a serene shoreline and an ideal napping place.

Marching west, the AT begins one last major ascent. Slither up the increasingly rocky footpath. In 0.6 mile, arrive atop Third Mountain's Monument Cliff. The scenery north to Long Pond and the mountains surrounding Moosehead Lake are awe-inspiring. Savor the moment before returning to the journey.

Dropping steadily over rock and past ledges, the well-trodden route arrives at a four-way intersection in 0.8 mile. Turn right onto the 1.4-mile Third Mountain Trail. This straightforward descent becomes easier with each step. Parallel a small stream before arriving at a trailhead along Chairback Mountain Road. Continue straight onto a much wider corridor and descend 0.2 mile.

Turn right onto the Long Pond Trail. Popular with cross-country skiers, it leads easily 0.5 mile to a dirt road. Follow this road left and drop 0.1 mile to AMC's Gorman Chairback Lodge. Available for overnight use, this traditional Maine sporting camp is a great base for exploring the area. Stay right at the lodge and follow the road as it wraps around a building. At a junction where the Lodge to Lodge Trail leaves left toward Little Lyford Pond, stay right on the Henderson Brook Trail. This wide path heads 0.3 mile back to Chairback Mountain Road. Bear left on the road; the parking area is 0.3 mile away.

ALTERNATING YOUR HIKE

Consider staying at the Gorman Chairback Lodge to begin and end the hike from your accommodation. A good shorter day-hike alternative is to park at the Third Mountain trailhead. Combine this path and the AT for a 4-mile round-trip trek to Monument Cliff.

112 Niagara Falls

RATING/ DIFFICULTY	ROUND-TRIP	ELEV GAIN/ HIGH POINT	SEASON
**/2	2.8 miles	200 feet/ 1090 feet	May–Oct

Map: USGS Doubletop Mountain; **Contact:** Baxter State Park; **Note:** Fee for non-Maine residents; **GPS:** 45.883581, -69.032689

Daicey Pond Campground is the perfect Baxter State Park trailhead when the weather is less than ideal, to recover after a more rigorous adventure, or to use as an early morning journey before heading back to civilization. This mostly level route to scenic waterfalls also features mountain views. If time permits, extend your hike by traveling around the ponds to the east and the prime moose habitat that abounds.

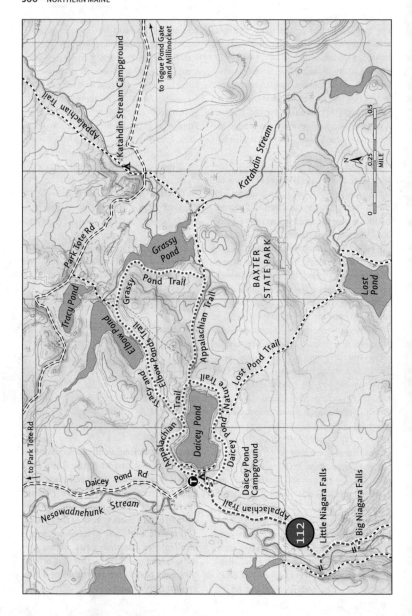

GETTING THERE

From Route 11 in downtown Millinocket, follow the roads (well signed) that lead 17 miles north to Baxter State Park's southern entrance at Togue Pond Gate. Once in the park, follow Park Tote Road 9.8 miles west. Turn left onto Daicey Pond Road. In 1.4 miles, reach the Appalachian Trail parking area.

ON THE TRAIL

Head south along the Appalachian Trail. Rise 0.1 mile to an intersection and stay right on the main corridor. Across mostly level terrain, the path parallels the slow-moving Nesowadnehunk Stream. The easy-to-follow route allows optimum exploration for signs of bird and animal life. In addition, scan the forest floor for colorful wildflowers and mushrooms.

In 0.8 mile, the route reaches two spurs that diverge right. The first leads to the edge of the stream, just below an old dam used during a past timber-harvesting era. Above the dam, there are picturesque scenes of Mount OJI, a peak with slides that once resembled those three letters. Keep your eyes open for spotted sandpipers. They often bob up and down while searching for food in the bubbling stream.

The second spur diverges right a few dozen feet beyond the first. This path leads to the edge of Little Niagara Falls, an impressive cascade. The open ledges here provide a wonderful location to hang out, enjoy lunch, and soak in the sun's warm rays.

Rejoin the trek south along the Appalachian Trail. The path becomes a bit rougher over the next 0.3 mile as it descends moderately through the darker forest. Reach a side trail and turn right. It leads 0.1 mile back to the alluring stream. This time find yourself at the edge of Big Niagara Falls, a series of cascades that wind through the smooth granite ledges, forming pools, chutes, and falls. The soothing roar of the tumbling water is the perfect backdrop to lose yourself in this incredible wilderness area. Retrace your steps to return to the trailhead.

EXTENDING YOUR HIKE

Consider adding a loop around Daicey Pond or even a second loop to Grassy and Elbow ponds. This area is often frequented by moose. The well-marked trails lead to serene forested oases and quiet pond-side vistas. The Daicey Pond Nature Trail is

Big Niagara Falls

nearly 1.5 miles. Continuing onto the second loop adds an additional 2 miles. The view east across Daicey Pond provides one of the finest views of Mount Katahdin.

113 Brothers and Coe

RATING/ DIFFICULTY	LOOP	ELEV GAIN/ HIGH POINT	SEASON
****/5	10.9 miles	4000 feet/ 4143 feet	May–Oct

Maps: USGS Doubletop Mountain and USGS Mount Katahdin; **Contact:** Baxter State Park; **Note:** Fee for non-Maine residents; **GPS:** 45.939251, -69.041376

This loop over Baxter State Park's second-highest ridge travels through quiet mountain forests and up slide-scarred slopes to reach barren summits with 360-degree views of boundless lakes and peaks across northern Maine. While the route is challenging, venture here for its alluring solitude and remoteness, traits often overlooked by the many park visitors choosing nearby Mount Katahdin.

GETTING THERE
From Route 11 in downtown Millinocket, follow the roads (well signed) that lead 17 miles north to Baxter State Park's southern entrance at Togue Pond Gate. Once in the park, follow Park Tote Road left 13.2 miles to the parking area on the right.

ON THE TRAIL
Start on the Marston Trail, which begins over flat terrain through a beautiful grove of mature maple trees. At 0.2 mile, the route swings right and begins a steady climb near a tumbling mountain stream. The climb moderates as the trail crosses a few small brooks. At 1.3 miles, turn right onto the Mount Coe Trail.

Leading 1.9 miles to the summit of Mount Coe, the trail quickly emerges onto the base of a seemingly endless slide. Following the slide, the trail methodically climbs loose rocks and gravel, surrounded by ever-expanding beauty. As the valley narrows, stay close to the small brook. After crossing it a few times, the trail begins to climb more aggressively. Swing left and rise steeply straight past a junction with the OJI Link Trail.

Carefully follow the blue blazes, which eventually lead to the left side of the slide. The trail is extremely challenging and very exposed (use extra caution if it's wet or icy), but the views are incredible. At the top of the slide, reenter the woods and continue the aggressive climb 0.2 mile to the open summit. Perched high above the impenetrable boggy area known as the Klondike, Mount Coe provides mesmerizing shots of Mount Katahdin.

Descend the very narrow ridgeline north over small open knobs before dropping into the balsam-scented forest. Through the quiet surroundings, follow the trail as it winds down, around, and eventually up to a signed junction 1.2 miles from Mount Coe. To the right, follow the 0.3-mile spur to the 3930-foot summit of South Brother and exceptional views in all directions. Watch your step along the way; the path leads over and around a series of large boulders and ledges.

Return to the Mount Coe Trail and turn right. Descend gradually 0.7 mile into a flat saddle to an intersection with the Marston Trail. Before returning to the parking area, stay straight and head toward North

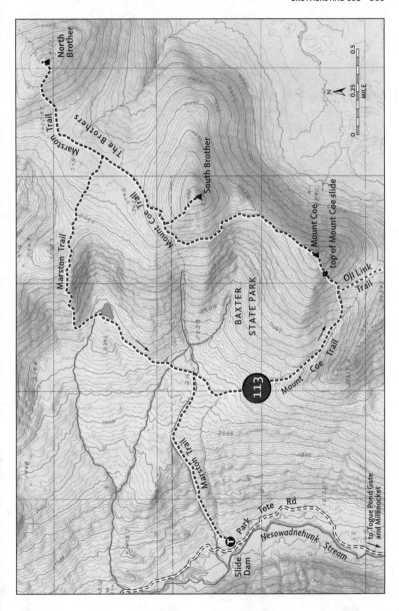

North Brother

Marston Trail

The Brothers

South Brother

Mount Coe Trail

Marston Trail

Mount Coe

top of Mount Coe slide

Oji Link Trail

BAXTER STATE PARK

113

Mount Coe Trail

Marston Trail

Park Tote Rd

Nesowadnehunk Stream

to Togue Pond Gate and Millinocket

Slide Dam

T

N

0   0.25   0.5

MILE

Views abound from North Brother.

Brother's barren summit. The 0.8-mile journey crosses a number of wet areas but soon climbs steadily up drier, rockier terrain. The last stretch leads across a treeless alpine zone where fragile flowering plants are on display throughout the summer. A wooden sign marks the rocky 4143-foot summit, an optimal location to view much of Baxter State Park as well as lakes and forests as far as the eyes can see.

Return to the upper junction with the Mount Coe Trail. Turn right and follow the Marston Trail 1.6 miles to a small pond tucked away in a large cirque nestled in the side of the mountain. The route there begins gradually but eventually switchbacks down a steep slope with occasional views. As the trail levels off, turn left and cross a small stream. Ascend quickly to the pond's shore and rest your legs. From here, enjoy a more relaxing 0.8-mile stroll, returning to the lower Mount Coe Trail junction. Stay right to reach the trailhead in 1.3 miles.

114 Traveler Mountain

RATING/ DIFFICULTY	LOOP	ELEV GAIN/ HIGH POINT	SEASON
*****/5	10.9 miles	4050 feet/ 3541 feet	May–Oct

Map: USGS The Traveler; **Contact:** Baxter State Park; **Note:** Fee for non-Maine residents; **GPS:** 46.108879, -68.900816

Dominating the skyline in the northern half of Baxter State Park, Traveler Mountain is the state's highest volcanic peak. Heading up steep slopes and across exposed rocky terrain, this very strenuous loop is not for the ill prepared, nor is it recommended during inclement weather. However, those who can complete this circuit under blue skies will enjoy scenery as raw and spectacular as any other locale in New England.

GETTING THERE

From the junction of Routes 159 and 11 in Patten, follow Route 159 west. Drive 26 miles (in 11.5 miles Route 159 ends, but stay straight on the paved road) to Baxter State Park's northern entrance at Matagamon Gate. Once in the park, follow Park Tote Road 6.9 miles west and then turn left. Continue 2.1 miles to the South Branch Pond Campground. Day-use parking is on the left before the ranger station.

ON THE TRAIL

It is wise to get an early start when tackling this challenging loop. Based on the terrain, the best option is to hike in a counterclockwise direction. Find the start of the Pogy Notch Trail at the campground's eastern

end. The North Traveler Trail quickly departs left; this route will be used on the descent. Enjoy the easy start. The Pogy Notch Trail parallels the scenic shore of Lower South Branch Pond and reaches the Howe Brook Trail in 0.9 mile. Cross Howe Brook's rocky streambed. A brief climb leads to views of Upper South Branch Pond and the beginning of the Center Ridge Trail.

Turn left as the hike initiates a grueling 2.3-mile ascent to the 3254-foot Peak of the Ridges summit. Rising more than 2000 feet, the route is very steep and incredibly rocky. Climb up the forested slopes 0.5 mile to the first of many promontories. The views of the two ponds below are stunning. Return to the forest before emerging onto an immense talus slope. Plod your way through thinning

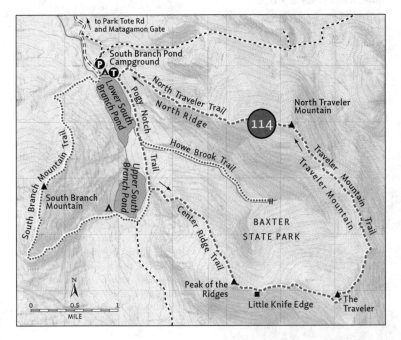

vegetation to the Peak of the Ridges' narrow summit and marvel at the spectacular views south to Mount Katahdin. If the weather is questionable, the day is getting late, your water supply is low, or you just do not feel right, turn back here.

The loop continues east and for 4.5 miles traverses remote and rugged terrain. In 0.1 mile, the rocky trail leads up and across Little Knife Edge. Watch your footing on this scenic knoll and carefully make your way to less precarious surroundings.

Still more than 1 mile from the summit of Traveler Mountain, descend into a saddle and then briefly enter the boreal forest. After emerging onto and then crossing a massive scree slope, reenter the forest one last time.

Hikers navigate Little Knife Edge.

Back into the open, the trail winds up loose rocks to the barren 3541-foot summit. The 360-degree views as far as the eyes can see and sense of isolation are amazing.

While this is not yet the loop's halfway point, the most difficult sections are behind you. Do not relax; it is still 3 miles to North Traveler. Descending to the northeast, the lightly traveled route can be a bit difficult to follow at first. Take your time, follow the series of cairns used to mark the trail, and enjoy the scenery. Back in the forest, the corridor becomes more obvious. The moss-bordered path winds through the welcoming shade of dense evergreens. A little more than a mile along the ridge, ascend a series of open peaks. Drop off the final one into a picturesque birch forest. It is time to begin the day's last climb.

Ledges and loose rocks lead to the 3152-foot summit of North Traveler. The most easily accessible of the Traveler peaks, it provides a great perspective of the day's journey. Follow the popular North Traveler Trail 2.8 miles west back to the trailhead. Over the first 2 miles the route drops steadily. It remains mostly in the open and features seemingly endless vistas. The final stretch to the Lower South Branch Pond's blue waters below is steep and occasionally traverses loose rocks. Enjoy one last view north to Mount Katahdin before carefully returning to the quiet campground below—the perfect spot to spend the night after a fabulous day in Baxter State Park.

SHORTENING YOUR HIKE

Exploring the Howe Brook Trail is a good poor-weather alternative. It rises past cascades to a secluded waterfall 2.9 miles from South Branch Pond Campground. For a less demanding mountain climb, complete the 5.6-mile round-trip hike to the summit of North Traveler or consider the nearby 6.8-mile loop over South Branch Mountain. Each of these three hikes begins at the same trailhead.

115 Mount Katahdin

RATING/ DIFFICULTY	LOOP	ELEV GAIN/ HIGH POINT	SEASON
*****/5	11.7 miles	4500 feet/ 5268 feet	Late May– Oct

Map: USGS Mount Katahdin; **Contact:** Baxter State Park; **Notes:** Fee for non-Maine residents, Togue Pond Gate opens at 5:00 AM; **GPS:** 45.919136, -68.857443

Rising high above the flat valleys and lesser peaks surrounding it, Mount Katahdin's headwalls and deep ravines are like no other in New England. Its rugged beauty has lured visitors—experienced Appalachian Trail hikers and novices alike—for centuries. Many of these visitors have underestimated the physical and natural challenges the mountain presents. Approach Katahdin prepared for whatever the mountain has in store to successfully complete this incredible journey. A trek to the top of Maine is an experience you will remember for a lifetime.

GETTING THERE
From Route 11 in downtown Millinocket, follow the roads (well signed) that lead 17 miles north to Baxter State Park's southern entrance at Togue Pond Gate. Once in the park, follow Roaring Brook Road right and drive 8.1 miles to Roaring Brook Campground. Securing a parking space can be difficult. There are two ways to reserve a spot: stay in the campground overnight, or reserve one of a limited number of parking spaces in advance for a small fee. The remaining day-use spaces are filled on a first-come, first-served basis.

ON THE TRAIL
Of Katahdin's three trailheads, the one at Roaring Brook is the most popular, but this circuit will also venture to one of the mountain's less-traveled locations. After registering at the ranger station, where weather updates and other useful information are available, head up the well-used Chimney Pond Trail, a 3-mile route that divides into three relatively equal sections.

The first third of the hike, while rocky, climbs modestly, making it a nice way to loosen the legs. After crossing a long wooden bridge over a small brook, turn left and begin a steadier ascent up rougher terrain. As the incline eases, reach a spur right to a scenic view of the mountain. Ahead, a second spur ends at the shore of Lower Basin Pond, where a more stunning vista, and perhaps a moose, can be found. The final stretch is challenging at first but moderates significantly as it approaches Chimney Pond and awe-inspiring views of Katahdin's most rugged slopes.

Before pushing ahead, register at the Chimney Pond Ranger Station. If the weather is uncooperative, the park may close high-elevation trails. With a good forecast, join the 1.8-mile Cathedral Trail. It and the slightly less challenging Saddle Trail depart near the ranger station. The two quickly divide. Stay left on the Cathedral Trail. Proceed 0.4 mile to the base of a large boulder field and start of the alpine zone. Here the real adventure begins.

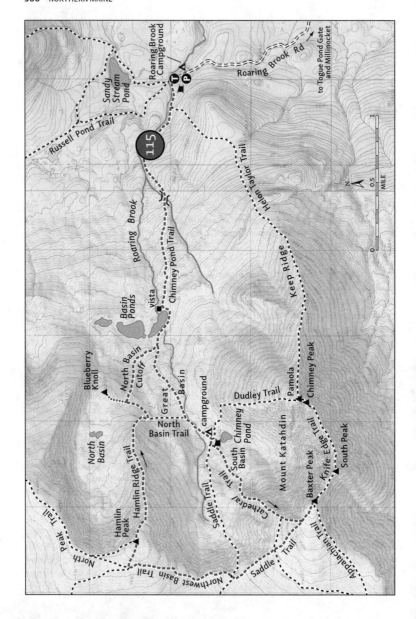

Roaring Brook Campground

Roaring Brook Rd

to Togue Pond Gate and Millinocket

Roaring

Sandy Stream Pond

Russell Pond Trail

115

Roaring Brook

Helon Taylor Trail

Chimney Pond Trail

vista

Keep Ridge

Basin Ponds

Blueberry Knoll

North Basin Cutoff

Great Basin

North Basin

North Basin Trail

campground

Dudley Trail

Pamola

Chimney Peak

Hamlin Ridge Trail

Hamlin Peak

North Peak

Saddle Trail

South Basin Trail

Chimney Pond

Cathedral Trail

Mount Katahdin

Baxter Peak

Knife Edge Trail

South Peak

Northwest Basin Trail

Saddle Trail

Appalachian Trail

N

0   0.5   1

MILE

Cathedral Trail panorama

Rising at an intimidating angle, the rigorous trail is incredibly demanding. Take your time and use caution not to dislodge any rocks onto fellow hikers below. Fortunately, the Cathedral Trail is as beautiful as it is challenging. Ascend up and over three separate pinnacles reminiscent of large houses of worship. Each step leads to more expansive views. Beyond the third cathedral, the terrain becomes slightly easier. Stay left where a cutoff trail departs right, and ascend one last pitch to the Saddle Trail. Turn left and, in 0.2 mile, reach the top of Maine. Few places in New England rival its beauty.

Not surprisingly, Katahdin's 5268-foot Baxter Peak is a popular destination. Snap your photos and enjoy the scenery. Now it is time to leave the dozens of fellow hikers behind and find solitude. Head northwest along the Saddle Trail. It descends straightforwardly for 1.1 miles. If the weather is pleasant, the biggest danger is slipping on loose rock, because it is too hard to take your eyes off the distant landscapes.

Near the ridge's low point, the Saddle Trail swings right toward Chimney Pond (an easier end to the day if the weather is bad or the legs are too tired). Stay straight and join the Northwest Basin Trail. Immediately notice the narrower path and thicker alpine vegetation. Rising steadily 0.9 mile, this lightly used trail heads up the western side of Katahdin's Hamlin Peak to a four-way intersection. The routes straight and left lead deep into the heart of the park's wilderness area. Turn sharply right and hike 0.2 mile to reach Maine's second-highest summit. From this stunning perspective, the distant crowds on Baxter Peak are now a faded memory as you stand atop 4756-foot Hamlin Peak.

Remain on the Hamlin Ridge Trail. It descends steeply 1.5 miles down a narrowing spine dividing the mountain's North and South basins. Difficult in places, the scenic trail can be safely navigated with a bit of caution. While traversing the less rugged sections, be sure to enjoy the panorama east to Katahdin Lake. After the final vista, the trail drops rapidly into the shady forest.

At a junction with the North Basin Trail, turn left. The level terrain is a welcome sight for sore legs. In 0.2 mile, swing right onto the 0.7-mile North Basin Cutoff. If you have not had enough, follow the North Basin Trail straight 0.2 mile to Blueberry Knoll's secluded vista. The North Basin Cutoff is rocky in places, but not difficult. Upon reaching the Chimney Pond Trail, turn left and hike 2.1 miles back to Roaring Brook Campground. It will seem longer on the descent, but cherishing your day on Katahdin will ease the pain.

Appendix I:
Contact Information

Acadia National Park
PO Box 177
Bar Harbor, ME 04609
(207) 288-3338
www.nps.gov/acad/index.htm

Appalachian Mountain Club
5 Joy Street
Boston, MA 02108
(207) 899-0150
www.outdoors.org

Appalachian National Scenic Trail
PO Box 50
Harpers Ferry, WV 25425
www.nps.gov/appa/index.htm

Audubon Society of Rhode Island
12 Sanderson Road
Smithfield, RI 02917
(401) 949-5454
www.asri.org/index.php

Baxter State Park
64 Balsam Drive
Millinocket, ME 04462
(207) 723-5140
http://baxterstateparkauthority.com

Belknap Range Conservation Coalition
PO Box 151
Gilmanton, NH 03837
http://belknaprange.org

Cape Cod National Seashore
99 Marconi Site Road
Wellfleet, MA 02667
(508) 771-2144
www.nps.gov/caco/index.htm

Cobscook Trails
www.cobscooktrails.org

Connecticut Department of Energy and Environmental Protection
79 Elm Street
Hartford, CT 06106
(860) 424-3000
www.ct.gov/deep/site/default.asp

Dartmouth Outing Club
Dartmouth College
c/o Gift Recording Office
6066 Development Office
Hanover, NH 03755
http://outdoors.dartmouth.edu/doc

Downeast Coastal Conservancy
PO Box 760
Machias, ME 04654
(207) 255-4500
www.downeastcoastalconservancy.org

Equinox Preservation Trust
PO Box 986
Manchester, VT 05254
(802) 366-1400
http://equinoxpreservationtrust.org

Green Mountain National Forest
Supervisor's Office
231 North Main Street
Rutland, VT 05701
(802) 747-6700
www.fs.usda.gov/greenmountain

Lakes Region Conservation Trust
PO Box 766
Center Harbor, NH 03226
(603) 253-3301
http://lrct.org

Mahoosuc Land Trust
18 Mayville Road
PO Box 981
Bethel, ME 04217
(207) 824-3806
www.mahoosuc.org/index.html

Maine Audubon
20 Gilsland Farm Road
Falmouth, ME 04105
(207) 781-2330
http://maineaudubon.org

Maine Bureau of Parks and Lands
Department of Agriculture, Conservation,
   and Forestry
22 State House Station
18 Elkins Lane
Augusta, ME 04333
(207) 287-3821
www.maine.gov/dacf/parks/index.shtml

Maine Coast Heritage Trust
1 Bowdoin Mill Island, Suite 201
Topsham, ME 04086
(207) 729-7366
www.mcht.org

**Maine Coastal Islands National
   Wildlife Refuge**
PO Box 1735
9 Water Street
Rockland, ME 04841
(207) 594-0600
www.fws.gov/refuge/maine_coastal
   _islands

**Marsh-Billings-Rockefeller National
   Historical Park**
54 Elm Street
Woodstock, VT 05091
(802) 457-3368
www.nps.gov/mabi

**Massachusetts Department of
   Conservation and Recreation**
251 Causeway Street, Suite 900
Boston, MA 02114
(617) 626-1250
www.mass.gov/eea/agencies/dcr/

Meriden Land Trust
PO Box 1745
Meriden, CT 06450
http://meridenlandtrust.com

Missisquoi National Wildlife Refuge
29 Tabor Road
Swanton, VT 05488
(802) 868-4781
www.fws.gov/refuge/missisquoi

**Mount Agamenticus Conservation
   Program**
186 York Street
York, ME 03909
(207) 361-1102
http://agamenticus.org

The Nature Conservancy
New Hampshire Chapter
22 Bridge Street, 4th Floor
Concord, NH 03301
(603) 224-5853
www.nature.org

Rhode Island Chapter
159 Waterman Street
Providence, RI 02906
(401) 331-7110
www.nature.org

Vermont Chapter
21 State Street, Suite 4
Montpelier, VT 05602
(802) 229-4425
www.nature.org

New Hampshire Audubon
Statewide Headquarters, McLane Center
84 Silk Farm Road
Concord, NH 03301
(603) 224-9909
www.nhaudubon.org

**New Hampshire Division of Forest
   and Lands**
PO Box 1856
Concord, NH 03301
(603) 271-2214
www.nhdfl.org

**New Hampshire Division of Parks
   and Recreation**
172 Pembroke Road
PO Box 1856
Concord, NH 03302
(603) 271-3556
www.nhstateparks.org

**Rhode Island Department of
   Environmental Management**
235 Promenade Street
Providence, RI 02908
(401) 222-6800
www.dem.ri.gov/index.htm

Rhode Island National Wildlife Refuge
1040 Matunuck Schoolhouse Road
South Kingstown, RI 02879
(401) 364-9124
www.fws.gov/refuge/Trustom_Pond

Sandy Neck Beach Park
Marine and Environmental Affairs
1189 Phinneys Lane
Centerville, MA 02632
(508) 362-8300
www.town.barnstable.ma.us
    /sandyneckpark

Tiverton Land Trust
PO Box 167
Tiverton, RI 02878
(401) 625-1300
www.tivertonlandtrust.org

The Trustees of Reservations
572 Essex Street
Beverly, MA 01915
(978) 921-1944
www.thetrustees.org

University of Massachusetts, Amherst
Department of Environmental
    Conservation
Room 225
160 Holdsworth Way
Amherst, MA 01003
(413) 545-2665
http://eco.umass.edu/facilities/our-
    forest-properties/mt-toby

Vermont Department of Forests, Parks, and Recreation
1 National Life Drive, Davis 2
Montpelier, VT 05620
(888) 409-7579
www.vtfpr.org

Vermont Fish and Wildlife Department
1 National Life Drive, Davis 2
Montpelier, VT 05620
(802) 828-1000
www.vtfishandwildlife.com

Wells National Estuarine Research Reserve
342 Laudholm Farm Road
Wells, ME 04090
(207) 646-1555
www.wellsreserve.org

White Mountain National Forest
71 White Mountain Drive
Campton, NH 03223
(603) 536-6100
www.fs.usda.gov/whitemountain

Williamstown Rural Lands Foundation
671 Cold Spring Road
Williamstown, MA 01267
(413) 458-2494
www.wrlf.org

Appendix II: Conservation and Trail Organizations

Appalachian Mountain Club
    5 Joy Street
    Boston, MA 02108
    (617) 523-0636
    www.outdoors.org

Appalachian Trail Conservancy
    PO Box 807
    Harpers Ferry, WV 25425
    (304) 535-6331
    www.appalachiantrail.org

Audubon Society of Rhode Island
    12 Sanderson Road
    Smithfield, RI 02917
    www.asri.org/index.php

Connecticut Recreation and Parks Association
    1800 Silas Deane Highway, Suite 172
    Rocky Hill, CT 06067
    (860) 721-0384
    www.crpa.com

Friends of Acadia
    43 Cottage Street
    PO Box 45
    Bar Harbor, ME 04609
    (800) 625-0321
    www.friendsofacadia.org

Friends of the Wapack
    PO Box 115
    West Peterborough, NH 03468
    www.wapack.org

Green Mountain Club
    4711 Waterbury-Stowe Road
    Waterbury Center, VT 05677
    (802) 244-7037
    www.greenmountainclub.org/

Maine Appalachian Trail Club
    PO Box 283
    Augusta, ME 04332
    www.matc.org

Maine Audubon
    20 Gilsland Farm Road
    Falmouth, ME 04105
    (207) 781-2330
    http://maineaudubon.org

Maine Coast Heritage Trust
    1 Bowdoin Mill Island, Suite 201
    Topsham, ME 04086
    (207) 729-7366
    www.mcht.org

New Hampshire Audubon
    84 Silk Farm Road
    Concord, NH 03301
    (603) 224-9909
    www.nhaudubon.org

Randolph Mountain Club
    PO Box 279
    Gorham, NH 03581
    www.randolphmountainclub.org/index
        .html

Rhode Island Land Trust Council
    PO Box 633
    Saunderstown, RI 02874
    www.rilandtrusts.org/index.htm

Society for the Protection of New Hampshire Forests
    54 Portsmouth Street
    Concord, NH 03301
    (603) 224-9945
    www.spnhf.org

The Nature Conservancy
    4245 North Fairfax Drive, Suite 100
    Arlington, VA 22203
    (703) 841-5300
    www.nature.org

    Connecticut Chapter
        55 High Street
        Middletown, CT 06457
        (860) 344-0716

Maine Chapter
14 Maine Street, Suite 401
Brunswick, ME 04011
(207) 729-5181

Massachusetts Chapter
205 Portland Street, Suite 400
Boston, MA 02114
(617) 227-7017

New Hampshire Chapter
22 Bridge Street, 4th Floor
Concord, NH 03301
(603) 224-5853

Rhode Island Chapter
159 Waterman Street
Providence, RI 02906
(401) 331-7110

Vermont Chapter
27 State Street, Suite 4
Montpelier, VT 05602
(802) 229-4425

The Trustees of Reservations
251 Causeway Street, Suite 600
Boston, MA 02114
(617) 626-1250
www.thetrustees.org

Trust for Public Land
New England Regional Office
33 Union Street
Boston, MA 02108
(617) 367-6200
www.tpl.org

Vermont Land Trust
8 Bailey Avenue
Montpelier, VT 05602
(802) 223-5234
www.vlt.org

INDEX

A

Acadia Mountain 262–264, 270
Acadia National Park 240, 254–265, 310
Adirondack Mountains 157–158, 160, 164, 168, 173
Agamenticus, Mount 240–242
Ames Mansion 72
Androscoggin Riverlands State Park 274–276
Appalachian Mountain Club 219–220, 229, 297–299, 310, 313
Appalachian Trail 122–130, 133–134, 136–138, 147–148, 150–153, 159, 200, 205–206, 229, 231–232, 274, 288–292, 297–302, 308
Arethusa Falls 217–219
Avalon, Mount 220–222
Avery, Myron 290
Avery Peak 290–292

B

Baker Pond 106–107
Balancing Rock 181–182
Bald Knob 192–193
Balsams Grand Resort 237–238
Basin, The 205–206
Baxter State Park 274, 299–310
Bay Circuit Trail 69–71, 80–81
Bearberry Hill 33–34
Beech Cliff 263–264
Beech Mountain 263–265
Belknap Mountain 189–190
Belknap Mountain State Forest 188–189
Belknap Range Trail 189–190
Bentley Loop 37–38
Bigelow Mountain Preserve 290–292
Billings Park 162–163
Blackstone River and Canal Heritage State Park 67–69
Blueberry Mountain 279–280
Bomoseen State Park 155–156
Boojum Rock 75–76
Borestone Mountain Sanctuary 295–297
Boulder Loop Trail 209–210
Bradbury Mountain State Park 245–247
Bradley Palmer State Park 79–81
Bromley Mountain 147–148
Brownsville Rock 146–147

C

Camden Hills State Park 249–251
Camels Hump 166–169, 179, 184
Cape Cod National Seashore 33–34, 310
Cape Lookoff Mountain 164–165
Cardigan, Mount 193–195
Cardigan Mountain State Park 194
Caribou Mountain 281–283
Caribou–Speckled Mountain Wilderness 279–282
Carpenters Rocks 63
Castle in the Clouds Conservation Area 190, 192
Chairback Mountain 299
Champlain, Lake 168–172
Champlain Mountain 254–256
Chauncey, Mount 89–91
Chester–Blandford State Forest 95–97
Chief Waternomee (Abenaki) 197
Chimney Pond 307–308
Chocorua, Mount 208, 210–212
Civilian Conservation Corps 96, 142, 184
Coe, Mount 302–303
Connecticut River 98–100, 146, 186
Coolidge State Forest 159–160
Crawford Notch State Park 217–222
Crescent Lake 90–91

D

Daicey Pond 299–302
Dartmouth Outing Club 197–199, 310
Diana's Baths 213–214
Discover Hamilton Trail 79–81
Dixville Notch State Park 237–238
Dodge Point Preserve 247–249
Donnell Pond Public Reserve 266–268
Dorr Mountain 256–259
Dumplings, The 143–144

E

Eagle Cliff 263–264
East Head Reservoir 38
Elmore, Lake 181–182
Elmore Mountain 180–182
Elmore State Park 180–182
Equinox, Mount 138–140
Equinox Preserve 138–139, 310
Equinox Resort & Spa 138

F

Falls Brook Falls 91–93
Field, Mount 220–221
Franconia Falls 201–202
Franconia Notch State Park 203–207
Frankenstein Cliff 218
Fresh Pond 252–253

G

Gerrys Falls 146
Giuffrida Park 89–91
Glen Lake 154–156
Goat Hill 67–68
Grace, Mount 102–105
Great Bay 82–84
Great Brook Farm State Park 77–79
Great Swamp Wildlife Reservation 43–45
Green Hills Preserve 215–217
Green Mountain Club 173, 313
Green Mountain National Forest 136–137,
    147–154, 159, 163–165, 310
Greylock, Mount 132–134, 142
Groton State Forest 182–183
Gunstock Mountain 189

H

Hadlock Ponds 260–261
Hamilton Falls 143–144
Harmon Hill 136–138
Hitchcock Fall 227–228
Holbrook Island Sanctuary 252–254
Hollingsworth Trail 269–270
Holyoke, Mount 98–99
Horrid, Mount 163–165
Hunger, Mount 178–179

I

Ice Beds 153–154
Imp Face 232–233

J

Jamaica State Park 142–144
James L. Goodwin State Forest 55–57
Jay Peak 175–177
Jay, John (chief justice) 175
Jefferson, Mount 224–227
Jefferson, Thomas (president) 224
Joanne Bass Bross Preserve 108–109
John H. Chafee Nature Preserve 46–47
Joseph Battell Wilderness 164–165

K

Kancamagus Highway 200–201, 207–210,
    215

Katahdin, Mount 292, 302, 307–309
Kees Falls 282
Kennebec Highlands 277–279
Kettle Pond 183–184
Killington Peak 152, 159–160
King Philip's War 43, 102
Kinsman Falls 205

L

Lake Champlain 168–172
Lake Elmore 181–182
Lake Solitude 113–114
Lake Winnipesaukee 189, 193
Lakes Region Conservation Trust 189, 310
Lamentation, Mount 89–91
Leach Pond 70–71
Lincoln Woods 200–202
Little Jackson Mountain 285–288
Little Knife Edge 305–306
Little Moose Pond Public Reserve 292–294
Little Purgatory 65–66
Little Rock Pond 150–152
Lonesome Lake 205–206
Long and Ell Ponds Natural Area 47–49
Long Trail 130, 137, 147–148, 150–153, 159,
    164–168, 173–177
Lookout Rock 68–69

M

Madison, Mount 227–230
Mahoosuc Land Trust 283–285, 310
Maine Audubon 295–297, 310, 313
Maine Coast Heritage Trust 270–272, 311,
    313, 319
Maine Coastal Island National Wildlife
    Refuge 268–270, 311
Mansfield, Mount 169, 173–175, 179, 182
Mansfield Hollow State Park 59–62
Maquam Bog 172
Marsh–Billings–Rockefeller National Historic
    Park 161–163, 311
Mattabesett Trail 89–91
Metacomet Trail 93–95
Middle Sister 210–213
Middlebury College 164
Middlesex Fells Reservation 74–76
Miles Standish State Forest 36–38
Misery, Mount 52–54
Missisquoi National Wildlife Refuge
    170–172, 311
Monadnock, Mount (NH) 101, 110–111
Monadnock, Mount (VT) 184–186
Monadnock–Metacomet Trail 98–99,
    103–105

Moosilauke, Mount 197–200, 204
Mount Agamenticus 240–242
Mount Ascutney State Park 145–147
Mount Avalon 220–222
Mount Cardigan 193–195
Mount Chauncey 89–91
Mount Chocorua 208, 210–212
Mount Coe 302–303
Mount Equinox 138–140
Mount Field 220–221
Mount Grace 102–105
Mount Greylock 132–134, 142
Mount Holyoke 98–99
Mount Horrid, Great Cliff 163–165
Mount Hunger 178–179
Mount Jefferson 224–227
Mount Katahdin 292, 302, 307–309
Mount Lamentation 89–91
Mount Madison 227–230
Mount Mansfield 169, 173–175, 179, 182
Mount Misery 52–54
Mount Monadnock (NH) 101, 110–111
Mount Monadnock (VT) 184–186
Mount Moosilauke 197–200, 204
Mount Olga 141–142
Mount Osceola 195–197
Mount Pemigewasset 203–204
Mount Shaw 191–193
Mount Sunapee State Park 112–114
Mount Toby 100–101
Mount Tom 161–163
Mount Washington 223, 229–232

N

Nash Stream Forest 234–235
Nature Conservancy, The 49–52, 82–84,
    109, 157, 178, 215–216, 311, 313–314
Nayantaquit Trail 57–59
Nehantic Trail 52–54
Nelson Crag 231–232
New Hampshire Audubon 110, 311, 313
Niagara Falls 299–302
Nickerson Hill 58
Nipmuck Trail 60–61
Niquette State Park 168–170
Noanet Woodlands 72–74
North Brother 302–304
North Moat Mountain 213–215
Norumbega Mountain 259–261

O

Olga, Mount 141–142
Osceola, Mount 195–197
Owls Head Mountain 182–183

P

Pachaug State Forest 52–54
Pack Monadnock 107–111
Pamet Trail 33–34
Pardon Gray Preserve 38–40
Peaked Mountain 216–217
Pemigewasset, Mount 203–204
Pemigewasset Wilderness 200, 202
Penwood State Park 93–94
Percy Peaks 234–236
Petit Manan 268–270
Pigeon Hill Preserve 270
Pine Acres Pond 55–57
Pinnacle, The 94–95
Pisgah State Park 105–107
Pogue, The 161–163
Potash Mountain 207–208
Presidential Range 196, 222, 232,
    280
Purgatory Chasm 64–66
Putnam State Forest 178–179

Q

Quinnipiac Trail 86–88

R

Rattlesnake Ledge 51
Robert Frost Trail 100–101
Rock Circuit Trail 75–76
Rome Point 45–47
Roosevelt, Franklin (president) 107
Rumford Whitecap Preserve
    283–285

S

Sanderson Brook Falls 97–98
Sandy Neck Beach Park 34–35, 311
Shaw, Mount 191–193
Sieur de Monts Spring 254, 257
Sleeping Giant State Park 86–89
Smugglers Notch State Park
    173–174
Snake Mountain 157–158
Solitude, Lake 113–114
South Brother 302–303
Speckled Mountain 279–281
Stark, Molly 141
Stone, Harlan Fiske (chief justice) 107
Sugarloaf Mountain 288–290
Sugarloaf Trail 222–223
Sunapee (Mount) State Park 112–114
Sunapee-Ragged-Kearsarge Greenway 86,
    112–113
Sweet Trail 82–84

T

Table Rock 237
Teapot Dome Scandal 79
Tillinghast Pond 50–52
Titans Piazza 99
Toby, Mount 100–101
Tom, Mount 161–163
Tophet Swamp 79
Traveler Mountain 304–306
The Trustees of Reservations 72–74, 312
Trustom Pond National Wildlife Refuge 41–43
Tumbledown Pond 287
Tumbledown Public Reserve 285–288
Tunk Mountain 266–268
Tunxis State Forest 91–92

W

Wapack National Wildlife Refuge 108–109
Wapack Trail 86, 107–110
Washington, Mount 223, 229–232
Waternomee (Abenaki chief) 197
Weetamoo Woods 38–40
Wells Reserve 242–244, 312
Wells State Park 62–64
White Mountain National Forest 112, 160, 166, 168, 173, 177, 179, 188, 195, 197, 207–209, 211–212, 220–225, 228, 231, 279–282, 312
White Rocks Cliff 152–154
White Rocks National Recreational Area 152–153
Wickaboxet Management Area 51
Willard Pond 110–112
Winnipesaukee, Lake 189, 193

About the Author

Author and son, Vermont Long Trail (Photo by Maria Fuentes)

Jeffrey Romano has been hiking for more than forty years. A lifelong resident of New England, Jeff has lived in Connecticut, New Hampshire, Vermont, and Maine. In addition to scaling New England's one hundred highest peaks, he has hiked extensively throughout the wild places of all six states.

Born in Connecticut, Jeff grew up in southern New Hampshire. He earned a BA in politics from Saint Anselm College and a JD from Vermont Law School. Jeff has worked on a handful of political campaigns and for a number of nonprofit organizations. He currently coordinates public policy activities for Maine Coast Heritage Trust, a statewide land trust that focuses on the conservation of Maine's unique coastline. When not in his office or in the Maine State House in Augusta, Jeff is often with his family on one of New England's many hiking trails. An avid bird-watcher, he lives in Hallowell with his wife, Maria, and their son, Anthony. Jeff is also the author of *Best Loop Hikes: New Hampshire's White Mountains to the Maine Coast* and *100 Classic Hikes: New England*, both published by Mountaineers Books.

recreation · lifestyle · conservation

MOUNTAINEERS BOOKS is a leading publisher of mountaineering literature and guides—including our flagship title, *Mountaineering: The Freedom of the Hills*—as well as adventure narratives, natural history, and general outdoor recreation. Through our two imprints, Skipstone and Braided River, we also publish titles on sustainability and conservation. As a 501(c)3 nonprofit, we are committed to supporting the environmental and educational goals of our organization by providing expert information on human-powered adventure, sustainable practices at home and on the trail, and preservation of wilderness.

The Mountaineers, founded in 1906, is a nonprofit outdoor activity and conservation organization whose mission is "to explore, study, preserve, and enjoy the natural beauty of the outdoors." One of the largest such organizations in the United States, it sponsors classes and year-round outdoor activities throughout the Pacific Northwest, including climbing, hiking, backcountry skiing, snowshoeing, bicycling, camping, paddling, and more. The Mountaineers also supports its mission through its publishing division, Mountaineers Books, and promotes environmental causes through educational activities and sponsorship of legislation. For more information, visit The Mountaineers Program Center, 7700 Sand Point Way NE, Seattle, WA 98115-3996; phone 206-521-6001; www.mountaineers.org; or email info@mountaineers.org.

All of our publications are made possible through the generosity of donors and through sales of more than 600 titles on outdoor recreation, sustainable lifestyle, and conservation. To donate, purchase books, or learn more, visit us online:

MOUNTAINEERS BOOKS
1001 SW Klickitat Way, Suite 201 • Seattle, WA 98134
800-553-4453 • mbooks@mountaineersbooks.org • www.mountaineersbooks.org

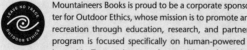

Mountaineers Books is proud to be a corporate sponsor of The Leave No Trace Center for Outdoor Ethics, whose mission is to promote and inspire responsible outdoor recreation through education, research, and partnerships · The Leave No Trace program is focused specifically on human-powered (nonmotorized) recreation · Leave No Trace strives to educate visitors about the nature of their recreational impacts and offers techniques to prevent and minimize such impacts · Leave No Trace is best understood as an educational and ethical program, not as a set of rules and regulations · For more information, visit www.lnt.org, or call 800-332-4100.